PROFESSIONAL
INVESTIGATOR'S
MANUAL

PROFESSIONAL
INVESTIGATOR'S
MANUAL

This text contains excerpts from the *Protection of Assets Manual (POA)* edited and expanded specifically for investigators and those studying for the PCI® examination.

ASIS International | 1625 Prince Street | Alexandria, VA 22314 USA | *www.asisonline.org*

PREFACE

This *Professional Investigator's Manual* would not be possible without the collaboration of many contributors whose experience, guidance, and wisdom are reflected throughout the finished work. The breadth and depth of this manual appeals to those interested in understanding what investigators do, as well as those starting out in the profession and veteran investigators seeking to hone their skills or seek professional credentials through certification.

The editors, writers, and many professional colleagues conducted months of research to prepare the first draft of this manual. The draft was subjected to a peer review wherein an additional group of professionals offered constructive criticism, modified existing content, and recommended additional depth in some areas so that the finished publication is a comprehensive work.

Our hope is that the *Professional Investigator's Manual* becomes an important source of professional insight for those who read it and that it stimulates serious dialogue between and among security professionals.

With all these objectives in mind, we present to you the *Professional Investigator's Manual*, in the sincere belief it will enhance your knowledge in the world of investigations.

Michael E. Knoke, CPP
Managing Editor
March, 2010

CONTRIBUTORS

The success of this publication is directly related to the peer review process recognized by most professions. Security professionals, members of Academia and other subject matter experts were involved in contributing current information, conducting research, reviewing submissions, and providing constructive comments so that we are able to provide a publication that is recognized as the "go to" reference for security professionals worldwide.

It is with sincere appreciation that I wish to thank the below named individuals who contributed to the *Professional Investigator's Manual.*

Michael E. Knoke, CPP
Managing Editor

Edward P. De Lise, CPP
Assistant Editor

Peter E. Ohlhausen
Technical Editor

Eva Giercuszkiewicz
ASIS Project Manager

Evangeline Pappas
ASIS Production Manager

George J. Barletta, CPP

Henri A. Berube

Martin T. Biegelman, J.D.

Patrick C. Bishop, CPP

Joseph P. Buckley, III

James P. Carino, Jr., CPP

Richard E. Chase, CPP

Bruce Dean, CPP

Clifford E. Dow, CPP

Cheryl D. Elliott, CPP, PCI

Eugene F. Ferraro, CPP, PCI

Richard H. Frank, CPP

Michael Flachs, CPP

Frederick G. Giles, CPP

Christopher Giusti, CPP

Jeffrey L. Gwynne, Ph.D.

William T. Hill, CPP

Mark D. Hucker, CPP

W. Geoffrey Hughes, PCI

Diane Horn Kaloustian, CPP

Terrence J. Korpal

James M. Kuehn, CPP

Roger B. Maslen, CPP

Edward F. McDonough, Jr., CPP

J. Harm Oosten, CPP

Kevin E. Peterson, CPP

Karl S. Perman

John D. Rankin, CPP

David L. Ray, LL.B.

Ty L. Richmond, CPP

Lisa M. Ruth

Gregory L. Sanders, CPP

Dennis Shepp, CPP, PCI

Shari F. Shovlin

Pamela M. Stewart, PCI

Fritz Weidner, PCI

Allan R. Wick, CPP, PSP

Richard Y. Yamamoto, CPP

CONTENTS

TABLE OF FIGURES

Background:
Historical Perspectives

It is important to understand the historical foundation of the investigative process in order to place today's approaches, tools, techniques, organizational structures, and relationships in context. The practice of investigation has long been carried out as both a public sector and a private sector function. The following summary of the origins and development of investigating is based on *An Introduction to Public and Private Investigations* (Dempsey, 1996, pp. 84–92) and on "Our History" (Securitas Security Services USA, 2004).

Before Public Investigating

Little is known about the very early history of policing or investigating. In a well-known fictional view of 14th century investigation, *The Name of the Rose*, Italian philosopher and historian Umberto Eco depicts a senior Roman monk teaching his protégé in investigative techniques, including interviews and scene examination, in order to solve the murders of fellow monks. Franciscan monks often investigated alleged crimes to avoid subjecting the parties to the Inquisition.

The name of the book's central character, William of Baskerville, alludes to the fictional detective Sherlock Holmes, the main protagonist in Sir Arthur Conan Doyle's *The Hound of the Baskervilles*, and to William of Ockham, who stated the principle (known as Ockham's Razor) that one should always accept as most likely the simplest explanation that covers the facts. *The Name of the Rose* describes the scholastic method, which was very popular in the 14th century. The main character demonstrates the power of deductive reasoning, keeps an open mind, collects facts and observations, and follows his intuition regarding what to investigate. The story also demonstrates the importance of chance in any investigative endeavor. Nevertheless, William could not have solved the cases if he had not prepared a framework of facts and interconnections, which the chance discovery then made meaningful.

Policing—maintaining order and dealing with lawbreakers—had always been a private matter. Citizens were responsible for protecting themselves and investigating crimes committed against themselves. Modern-style police departments did not appear until the 14th century in France and the early 19th century in England.

There was no official or organized police or law enforcement investigative process in Europe until well into the 19th century. Neither were there any official investigative agencies. Even with the advent of formal police departments, the police were primarily concerned with the prevention of crime by conspicuous uniformed police patrol. If a crime was reported or discovered, the police merely took a report. Private individuals served as some of the earliest investigators of crimes.

Thief-Takers. Before formal police departments developed, individuals called thief-takers served as a form of private police in 16th, 17th, and 18th century France and England. Thief-takers had no official status but were paid by the king for every criminal they arrested, much like bounty hunters of the American West.

The major role of thief-takers was to combat robbery by highwaymen. By the 17th century, highwaymen like Jack Sheppard and Dick Turpin made traveling through the English countryside so dangerous that no coach or traveler was safe. In 1693, an Act of Parliament established a monetary reward for the capture of any highwayman or road agent. The thief-taker was paid upon the conviction of the highwayman and also received the highwayman's horse, arms, money, and property.

The thief-taker system was later extended to cover offenses other than highway robbery, and soon a sliding scale of rewards was established. Arresting a burglar or a footpad (street robber), for example, was worth the same as catching a highwayman, but catching a sheep stealer or a deserter from the army brought a much smaller reward. In some areas, homeowners joined together and offered supplementary rewards for the apprehension of a highwayman or footpad in their area. In addition, during serious crime waves Parliament granted special rewards for thief-takers to arrest particular felons.

Bow Street Runners. Henry Fielding, the 18th century novelist best known for writing *Tom Jones*, can also be credited with laying the foundation for the first modern police force. In 1748, during the heyday of the English highwayman, Fielding was appointed magistrate in Westminster, a city near London. He moved into a house on Bow Street, which also became his office. In an attempt to decrease the high number of burglaries, street and highway robberies, and other thefts, Fielding established relationships with local pawnbrokers. He would provide them with lists and descriptions of recently stolen property and ask them to notify him should such property be brought into their pawnshops. He then placed the following ad in the London and Westminster newspapers:

> All persons who shall for the future suffer by robber, burglars, etc., are desired immediately to bring or send the best description they can of such robbers, etc., with the time and place and circumstances of the fact, to Henry Fielding Esq., at his house in Bow Street.

Fielding's actions brought about what can be called the first official crime reports. Fielding was able to gain the cooperation of the High Constable of Holborn and several other public-spirited constables. Together they formed a small investigative unit, which they called the Bow Street Runners. These were private citizens who were not paid by public funds but who were permitted to accept thief-taker rewards.

19th Century Investigating

The first official publicly funded governmental police investigating units emerged in the 19th century. Such units first appeared in France and England. Investigation then began to take place in the United States, both in urban centers and on the frontier.

France. The French led the way in developing specialized detectives when the king's chief minister, Cardinal Mazari, hired 100 exempts (investigators) in 1645. The leaders of the French Revolution felt repugnance for the system of the old regime and abolished the detective branch, but a new one was created by Napoléon Bonaparte in 1817.

The Police de Sûreté (security police), France's new police detective bureau, was created in Paris in 1817 under the leadership of the notorious French criminal and police informant Eugène Vidocq (1775–1857). In 1809, Vidocq, while serving a prison sentence, offered his services as an informer to the Paris police. The prefecture of the Paris police assigned him to inform on fellow prison inmates. In return for his information he was allowed to escape custody. In 1817, Vidocq, under police authorization, formed the first Paris police detective bureau. Vidocq served as chief of the Sûreté from 1817 to 1827.

The first Paris police detective bureau consisted of four detectives and increased over several years to 28 members. Between January and December 1817, with only 12 members, the squad made 772 arrests. Those arrested included 15 murderers, 108 burglars, 5 armed robbers, and more than 250 thieves of various descriptions.

Vidocq, whose maxim was "it takes a thief to catch a thief," was responsible for what has become known as the French method of detective work. Detectives of the Sûreté routinely employed clandestine methods against both political and criminal suspects and retained a large number of spies and informers. It was Vidocq's contention that major crimes and criminals were best handled by criminals themselves, and he quickly hired about 20 ex-convicts he had known in prison. These men formed the basis of the newly expanded Sûreté. Vidocq would then arrest his own men on bogus charges and send them to prison, where they served as spies, gathering information on crimes and criminals inside and outside of prison. When they had collected enough useful information, Vidocq arranged for his men to escape prison, or he had them feign their own deaths. They were carted from prison in coffins, only to rise again to serve the Sûreté once more.

After 10 years as head of the detective bureau, Vidocq resigned. He then began his own private investigations business. Thousands of crime victims asked for his help in regaining their stolen property. Vidocq also formed a "trade protection society"—a forerunner of today's credit reporting agency. For a fee, any shopkeeper or business establishment could obtain the particulars regarding the financial solvency of new customers. At one time, more than 8,000 shopkeepers subscribed to the service.

England. London's first large-scale, organized police department, the London Metropolitan Police, was created through the efforts of Sir Robert Peel, who successfully managed to have the Metropolitan Police Act of 1829 passed by Parliament. London's first officers were nicknamed "bobbies" after him.

Because the bobbies were housed in a building that had formerly been occupied by Scottish royalty, the home of the London Metropolitan Police became known as Scotland Yard. The early London police rarely engaged in criminal investigations because they did not wish to work in plainclothes, deal with criminal informants, or engage in covert operations. The police felt the public would turn against them if they operated like spies, the image of detectives in France.

One commentator gives the following explanation as why to England, with its emphasis on community-based policing, tried to avoid a French-style approach to investigating (Repetto, 1978, p. 29):

> Whereas the detective's clientele were mostly criminal and his contacts necessarily furtive, detective and thief were, in fact, fellow craftsmen who shared a great many of the same perceptions and values. Both recognized that criminal behavior was normal in some milieus and viewed arrest and punishment as part of the game. Given the intimacy and shared values, it was inevitable that deals would be struck, ranging from outright corruption to the exchange of information for favors. Indeed, most policemen and some judges believed without such deals the detectives could not function. The public, however, could not be told that the detectives worked through informers and deals, since in many cases these skirted the law and public morality.

High crime rates forced the London police to open a detective branch at Scotland Yard in 1842. Under London police commissioner Richard Mayne, the detective force numbered no more than 16 men, and its operations were restricted by Mayne's distrust of clandestine detective methods. In 1867, Irish rebels blew up a wall of Clerkenwell Prison, killing four people and injuring 40. The detective branch was criticized for failing to respond to prior warnings of the event. In 1868, as a result of the Clerkenwell incident, the number of headquarters detectives was increased to approximately 40, and an additional 180 detectives of all ranks were assigned to various local division headquarters.

In 1877, three of the four chief inspectors of the headquarters detectives were convicted of accepting bribes. A formal investigation was undertaken by a government commission, and the following year the Criminal Investigation Division (CID) was created and placed in charge of both headquarters and division detectives. When Howard Vincent, a London lawyer, heard of the government investigation of the detectives, he rushed to Paris to study the French Sûreté, whose detectives routinely employed clandestine methods against both political and criminal suspects and retained a large number of spies. Vincent reported his findings to the Home Secretary and talked himself into appointment to the well-paid directorship of the CID. Under his regime, the CID was severely criticized for using French methods.

The early years of the CID saw much activity by Irish nationalists. Because revolution in Ireland was blocked by the Royal Irish Constabulary and the army, the rebels turned to a terror campaign in England. During the years 1883-1885 they bombed railroads, subways, the Tower of London, and even Scotland Yard itself. A special squad of CID detectives was formed to deal with the terrorists and came to be known as the Special Branch of the CID. In 1887, detectives intercepted an Irish-American terrorist and broke up a plot to plant a bomb in Westminster Abbey during Queen Victoria's jubilee ceremony. After that incident the movement receded, but the Special Branch remained in existence and is still a force in British policing.

United States. The American criminal justice system owes its heritage to the English experience. Discussion of 19th century investigating in the United States must distinguish between public investigating in the East, private investigating on the American frontier, and federal investigating in general.

America's early police departments formed in the mid-1800s on the East Coast, then quickly spread to cities in the Midwest. Like London's police department, these departments concentrated mostly on uniformed patrol to deter crime. Many of America's early public detectives, such as Francis Tukey in Boston and Allan Pinkerton in Chicago, were appointed to their positions by mayors in response to public pressure to halt an increase in crime. Tukey, appointed as Boston's new marshal in 1846, hired three officers to serve as Boston's first detective bureau. They recovered $16,000 worth of stolen property in 1850 and $62,000 in 1860. Chicago appointed Allan Pinkerton as its first detective in 1849. Philadelphia started its first detective bureau in 1859 under Chief of Detectives Wood. During its first year, the eight-man unit arrested 481 suspects and recovered $25,000 in stolen property.

In 1857, the New York City Police Department, under the supervision of Captain George Walling, designated 20 police officers as detectives. Walling divided the detective force into squads responsible for specific crimes. Each squad maintained records of complaints and arrests. Each detective was required to submit daily reports on the progress and disposition of cases.

The Detective Bureau of New York was formally established by the New York State legislature in 1882. American detectives were originally recruited directly from civilian life, often from the criminal underworld. However, they frequently became involved in scandals. Therefore, it soon became necessary to select detectives from the uniformed patrol force.

On the American frontier there was no real law enforcement except for the town marshal, appointed by the town's mayor, and the elected county sheriff. Private police were much more effective than public law enforcement agencies on the frontier. Although they often acted in the same manner as the English thief-takers, keeping a percentage of the stolen property they recovered, America's private police were much more professional and honest than early England's.

Allan Pinkerton could be called America's founder of criminal investigation. Born in Glasgow, Scotland, in 1819, Pinkerton immigrated to the United States and settled in the small town of Dundee, Illinois, near Chicago. His volunteer assistance in cracking major counterfeiting cases caught the attention of the Cook County sheriff, who later asked Pinkerton to come to Chicago and serve as a deputy. Within a year, he had risen to become Chicago's first full-time detective. He also served as a special U.S. agent investigating mail thefts.

In the early 1850s, Pinkerton left his job with the city to found a private detective agency—one of the first of its kind—in partnership with Chicago attorney Edward Rucker. Their agency, the North-Western Police Agency, was an immediate success.

Pinkerton pioneered numerous investigative techniques, such as shadowing or suspect surveillance and undercover operations. His agency was the first to hire a female detective, Kate Warne, in 1856. Pinkerton also established and enforced a code of ethics for his employees, prohibiting them from accepting gratuities or rewards and removing politics from his operations. He believed that the job of a criminal investigator was to collect facts in order to identify the guilty party, locate them, and provide evidence of their guilt.

Another Pinkerton innovation—the mug shot—soon spread to police and other detective organizations. By the 1870s his agency had the largest collection of mug shots in the world. It also established a system whereby field agents around the country would diligently clip newspaper stories about criminals, add notations, and send them to a central office where they were incorporated into a criminal database.

Pinkerton later offered his services to the federal government. He was assigned to protect President Lincoln and is credited with detecting and preventing at least one assassination plot. In addition, he developed both intelligence and counterintelligence capabilities during the Civil War. He operated an espionage unit that gathered military intelligence, and he personally conducted several undercover missions. On one occasion he posed as a Confederate supporter and was given a personal tour of enemy lines by a top-ranking officer. Later, his firm worked to track down embezzlers who cheated on government contracts.

Among Pinkerton's other major accomplishments were establishing the practice of handwriting examination in U.S. courts and proposing a plan to centralize criminal identification records. He also advanced the cause of international police cooperation by sharing information with Scotland Yard and the French Sûreté.

In competition with the Pinkerton Agency during the latter part of the 19th century was the Rocky Mountain Detective Association, which pursued and apprehended bank and train robbers, cattle thieves, murderers, and the road agents who plundered highways and mining communities throughout the Southwest and Rocky Mountain areas.

Also in competition with Pinkerton was Wells, Fargo & Co., started in 1852 by Henry Wells and William G. Fargo as a banking and stock association designed to capitalize on the emerging shipping and banking opportunities in California. It operated as a mail-carrying service and stagecoach line out of more than 100 offices in the Western mining districts. Because it transported millions of dollars' worth of gold and other cargo, the company created its own guard organization to protect shipments. The firm's private security employees were generally effective in preventing robberies and thefts. When criminals succeeded in robbing the company's banks and carriers, they were relentlessly hunted down.

On the federal side, the U.S. government has employed investigators to detect revenue violations since the country's earliest days. In 1789, the government appointed investigators, known collectively as the Revenue Cutter Service, to prevent smuggling. In 1829, the Post Office Department appointed investigators to investigate mail theft. In 1865, the Congress created the United States Secret Service to combat the counterfeiting of U.S. obligations, such as currency, bonds, and stamps. In 1903, two years after the assassination of President McKinley, the Secret Service assumed the responsibility of guarding the President.

20TH CENTURY INVESTIGATING

The 20th century saw the spread of public investigating to most local police departments in the United States. It also saw the further development of investigating units at the federal level, particularly the Federal Bureau of Investigation (FBI) and the Treasury Department's Narcotic Bureau, now known as the Drug Enforcement Administration (DEA). The 20th century also witnessed the increased use of science in investigating crime and the use of academic research to study police investigations and establish new methods of investigating crimes.

Private investigating also flourished. For example, the William J. Burns Detective Agency was founded in 1909. Burns was a well-known and highly experienced crime watchdog as well as a man of great integrity. In fact, he had a reputation as the greatest detective the U.S. had ever produced. Under his leadership, the company grew from a small detective agency to the second-largest security provider in the United States. In 1921, he was appointed director of the newly formed Bureau of Investigation, which later became the FBI.

INVESTIGATIONS MANAGEMENT

1.1 THE NATURE OF INVESTIGATION MANAGEMENT

A commonly accepted definition of *investigation* is a systematic and thorough examination or inquiry into something or someone (the collection of facts and information) and the recording of that examination in a report (Dempsey, 1996, p. 3). This definition applies equally in both the public and private sectors and clearly covers the broad range of investigations, from background checks to administrative inquiries to criminal matters. *Management* is defined as the act of conducting or supervising something or "the judicious use of means to accomplish an end" (Merriam-Webster, 2009).

The primary purpose of any investigation—particularly in the corporate or organizational setting—generally falls within one or more of the following categories (Webster University, 2004):

- thoroughly documenting incidents (such as those reported to security staff or officers)

- identifying the cause of undesirable situations (e.g., notable losses, sudden decrease in income or market share, unexplained shrinkage, inventory discrepancies, defalcation {failure to properly account for money held in a fiduciary capacity}, etc.) where nefarious activity is suspected

- documenting and correlating facts surrounding any situation or allegation

- identifying suspects involved in a crime or act of misconduct

- compiling information that proves or disproves an allegation or that implicates or exonerates an individual suspected of committing a crime or misconduct

- allowing a decision to be made, often with respect to a level of trust or suitability determination, regarding an individual (e.g., in a personnel security clearance) or an organization (e.g., a potential partner firm or acquisition target)

From a management perspective, it is important to consider the purpose of the investigation at both the case level and the strategic level. At the case level, the purpose sets the context within which the investigation will be conducted and help keep the people working on (and managing) the particular case focused. At the strategic level, the purpose of an investigation dictates the necessary planning, organizing, equipping, staffing, and preparation. Unit managers and security directors need to consider all possible purposes they may face, even though the majority of cases may fall clearly into one category. Although they should focus their resources and approaches on the most prevalent types of cases, they should also give forethought to other possibilities.

1.1.1 QUALITIES OF AN EFFECTIVE INVESTIGATION

Five attributes characterize an effective and reliable investigation: objectivity, thoroughness, relevance, accuracy, and timeliness. It is management's role to ensure these qualities are present at both the strategic level (having in place a system that facilitates investigations characterized by these qualities) and on an individual case basis (through effective case review and quality control).

The investigative process involves both science and art. Much of the art manifests itself in the qualities below. The cornerstone of each quality is summarized in italics as an introductory statement.

> **Objectivity:** *Remaining objective and focusing on the use of a rational investigative hypothesis while carefully avoiding the interjection of prejudgment.*

This can be one of the most difficult requirements for the investigator—even for the experienced professional—because it defies human nature. Many investigations are founded on a working hypothesis, which may be developed at the outset or later and may change one or more times. The hypothesis is appropriately used as a tool as long as it remains within the bounds of objectivity.

According to a *Security Management* article, this means not jumping to conclusions—even in the face of what seems to be overwhelming and conclusive evidence—without first independently corroborating the facts. Failure to corroborate evidence is a common mistake of inexperienced investigators, but it can happen to anyone. The overall goal is to allow the facts to speak for themselves in a concise, accurate, and professional manner (Albrecht, 2004, p. 78).

To aid in maintaining objectivity, every investigator should consciously recognize his or her personal prejudices and neutralize the effects of those prejudices on investigative activities, including the formation of the hypothesis. In other words, the professional investigator must ensure that the investigative findings form the basis for his or her impressions, not the reverse.

In addition, investigators' approach and demeanor is of critical importance to the successful outcome of a case. First and foremost, the investigator must project an air of objectivity. This is accomplished by choosing words and phrases carefully during the investigative process and by avoiding facial expressions and body language that might project an inappropriate attitude or prejudgment.

> **Thoroughness:** *Following all relevant leads to their logical conclusion and focusing on corroboration of all key investigative findings.*

A thorough investigation involves checking all leads and checking key leads more than once to ensure consistency. Corroborating important aspects through different sources is a proven means of achieving thoroughness. The different sources should also be different types of sources to the greatest extent possible. Various types of sources for a particular piece of information might be interviewees or witnesses, subject matter experts, physical evidence, electronic evidence, public records, surveillance results, open sources, databases, etc.

In the course of an investigation, leads often generate other leads, some of which may appear to be superfluous; however, these secondary and tertiary leads can be of great value in either a direct or corroborative sense. In the interest of thoroughness, a balance must be drawn between an effort to follow every possible lead to its logical conclusion and gathering so much information that it confuses the outcome or becomes counterproductive. This is not an easy balance to find. That is why independent case management is an important function in both the public and the private sectors. This balance is of special concern since there is often pressure to truncate an investigation due to time constraints (frequently, impatience) or resource constraints, particularly in the corporate setting.

> **Relevance:** *Effectively determining the relevance of information, considering an adequate spectrum and depth of details without gathering so much data as to confuse the facts of the case and bog down the investigation or possibly even obscure the truth.*

Relevance means that the information in question pertains to the subject of the investigation in some way and is at the appropriate level of detail. Another difficult aspect of the investigator's job is to determine relevance and the necessary level of detail (i.e., how deep to dig).

The spectrum of details pertains to how wide a net the investigator needs to cast in order to gather all relevant information. For example, in investigating an office building theft problem, should the investigator spend any time or energy looking into a construction project at a neighboring building? The answer is "perhaps." Several years ago, numerous child sexual abuse incidents took place in a particular neighborhood. Investigators were unable to identify any suspects until one investigator noticed that the timeframe of the reported incidents coincided exactly with the start and end dates of a local construction project. The prime suspect was then identified from among the construction crew members, and he later confessed.

The other key determinant is the depth of details. This can be illustrated by the somewhat humorous example of a request for a person to describe what he or she did yesterday. One response may be too detailed: "I got out of bed, brushed my teeth, washed my face, then I shaved, got a bowl of cereal, ate breakfast, put my bowl in the kitchen sink…" By contrast, another account might state, "I got up, went to work, and came home." Obviously, the appropriate level or depth of detail lies somewhere between those extremes.

Investigators deal with this issue daily. The appropriate depth of detail is difficult to achieve with some interviewees, especially those who may be less intelligent or very intelligent (e.g., scientists and engineers) or people who are nervous, in a hurry, attempting to hide something, or simply very quiet or very talkative. A skilled interviewer can help guide the conversation toward the proper depth of detail without diminishing the value of the information provided.

Another aspect of relevance is cause and effect. For example, the subject of a personnel background investigation may have a poor credit rating. Rather than simply reporting a potential weakness in the applicant, the investigator should attempt to determine and verify the cause of the credit rating. The subject may have been a victim of identity theft or may have suffered the loss of a close relative and been saddled with large secondary financial debts until the estate could be settled. In either case, the issue might be completely resolved at the time of the investigation, thereby eliminating the potential weakness. Similar cause-and-effect relationships can arise and become extremely relevant in any type of investigation.

> **Accuracy:** *The credibility of a source, whether human, physical or electronic evidence, or the result of observation or surveillance.*

Eyewitness accounts are among the least accurate forms of investigative information. As a university director of forensic psychology observes, "[G]iven the nature of memory, eyewitness testimony can never be totally accurate or reliable" (Cassel, 2000, p. 2).

The mental processes that collect and sort data from the human senses often produce errors. The mountain seen in the clear air of Arizona may appear to be half a mile away but in reality is three miles away. Was the person seen leaving a crime scene short and fat, medium height, running with a limp, wearing a long coat, wearing no coat? Witnesses frequently report conflicting data.

Another example of this phenomenon can be taken from a recent surveillance training exercise in which the author was a role player. He was described by one observer as "a short, chubby male with a green golf shirt, light brown hair, and a mustache." Another observer on the same exercise described him as "a thin male of medium height wearing a blue T-shirt and having dark hair and a mustache."

In the corporate environment, most credible information on losses, sexual harassment, and other reportable incidents comes from employee tips. However, workers are also the source of many incorrect or misinterpreted tips (Albrecht, 2004, p. 80).

Sound investigative techniques dictate frequent tests for verification. This is similar to financial auditing where evaluation of the accuracy, timeliness and completeness of the recordings of business transactions are critical. If data are susceptible to physical measurement, they must be measured. If an informant is the only source of key data, the informant should be tested at least for consistency. In addition, the information itself must be tested for inherent contradictions. (For example, a person may claim to have traveled in an automobile from one place at a certain time and arrived at a destination at a certain later time, but examination of the distance and elapsed time indicates that the person would have needed to travel at 135 miles per hour to do so.)

All investigative input should be carefully evaluated. It should not be accepted at face value, even if it appears to be straightforward. For example, date/time stamps such as those on computers, cameras (still or video), and facsimile machines may be inaccurate if the internal clock on the device is set incorrectly. Similarly, an access control system record that indicates that a particular individual entered a certain door at a given date and time should be considered suspect. It must first be determined whether the system can be manipulated or spoofed and whether another individual could have used the first person's access card on that occasion.

Accuracy is also a key element in personnel background and preemployment investigations. Some individuals believe that information provided by personal (listed) references is of no value because they are friends and would only say good things about the subject. Actual experience shows that this is often not true. Personal references may gratuitously provide information unfavorable to the person who listed them. That fact, in itself, should cause the investigator to consider the possible motivations of the interviewee.

Timeliness: *The ability to complete an investigation quickly, but not too quickly, and to resist pressure by outside forces to inappropriately either rush or stall a case, thereby damaging the quality of the resolution.*

In investigations, it is important to:

- open an investigation as soon as possible,

- complete an investigation as quickly as possible, and

- avoid closing an investigation prematurely.

Although these aspects may sound contradictory, once again balance is the key. Regarding a quick beginning, "investigations should be conducted as soon as an incident is reported" or discovered (Rudewicz, 2004, p. 49). The most important reason for doing so is that the value of physical or electronic evidence diminishes rapidly. In addition, witnesses and others who possess relevant information provide the best information when the incident is fresh in their memory. Over time, their memory commonly begins to fade, or the information they provide may begin to be tainted by their rationalizations as they have more time to think about the incident and the implication of their answers to the investigator's questions. Their recollection may also be colored by media reports, conversations with other witnesses, or other input.

Once an investigation is under way, it should be completed in an expedient manner to conserve resources, allow operations to return to normal as soon as possible, and deter other potential wrongdoers. Finally, quick and decisive investigations reflect on the professionalism of the investigations or security staff, thereby enhancing their overall effectiveness.

However, care must be taken not to rush an investigation at the expense of quality, thoroughness, or accuracy. Investigators may be pressured to close a case due to time or resource constraints or because of publicity or political factors. Bowing to these pressures should be avoided whenever possible. The investigative unit chief or security director may need to educate upper management on the potential adverse impact of a rushed investigation, including the possibility of increased liability risk.

In addition, senior decision makers and corporate executives must be made aware that resolution is not achieved in all cases. They cannot assume that every case will be solved rapidly or at all. Such misconceptions can lead to unrealistic expectations of an IU or security department. Regular and timely communications between senior security or investigative managers and corporate or organizational decision makers will help minimize the problem of unrealistic expectations.

1.2 PUBLIC SECTOR VERSUS PRIVATE SECTOR INVESTIGATIONS

Although the tools, techniques, and processes are often similar, there is a fundamental distinction between the investigative function in the public sector (generally law enforcement) and in private security. Public sector organizations exist to serve and protect society in general. Their activities are often measured in terms of numbers of arrests and convictions. For example, public sector investigative units will focus their primary methods to address a series of robberies either in a proactive strategy with surveillance or a reactive strategy with assigning more manpower to solve cases. A crime scene investigation is an example of a reactive measure. Examples of public sector agencies with an investigative mission include law enforcement agencies at the federal, state, and local level; regional or special-purpose units (e.g., airport, transportation, or park authorities); intelligence and counterintelligence agencies; inspector general offices; and regulatory agencies that enforce regulations or administrative statutes.

The primary purpose of a private sector security organization, however, is to protect the interests of the employing enterprise. Private sector players generally fit into one of two categories: (1) internal investigative or security units within a company or organization, or (2) companies that provide investigative services or special expertise on a fee basis. This chapter focuses on internal private sector units but recognizes the essential contributions of special service providers and refers to them as well where appropriate.

The role of private security investigations, including those in the corporate arena, is growing. In many cases, the public law enforcement agency having jurisdiction decides not to investigate an incident because of its workload and other priorities. According to *An Introduction to Public & Private Investigations*, "Police power and resources are limited…and there are areas of criminal and non-criminal activity where conventional law enforcement is either ill equipped or otherwise prohibited from getting involved" (Dempsey, 1996, p. 75).

The distinction between the public sector and private sector has implications for legal authority, resource allocation, program management, and investigative outcomes. Rather than public good, the value of private sector investigative capabilities is frequently measured in terms of recovery, restitution, and risk reduction.

The interests of society and the interests of a given enterprise are not necessarily the same. If criminal activity occurs within the enterprise, for example, the public interest is served by the prosecution and imprisonment of the offender. However, the interest of the private sector enterprise may be best served by some combination of accepting restitution or taking administrative or employment action.

The investigative process should reflect this difference. For example, the public sector investigator is frequently required to meet a higher standard of proof than that required of the private sector investigator. The distinction flows from the particular rules of procedure in different courts. In criminal court the prosecutor must prove the case beyond a reasonable doubt, while in civil court the preponderance of evidence drives the verdict. Usually, a greater burden of proof is required for prosecution than for employee discipline, including termination of employment. In the private sector, the desired outcome of the case dictates the required burden of proof. However, even if restitution and termination of employment are an acceptable outcome, rather than prosecution, the organization must still conduct the investigation professionally and reach a reasonable conclusion.

Corporate investigations also tend to be broader in scope than those initiated by public law enforcement. Rather than focusing on a specific act or criminal violation, private sector investigations may further explore company policy violations and may even expand beyond individual violations to review systematic issues that may warrant changes in business processes or corporate policies related to the matter at hand (Garcia, 2002, p. 8).

Early in the private sector investigation, the enterprise should determine the acceptable outcome or outcomes of the case. This determination must consider the legal requirements in the jurisdiction, organized labor contracts in force or pending, public and investor relations, and the past practices of the enterprise in similar cases. In fact, it may be advisable in some instances to have clear-cut corporate policies on investigative outcomes and the resultant corporate action to be taken. Legal counsel should always be consulted in making these types of determinations. In the private sector, a formal relationship should be formed between the investigation and appropriate legal counsel (corporate counsel or outside retained counsel) to protect the investigation results, exhibits, and data from discovery by the opposing side in the case of litigation. (The information becomes *attorney work product*.) The investigator should communicate only through assigned counsel or with those approved by counsel.

Another difference between public and private sector investigative units (IUs) is that corporate investigators often focus on one type or a few particular types of investigations. For example, investigators at one company may spend 90 percent of their time on theft investigations. Another company's unit may focus primarily on safety violations, employee misconduct, sexual harassment, or property damage. Still, security directors and unit chiefs should be prepared to deal with other, unusual types of investigations as well (and on short notice) either by maintaining some level of internal capability (expertise, training, equipment, etc.) or by having outside resources they can call on when needed.

Finally, although corporate IUs generally deal with internal issues, they may also focus on external matters. This is true, for example, of Internet service providers, telecommunications companies, insurance companies, and utilities—organizations whose services are particularly susceptible to fraud or illegal use. Internal issues are generally created through the absence or weakness of internal controls. Many enterprises that deal with both internal and external investigations establish separate units for each. Doing so allows investigators to focus on a particular activity and to develop special expertise, liaison networks, and prosecutorial contacts. It also reduces confusion regarding investigative outcomes and processes. In some cases, organizations hire outside firms to conduct their external or internal investigations. In many jurisdictions, the public sector occasionally hires a private sector company to provide specific investigative expertise (such as forensic accounting) in a police investigation. Such an arrangement may point to a future expansion of cooperation between the public and private sectors.

1.3 MANAGEMENT ISSUES IN INVESTIGATIONS

This section examines management issues pertaining to security and criminal investigations in the corporate environment. Topics include organizing for investigations; managing investigations at the strategic, operational, and case levels; and a variety of related subjects, such as legal concerns and liaisons.

Like any other corporate or organizational function, managing investigations entails basic functions of management: planning, organizing, directing, coordinating, and controlling. *Figure 1-1* shows that all five of these functions apply at each level of investigative management: the strategic level, the operational level, and the case level.

	STRATEGIC	OPERATIONAL	CASE
PLAN	✓	✓	✓
ORGANIZE	✓	✓	✓
DIRECT	✓	✓	✓
COORDINATE	✓	✓	✓
CONTROL	✓	✓	✓

Source: Webster University, 2004

FIGURE 1-1

Investigative Management Functions at Each Level

The strategic level involves the high-level management of the entire unit and its relationship with the company's executive leadership. Legal counsel must be involved at this level to ensure the proper focus of the investigation as it relates to company policy and procedure or civil or criminal statute. This is also where the formal retention of the investigators should occur to establish attorney work product protection. Issues at this level include who will head the investigative function, where it will fit in the organizational structure, what its strategic goals and objectives will be, where it will focus its efforts, and how financial and personnel resources will be allocated to the function.

The operational level deals with the technical aspects of the investigative function and how the function works within its department. Such issues as case load, case assessment, quality control, investigative policies and procedures, reporting formats, liaison, team composition, supplies and equipment, evidence management, and outside contracts are considered at this level.

The case level involves individual investigations and the particular investigators, investigative techniques, and case management protocols associated with them (Webster University, 2004).

The IU chief[1] must think at all three of these levels while simultaneously considering factors that transcend the investigative management levels.

Goals and objectives are critical to the investigations functions at all three levels. Goals articulate long-term and overarching end states and may be stated in general terms. Goals should be consistent with the parent organization's strategic direction and should be incorporated into the IU's mission statement.

Objectives are based on the goals but are more specific and may be more short-lived. They are generally measurable and can be used to gauge the progress, success, or achievement of a unit. Specific, measurable goals are also known as metrics in modern organizations. Metrics can be used to evaluate the performance of individuals, teams, and organizations; however, they must be related to the overall goals rather than being viewed as an end in themselves. Moreover, any investigative strategies developed must be compatible with the organization's overall strategic business plan.

Investigative objectives tend to be tactical and specific to the short-term expectations of the project. When developing the tactical objectives for an investigative project, the IU chief should consult the organization's tactical business plan to ensure compatibility. For example, an allegation may arise from an undercover project. If an investigation is launched, its objectives should remain consistent with the objectives of the overall project. Changes to operational objectives need to be carefully considered and treated as change orders in project management terms.

A significant issue that transcends the three levels of investigative management is that of ethics. From an organizational perspective, publishing written standards of ethical behavior, adopting a zero tolerance policy for breaches of ethical behavior and imposing penalties on those who commit such breaches will have a major impact. Although ethical lapses have plagued both the public and the private investigative community throughout history, a lack of solid ethical standards can seriously damage the effectiveness of an IU or individual investigators. This is true primarily because investigators and IUs rely on their credibility and respectability in order to be effective in gathering, corroborating, and integrating facts.

Almost all human sources upon whom investigators depend—victims, witnesses, first responders, liaison contacts, subject matter experts, and informants—provide information based on some level of trust in the investigator or agency. A reputation for unethical behavior has a significant adverse impact on that trust relationship and therefore reduces the amount, accuracy, or candor of information provided. It can also

---

[1] The investigative unit chief is the person directly responsible for the investigative function in an organization and might also be called chief security officer, security director, director of investigations, or another title.

damage the respect a unit enjoys within the corporate structure and thus can affect how the IU is used and how its members are treated.

The following examples of unethical or dishonest behavior are unacceptable in professional investigations:

- selectively opening, closing, rushing, or stalling investigations based on a relationship between the investigator or unit and the victim, suspect, or other key player or based on a desire for personal gain

- improperly handling evidence in order to influence the outcome of an investigation

- improperly handling evidence or investigative information through incompetence

- fabricating evidence or investigative information

- making inappropriate threats or promises during an interview or interrogation

- compromising sensitive investigative information

- using scientifically unproven, unreliable, inappropriate, or unnecessarily heavy-handed investigative techniques

- mistreating liaison contacts (e.g., providing misleading or false information or inappropriately exploiting the relationship)

- lying during judicial or administrative proceedings

Any of the preceding activities should result in the harshest punishment for the offender. Such behavior by a member of an investigative team can damage any prior investigations upon which the person worked. Everything the investigator has done in an official capacity before the discovery of the unethical behavior is now suspect.

Besides diminishing effectiveness, unethical behavior can leave an organization open to civil or criminal liability. IU chiefs must make ethics an underlying pillar of their operations, procedures, and relationships, as well as instilling the importance of ethical behavior in investigative personnel. A *Security Management* article noted that experienced investigators know "they are more likely to solve a case with thoroughness and a dogged pursuit of the truth than from heavy-handed tactics or trickery" (Albrecht, 2004, p. 85).

The remainder of *Section 1.3* provides information on organizing and managing IUs and personnel, as well as some key issues that IU managers must consider.

ORGANIZING FOR INVESTIGATIONS

In organizations that have not previously had an IU or where the IU is being expanded, redesigned, or otherwise modified, one of the first decisions is how to organize the function. For small organizations with infrequent investigative needs, the use of an outside agency or contract service (outsourcing) is the logical choice. Many small organizations keep qualified investigative consultants or private investigators on retainer to respond quickly to various issues that require an investigative response. In this way, investigative expenses are generally limited to the cost of specific inquiries and are incurred only when the need arises.

In larger organizations or other environments with a constant need for investigative services, a full-time investigator or investigative staff may be justified. The rationale for an investigative capability depends, in part, on the organization's needs. Matters that require investigations in the corporate arena may include personnel background investigations (BIs), product safety or tampering issues, white-collar crimes (including procurement fraud, other types of fraud, and embezzlement), employee misconduct, theft and pilferage, information loss, due diligence, information technology (IT) systems abuse, and regulatory compliance.

Most medium-sized to large companies have enough work to keep an investigator or investigative staff busy, particularly as investigative needs and regulatory issues become increasingly complex in the 21st century. The primary goal of a compliance investigation is to provide guidance regarding possible or potential violations of regulatory requirements.

In almost all situations, cost is a major factor in the decision to outsource or maintain an internal investigative capability. Cost elements include personnel expenses, contracts and retainers, equipment, consumables, and office expenses. Return on investment can be demonstrated by using restitution figures. The cost-benefit analysis is a useful tool to determine whether to outsource the investigative unit.

Investigative budgets are difficult to predict accurately, as one or two major unexpected cases can result in substantial unplanned costs. The best approach is to base budget estimates on historical data, quantitative estimates of risk avoidance, support of organizational goals and factor in projected changes. Changes in the company (e.g., growth, new facilities, international expansion, new markets, etc.) or changes in applicable regulations can significantly impact IU budgets. If no historical information is available, attempts should be made to benchmark with companies that are similar in size, location and mission. Costs for equipment, supplies, outside services, travel (both local and out-of-area), administrative support, and contract or personnel management should also be factored in.

Outsourced investigations can be managed in a way that passes the charges for the investigation over to the business unit where or on whose behalf the investigation is performed. This cost then affects the budget of the user and only for the actual cost of services.

Figure 1-2 summarizes the major advantages and disadvantages of outsourcing investigative needs and maintaining an internal IU or capability.

	OUTSOURCING	INTERNAL
ADVANTAGES	• Ability to expand or reduce workforce according to actual needs • Responsibility for equipment, supplies, and training can be transferred to the contractor • Specialists and experts can be called in as needed • Can be more cost-effective • Minimizes overhead costs • Investigators may have a broader base of expertise and experience • Gives independent, outside objective appearance to investigation	• Company exercises complete control of the investigative process and people • Ability to maintain closer liaison with local agencies and internal contacts • Better ability to protect sensitive information and keep it inside the organization • Investigators usually have much greater familiarity with the organization, mission, culture, and structure
DISADVANTAGES	• Quality control is largely in the hands of the contractor • Investigators may not be as familiar with the client's company, mission, organization, and culture • Requires contract management effort	• High cost of maintaining an internal investigative capability • Need to maintain equipment that may not be used for a lengthy period • Need to maintain an investigative staff, including training, licensing, and personnel management • Especially if there is litigation, the investigation may be tainted as it has been conducted under company direction

Source: K. Peterson, 2004

FIGURE 1-2

Investigative Services—Outsourcing Versus Internal

1.3.1 FITTING THE INVESTIGATIVE MISSION INTO THE ORGANIZATION

Precisely where in an organization an IU fits—and how it is used—varies a great deal from one organization to the next. For example, many commercial firms maintain an IU as part of the security department or under the chief security officer (CSO), while others may not have a dedicated investigative capability. Optimally, the structure of an investigative function is the result of a needs assessment and a cost-benefit analysis. All too often, however, this important decision is made indiscriminately, arbitrarily, or in a vacuum. Senior security, assets protection, or risk management professionals should advise executive leaders on realistic investigative needs and the most effective structure for meeting those needs.

The following are among the most common structures for an investigative capability in companies and other organizations:

- a separate IU with the unit chief (or senior investigator) reporting to the corporate security director or CSO

- a separate IU with the unit chief (or senior investigator) reporting to the risk management or assets protection director

- a separate IU with the unit chief (or senior investigator) reporting to the legal department

- specialized investigations supported by internal audit or IT

- investigations performed by an independent function, such as an inspector general or equivalent, which reports directly to senior executive management

- investigations conducted by the security director personally since no dedicated IU or investigator exists

- security director oversight of an outsourced investigative capability, calling on an outside vendor as needed under a prearranged agreement

In larger or more geographically dispersed firms, regional IUs or personnel maybe established in order to conserve travel costs and time. This arrangement also allows for investigators who are familiar with local issues (culture, geography, procedures, laws, regulations, etc.) and provides an opportunity to work more effectively with local liaison contacts.

Companies may also establish separate investigative capabilities within different business units. For example, there may be one IU for the commercial division and one for the government division, or for the consumer products division and the business-to-business division.

Another key issue in organizing for investigations is to recognize particular focus areas for the IU. The primary need in some organizations is personnel screening, while others may focus on employee misconduct, external theft, or fraud prevention and detection. The IU should consider the primary focus areas when organizing the unit, hiring and training personnel, arranging office space, purchasing equipment and supplies, developing communication mechanisms, and establishing relationships. However, managers must recognize (and tell the executive leadership) that other types of investigations may and probably will arise. In other words, it should be no surprise that an IU primarily focused on BIs may suddenly have to deal with an assault or theft case. Investigators should be prepared for this eventuality—mentally and in terms of equipment, contacts, and possible outside investigative service vendors.

The lineup of liaison contacts, potential outside sources for investigative services, specialists, and equipment vendors should be tailored to the primary focus areas of the IU (but, as mentioned above, should include some flexibility). Whether the investigative capability of an organization consists of a dedicated unit, a single investigator, the security director alone, or another arrangement, a specific individual (with a backup) should be designated to manage these outside investigative resources. This provides continuity and facilitates rapid implementation of capabilities. Investigative needs generally arise on short notice and on a surge basis.

Two other issues concerning how the investigative mission fits into an organization are the reporting chain and the physical location of the investigative capability. The reporting chain for investigative information or results is critical and can affect both the outcome of specific cases and the effectiveness of the unit itself. Generally, the shortest reporting chain between the source of the information and the final decision maker is best. Many times, especially if litigation is expected or some culpability of the company is suspected, the investigator should deliver the report directly to and only to the legal counsel of record for the company. Doing so protects the overall investigation as attorney work product. Legal counsel can then maintain attorney-client privilege while advising the company.

The final decision maker might be the chief executive officer, chief operating officer, chief legal counsel, president, or some other official. It is important to identify the decision maker, establish a close working (and trust) relationship with him or her, and develop a formal reporting mechanism. In some situations, it may be advisable to establish an alternate or contingency reporting mechanism in case the identified decision maker is unavailable or is possibly involved in the investigative matter.

The reporting chain does not necessarily need to follow the day-to-day organization chart or supervisory chain. In some organizations, following a nonstandard path maybe uncomfortable or run counter to corporate culture. That is why an inspector general function, with a direct, independent reporting channel to the decision maker, may work best in some structures.

The physical location of investigators or the IU may also be a factor in some instances. The physical location should provide the unit with adequate access to the officials and departments with which it must interact most closely. These usually include the executive office, general counsel, human resources, internal audit, and security. On the other hand, the unit may operate more effectively if it is remote from departments that attempt to micromanage investigative activity.

The following are key considerations in selecting the physical location and layout of the IU:

- access to key information and people
- privacy
- the need to call people in or access them for interviews (if applicable)
- the need to move quickly around the facility (or to other facilities)
- the possible need to store large amounts of information or evidence
- secure storage space for equipment and supplies
- communications needs

Ideally, the UI would have a soundproof room with ample space for the investigation team to work together and post exhibits (pictures, maps, etc.). The room should have Internet access, telephones, and whiteboards, and it should be secured when not in use. Some teams refer such a location as a *war room*.

Finally, investigative functions and capability within an organization may expand or contract as the business environment evolves. For example, a company with IUs around the world may decrease the number of such units during corporate belt tightening. Similarly, the company may eliminate the regional units and consolidate investigative functions at corporate headquarters. Outsourcing of investigations in these regions can be a solution to this retrenchment.

The corporate response to criminal and unethical behavior may also change over time. Where, once, a company would aggressively pursue both internal and external allegations of wrongdoing, the new paradigm might be to address only cases that might lead to major restitution or recovery or that may have a high profile. Alternatively, a firm might choose to spend scarce investigative resources on particular types of activity, for example taking a heavy hand against IT-related abuses, while disregarding minor thefts or misappropriations. The economic downturn and resulting new corporate governance regulations have made minor thefts more significant. New government regulations have required companies to take swift and decisive action when they become aware of a violation of these regulations.

These variations, evolutions, or cycles of emphasis can occur as the financial health of an enterprise ebbs and flows, as an industry sector evolves, or as public awareness of an issue surfaces. For example, in the aftermath of the September 11, 2001, attacks on the World Trade Center and the Pentagon, much of the investigative focus at the FBI shifted from organized and economic crime to counterterrorism activities. Similarly, the emphasis within the corporate arena on fraud and financial mismanagement expanded significantly in the wake of the Enron and WorldCom scandals of 2001 and 2002. Those responsible for the investigative function within organizations must build in the agility to accomplish key investigative objectives in a dynamic environment.

1.3.2 OUTSOURCING INVESTIGATIONS

For a corporate investigative function, outsourcing can mean (1) complete outsourcing of the investigative function to an outside agency under contract or (2) contracting out for selected or specialized investigative support services as needed.

The decision to outsource and the outsourcing approach are usually based on a cost-benefit analysis and projected overall investigative needs. Almost without exception, organizations are cost-conscious, and many have only sporadic investigative requirements. In addition, some prefer an independent source when it comes to investigations. Another common reason for contracting out is an overall corporate policy that encourages outsourcing of peripheral services. Contracting for full-scope investigative services is less common than obtaining services on an as-needed basis. Outsourcing for specialized and expert services, however, is almost always an important part of the budget and the approach to meeting the organization's investigative needs.

The following are specialized services that are commonly called on to support corporate investigations:

- computer forensics
- forensic auditing
- handwriting analysis
- questioned document examination
- statement analysis
- forensic psychology
- forensic polygraph (where legal)
- technical surveillance or countersurveillance to provide a deterrent to criminal activity
- investigative project management (specialized projects, undercover work, labor disruptions, etc.)
- criminal behavioral science or profiling
- physical evidence collection
- laboratory services
- audio or video enhancement
- criminal intelligence analysis

- brand integrity investigations requiring geographic density
- international investigations with local knowledge or contacts

Whether a full-scope or a specialized service provider is needed, finding the right vendor or combination of vendors can be a challenge. Two key decisions concern the size of the preferred vendor and whether the required services will be distinct or bundled. A large, nationally or internationally recognized provider can bring a significant set of resources to the project. However, smaller firms also have advantages and frequently offer a more personalized service commitment or local experience. In addition, the use of smaller firms may be recommended for specialized or expert support services since the needed expertise maybe the specific forte and particular interest of the provider. There may also be a cost and availability variance between larger and smaller providers. One should be wary of smaller or local firms that boast of being expert in all aspects of investigations. It is extremely rare for a firm to have significant expertise in areas as diverse as computer forensics, ballistic analysis, BIs, and executive kidnapping cases.

Regardless of the size and scope of the preferred vendor, clear criteria for potential service providers should be established and enforced. It is recommended that vendors be preapproved through a vetting process. The following are some important questions to ask and consider in the vendor identification and selection process:

- Does the provider have a reputation for ethical and honest service?
- Does the provider have the demonstrated technical expertise necessary to meet the client's particular requirements?
- Is the provider licensed in all the geographic areas to which the client's investigative needs might lead?
- Are the provider's investigators trained and certified in the techniques and equipment to be used?
- Has the provider served other companies in the client's industry?
- Has the provider served other companies in the client's geographic area?
- Does the provider have the personnel and physical resources to respond to the client's short-notice, long-term, and high-demand investigative needs?
- Does the provider have a talented, experienced, and stable investigative workforce?
- What is the provider's billing structure (including peripheral, as-needed, and sub-contracted services as well as reimbursable expenses)?
- Does the provider maintain professional relationships with liaison contacts, agencies, and other firms (including potential subcontractors) that can enhance its operational effectiveness?
- What mechanisms does the provider employ for quality assurance and contract performance feedback?

- What mechanisms does the provider employ (both formal and informal) for communications with the client, on both a routine and non-routine basis?

- Is the provider known for safeguarding information and protecting the interests of its clients?

- For full-scope providers, does the firm have internal capabilities for specialized and as-needed support, such as surveillance, technical services, computer forensics, etc.?

- What is the professional background of the firm's principals and key personnel?

- What is the acquisition and merger history of the provider firm?

- What professional, civic, and business associations are the provider affiliated with?

- Does the vendor maintain adequate professional liability insurance coverage?

Identifying Potential Vendors. One source of information on potential service providers is word-of-mouth recommendations from colleagues and counterparts. This form of benchmarking can yield candid, valuable information.

Another excellent strategy is to use trusted information sources, such as the *Security Industry Buyers Guide* from ASIS International or membership-based networks like Intellenet (www.intelnetwork.org/locator.asp), which lists vetted private investigators and investigative services firms. In addition, most U.S. states and Canadian provinces and many nations around the globe have professional associations of private investigators and investigative firms. These associations generally impose a code of ethics and training and licensing requirements on their members and often have a vetting process. Associations can also help clients find qualified vendors in particular regions.

Once a vendor is selected, the IU chief should ensure that key provisions or clauses of the contract pass through to any consultants or subcontractors the vendor may use. This is especially important with respect to such issues as evidence handling, information protection, public release of information, licensing requirements, availability to testify, and liability matters.

Ultimately, the responsibility for ensuring the proper training and licensing of contract investigators lies with the hiring organization (i.e., the company issuing the contract). These issues should always be thoroughly explored and verified during the source selection process. Some less reputable firms have been known to loosely interpret applicable licensing, training, and weapons qualification requirements.

1.3.3 ESTABLISHING AN IU

There is no typical organizational structure for the investigative mission in the corporate environment. Factors such as the industry and the company's mission, size, and scope all play a role in determining how the investigative function looks and how fits in the organization. When establishing or reengineering an investigative function, the IU chief should use the information provided previously in this chapter as a starting point for the thought process. He or she should work with the executive leadership to ensure decisions are not made on an emotional, spur-of-the-moment, or uninformed basis. The structure and operation of an organization's investigative function can have a great impact on the financial and operational health of the organization.

Functional Charters and Policy Statements. The IU is given credibility and authority through a functional charter issued by the CEO or an equivalent officer. This concise document (often one page or less) states the purpose and direction of the investigative function within the organization and lays out the unit's strategic goals. It defines who is responsible for the investigative function, the nature and primary emphasis of the function, and the essential internal relationships with the rest of the organization.

The next level of definition for the unit is usually a policy statement. This document outlines procedures for initiating and conducting investigations, and it addresses reporting channels, coordination mechanisms, and disposition. The policy statement applies to other departments in the organization as well. For example, it advises the human resources department on how to request personnel BIs.

A third level of definition for the new or reengineered unit is a set of objectives. Unlike the functional charter and policy statement, the objectives will be revised on a fairly frequent (usually annual) basis. The objectives for the unit will include performance metrics and targets for areas of improvement over the subsequent period.

Developing a well-thought-out and mission-tailored functional charter, policy statement, and set of objectives at the outset of establishing an IU contributes immeasurably to both the smooth introduction and the long-term effectiveness of the unit.

The next step in the process is identifying and garnering appropriate resources for the unit based on the previously developed foundation documents. Resources can be categorized as human, physical, and other.

Human Resources

To estimate the appropriate size of the unit, it is necessary to consider the projected case load, nature of cases, geographic area covered, and administrative or other support needs. If staffing needs cannot be accurately projected or benchmarked, the best approach is to start small, using outsourced resources when required, and grow the unit over time if necessary.

The expected type of cases is a key determinant in unit size. For example, the caseload per investigator can normally be much higher for BIs than for complex procurement fraud cases. Therefore, a unit that handles mainly fraud cases will likely require a more robust (and experienced) investigative complement as well as additional administrative and support staff than a unit that focuses mainly on BI work.

Selecting professional personnel is an important aspect of setting up a proprietary IU. While information, interrogation, and instrumentation are referred to as the three "I's" of an investigator, the complexity and profile of typical investigations within a unit will dictate the qualifications, education, and experience required of successful candidates. Many positions in today's corporate environment require backgrounds in specialized fields, such as computer investigations, contract fraud, or financial crimes.

Historically, a large percentage of corporate investigative personnel come from a public sector investigative or law enforcement background. The primary advantages of such a background are experience, excellent training, and a proven record of performance. It also facilitates the development of close liaison relationships with law enforcement agencies and other first responders. However, an experienced public sector investigator or law enforcement officer may or may not fit well into the corporate environment. Candidates must be able to operate effectively in a business environment, interface with senior executive management, and interact well with corporate staff members at all levels and in all specialties. Among the differences are the lines of authority and jurisdiction, the investigative objectives (to some degree), and the nature of the relationships and coordination requirements. They should have the ability to use investigative tools such as scatter graphs to identify weaknesses in manual or computerized systems. In short, the transition from public sector law enforcement to corporate investigations is sometimes a difficult one and is often very personality-dependent.

Investigator Qualifications. Criteria should include both the professional qualifications and the personal traits of the individual. On the following pages are recommended qualifications and traits to consider when hiring or assigning investigative personnel (Webster University, 2004):

Professional Qualifications

Education. Formal education is a point to consider. Many investigative positions require at least a bachelor's degree. Although the formal education may not be specific to the investigative field, it does connote a general level of intelligence, maturity and discipline as well as knowledge of a breadth of topic areas. A college education familiarizes people with structures and processes of culture and society that foster insights in the events and circumstances that real-world investigators encounter in the course of their professional work. Education also demonstrates an investigator's ability to continue learning because specialists and experts will require specialized education—often including advanced degrees—in their particular field (e.g., forensic science, behavioral psychology, etc.).

Training. An important factor in evaluating candidates is the training they have received. A wide variety of courses are available in general investigative techniques and specific aspects of investigations. Sources range from public sector law enforcement agencies to colleges and commercial vendors. The level of training, currency of the training and the training source (i.e., agency or school) should be carefully considered.

Certification. Related certifications such as PCI (Professional Certified Investigator; ASIS International, www.asisonline.org/certification/pci/pciabout.xml) or CFE (Certified Fraud Examiner; Association of Certified Fraud Examiners, www.cfenet.com/cfe/) indicate a demonstrated level of knowledge as well as an individual's commitment to the field and effort to maintain currency. Professional certifications should be given significant weight in recruiting and considering applicants, and for advancement.

Experience (General). Actual investigative experience is frequently the most important qualification, and should be carefully considered. As a rule of thumb, candidates should possess two years experience actually conducting investigations, preferably a variety of types of investigations. General experience should include interviews and interrogations, evidence handling, liaison, surveillance, record searches, photography, reporting and presentation of cases. Often times, individuals equate police patrol experience to investigations. However, there is not a sufficient correlation unless specific and detailed investigative activity was included.

Experience (Specialized). Specific experience in the relevant industry, in the business environment or in an investigative specialty is generally a plus—sometimes a significant one. This allows the investigator to bring not only expertise to the new position, but also a valuable suite of lessons learned and best practices, many of which can be transferred to enhance the effectiveness of the unit. Of course some "specialist" positions will require specialized experience as well. Fairly detailed information about specialized experience should be requested from applicants for positions which require those skills.

Communications Skills. This is one of the most critical skills needed by an investigator. The ability to elicit information (the core of any investigation) from all sorts of people, both cooperative and uncooperative, with many different perspectives and at different levels is absolutely essential. In addition, the investigator must be highly effective at presenting information orally and in writing to senior executives, attorneys, prosecutors, law enforcement personnel, security professionals. They must be simultaneously concise and convincing, balancing facts with conclusions. Although communications skills are to some degree, a personal trait, they should more correctly be considered a professional qualification.

Personal Traits

High Ethical Standards. Personal suitability for the position is key. Candidates must have a demonstrated background of trustworthiness and professional ethics. This trait will permeate every aspect of the individual's relationship with the unit and everyone he/she comes in contact with as a representative of the organization.

Persistence. An important trait of the successful investigator is an appropriate level of persistence. The investigative process often leads to apparent dead ends or other frustrations. The ability to forge ahead toward a successful case resolution or objective despite obstacles proves to be of significant value.

Balance. At the same time, however, the individual must be able to draw an appropriate balance between aggressively pursuing a successful outcome and following established rules and protocols (so as not to threaten the legal basis of the case or unduly raise the liability risk to the organization).

Maturity. A mature and realistic view of self and surroundings is an important trait for anyone who deals with investigative matters, private information, legal issues and activities that can affect people's lives and careers—and the organization itself. It allows an individual to keep their activities in perspective and place information, events and situations within the appropriate context.

Ability to Deal Effectively with People. Despite our techno-centric society, people form the core of almost every investigation worldwide in both the public and private sector. The ability to deal with all types of people, in every role, in a highly effective manner is absolutely essential to an investigator.

Self-Motivating and Self-Starting. In most environments, investigators operate with very little direct management oversight (other than from a legal and regulatory perspective) and are expected to perform independently. The ability to motivate oneself in combination with an inherent inner drive is of extreme value.

Ability to Multitask. The ability to manage several activities simultaneously is an extremely useful attribute for an investigator. Each investigation has numerous elements—and often a large number of information inputs. In addition, most investigators are assigned several investigations at any given time.

Professional Demeanor. In all aspects of the investigative function including dealing with people, collecting and analyzing information and presenting facts and conclusions, the investigator must maintain a professional demeanor. To do otherwise will threaten his or her effectiveness as well as the unit's (and the organization's) credibility.

Good Observational Skills. Skill-in-observation (curiosity is most important) of people, places, activities and situations is a key element of any investigation and feeds the information base for a particular case as well as helping direct future investigative steps and direction. People with excellent observation, interpretation and correlation skills often make good investigators.

Flexibility. An individual who can operate smoothly in a wide variety of environments, is comfortable in a range of situations and can distinguish between when to yield and when to persist will be a far more effective investigator than an inflexible person.

Additional Perspectives. One highly experienced security professional suggests that the best investigators are people who have good math skills. In many respects, an investigation is an analytical process (Thompson, 2004). Another individual, a veteran federal investigator, names the traits of a good investigator in *Figure 1-3*.

• One who seeks the truth	• One who functions with minimal supervision
• One who is not in a rush to judge	• One who can convey detailed information
• One who is methodical and thorough	• One who has good recall
• One who is not too aggressive	• One who has good powers of observation
• One who abides by the rules of law	• One who wants to excel at law enforcement
• One who accepts challenges	• One who wants to succeed
• One who is impartial	• One who has patience
• One who is secure with him/herself	• One who has an understanding family
• One who has stamina	• One who is familiar with his/her community
• One who is a team player	• One who stays current on new/changing judicial procedures and current events

Source: Jackson, 1999

FIGURE 1-3

Traits of a Good Investigator

Physical Resources

Office Space. Although it may not be the first thing to come to mind when considering the needs of an IU, office space is an important issue. In today's office environment, many layouts are based on a cubicle model rather than private offices. This can be a serious concern for the IU, especially if the office space is shared with other departments or functions. If possible, private or semiprivate offices should be assigned for the investigative staff, who will also need file storage space, a production room (with a fax machine, copier, printers, mailing equipment, etc.), and an interview or meeting room. If cubicles are the only alternative, there should at least be a couple of private offices that can be used for interviews, file storage, team meetings, and private phone conversations.

In addition, complex investigations are usually facilitated by the use of a manual storyboard (e.g., a dry-erase board) or electronic software for tracking leads, posting investigative links (link analysis), and planning follow-on steps. This information, like other investigative data, must be protected from view by anyone not directly associated with the investigative team. Use of a war room may help.

Evidence Storage. Although not all units will have a need for evidence storage facilities—and if they do have a need, it may be sporadic—consideration should be given to preparing for either temporary or long-term evidence storage. Keys or lock combinations to the evidence storage area should be given to only a few individuals. In addition, most evidence storage rooms are outfitted with individual lockable containers. A separately zoned intrusion detection system is also appropriate in most circumstances.

Records and File Storage. Many investigative files are highly sensitive or confidential and are subject to both practical and legal access restrictions. In addition, files and records have widely varying retention requirements. Thus, it is important to ensure that adequate secure storage is available for records and that records are organized in such a way that they can easily be identified for retention and destruction (or disposition) at the appropriate time. All documents and evidence should be retained—in their original format—until all legal action, including appeals, is complete.

In some circumstances, records can more easily be stored electronically. Such storage requires less physical space and often results in more efficient retrieval, but some precautions are in order. Secure backup copies should be stored off-site and should be immediately accessible should the primary data, the computer system, or the IU facility become unavailable (e.g., due to cyber attack, natural disaster, or other catastrophe). In addition, even if investigative records and associated information are digitized, the original documents, photographs, and other items may need to be preserved in some instances. Items that may be needed as evidence (such as photographs and original written statements) must not be destroyed or disposed of.

Investigative Supplies and Equipment. Private sector IUs vary widely in the type and amount of equipment they require. Some units focus on investigations involving interviews and reporting. Other units may conduct equipment-intensive investigations requiring evidence collection and handling, technical equipment, and consumables.

Most IUs need at least a cursory evidence collection kit and some audio and visual recording equipment. A voice-activated digital recorder and digital camera often suffice. The unit should consider its needs realistically and outfit itself accordingly. In some firms, it may be possible to borrow audio or video recording and processing equipment from the audiovisual department or its equivalent.

Original evidence (of an audiovisual or IT nature) must not be compromised or questioned due to duplication, enhancement, or other technical manipulation. Investigative personnel must be thoroughly familiar with any equipment before employing it in an actual operation. Investigators should test it under different conditions (e.g., light levels, microphone locations, background noise, etc.) and practice its use.

Physical Investigative Aids. Although extensive crime laboratory equipment is not needed in most environments, some simple investigative aids are often helpful. Examples of items that are stocked at many corporate IUs include a latent fingerprint kit, evidence bags and containers, latex gloves, and evidence marking or identification materials. The marking and identification materials come in many forms, including substances that fluoresce under ultraviolet light, barcode labels, etching pens, and even radio-frequency identification (RFID) devices and global positioning system (GPS) tracking devices. Law enforcement and investigative supply firms offer various kits that combine a number of the required investigative aids at a reasonable cost.

Other Equipment. Consideration should also be given to the computer equipment needed to support the mission. In addition to administrative requirements, computers may be needed for digital records management as well as computer forensics work and electronic evidence storage. Other possible equipment needs for the unit include covert surveillance equipment such as photographic equipment for use during disability claims, vehicles, and communications systems. Covert surveillance equipment is no longer expensive and wireless technology makes installation easy and efficient. Some basic equipment should be available for quick deployment. If it is purchased, it should be properly maintained and any personnel who will be using it should be thoroughly trained.

If the unit will be assigned a vehicle, a low-profile vehicle, not marked with company markings, is preferable. Communications equipment might include cellular phones, personal digital assistants (PDAs, such as Blackberry wireless devices), and office telephones. In some instances, a telephone with a prefix different from that of other company phones might be appropriate. Secure communications devices might also be useful in some environments. Procedures should be established for the use of this type of equipment as well as for communications security.

Additional Resources

Other unit resources, both tangible and intangible, that must be planned for include the following:

Training. The investigative team will require a significant amount of training, and both time and money must be allotted for it. Training includes informal, internal training as well as attendance at courses and conferences. Training requirements for specialists is more substantial than for general investigators, but all unit members need some degree of recurring and upgrade training to remain current on investigative techniques and legal issues and to enhance their skills.

Relationships. Relationships and liaison contacts, both internal and external, should be viewed as a resource and must be deliberately developed. This is especially true when the investigative function is first established.

Communications. Effective channels for communications within the organization and with outside entities (such as law enforcement and other external liaison contacts) must be established. Procedures for information sharing, case briefings, support requests, and resource allocation should be clear and realistic. The communications channels that are developed will be both formal and informal and should include procedures for both routine and crisis situations.

Financial resources. Budgets and financial management are always important issues, particularly when establishing a new function or unit. Budgets should be carefully planned and based on the best possible projections. Within some organizational structures and cultures, it makes sense to collaborate with other departments (e.g., facilities, security, safety, legal, risk management, etc.) to leverage one another's budget allocations.

Information assets. The lifeblood of the investigative mission is information, and a wide variety of information assets must be established at the outset and maintained throughout the life of an IU. Among these assets are recruitment, handling and case wrap-up of informants, liaison contacts, databases (internal and external), access to key personnel within the organization, open source information, and operational data. In addition, the IU should establish (or arrange for access to) an employee hot line for complaints, allegations, tips, and other relevant information. An employee hot line is a cost effective way to obtain information with regard to employee malfeasance.

Geographic assets. Most organizations today span a large geographic area, and many operate globally. Having information sources, liaison contacts, contingency vendors, and other resources available to support investigations in each general area where the organization operates makes good business sense and creates efficiencies. Prearranging these relationships and pre-staging equipment, supplies, and perhaps investigative personnel can contribute greatly to efficient and successful investigative operations.

MANAGING INVESTIGATIONS

For both new and well-established investigative functions, numerous management issues warrant attention at both the strategic and day-to-day levels. This section addresses several important issues in four key subject areas: investigative functions, investigative resources, unit management, and case management.

1.3.4 INVESTIGATIVE FUNCTIONS

Most IUs focus on a particular function or set of functions. They may range from relatively simple activities such as documenting facts surrounding a security force response to a workplace incident to complex procurement fraud investigations. These functions are generally referred to as types of investigations, and frequently the unit's incident management system is organized according to incident types. The following are typical types of investigations in the corporate and organizational arena:

- incident or accident
- employee misconduct
- misuse or abuse of computer or IT system
- substance abuse
- due diligence
- regulatory compliance violation
- lifestyle or financial inquiries for corporate executives and personnel
- personnel security or background
- theft, pilferage, or misappropriation
- lapping (crediting one account with money from another account)
- assaults and crimes against persons
- property damage and vandalism
- inventory discrepancies or unexplained shrinkage
- sabotage
- industrial espionage
- copyright and proprietary information violations
- embezzlement or defalcation (appropriation of property by a person to whom it has been entrusted)
- fraud (general, procurement, insurance, travel, accounting, etc.)
- product tampering (actual and hoax)
- diverted or counterfeit product

- skimming (keeping some of the cash)

- communicating threats

- harassment (including sexual harassment)

- workplace violence (actual or potential)

- litigation support (varying according to whether the enterprise is the complainant or respondent in a particular case)

Other types of investigations are conducted in various industries and environments. In some sectors an IU may be employed to directly support the core mission of the organization. For example, a real estate firm may use its unit to determine the whereabouts of unknown property owners or conduct difficult title searches. Similarly, IUs are sometimes used to support market research, competitive intelligence, and other corporate functions. The bottom line in many organizations is that the IU is seen as a corporate resource and is employed in ways that support overall business objectives.

IU managers (and security directors where applicable) must understand how the investigative capability fits into the organization and how the executive leadership envisions its application (i.e., the big picture). Optimally, the investigations unit manager or security director plays a key role in defining that fit and the nature of the investigative functions. This role may vary from direct to subtle depending on the environment and leadership style, but wherever possible, investigations and security professionals should exert as strong an influence as possible, recognizing the overall business objective.

Section 1.4 provides more detailed information on some of the more significant types of investigations in the private sector. Among them are incident investigations (which are the most common type of investigation in many organizations), compliance investigations, background investigations, and substance abuse investigations. One particularly important but often neglected type is the due diligence investigation. Before entering into a new business relationship, a prudent organization will conduct an inquiry to verify the information provided by the proposed business associate. This activity is normally requested at the close of business negotiations and must be completed in a timely manner. The skilled investigator is able to confirm the assets, liabilities, legal problems, potential conflicts of interest, and any undisclosed affiliations or identities of the subject quickly.

1.3.5 INVESTIGATIVE RESOURCES

The principal resources of an IU are people, information, credibility, physical assets, and financial assets. The primary functional focus dictates how the unit is structured and how the resources are allocated and applied. For example, the focus affects what types of investigators are hired, what information acquisition mechanisms are put in place, how and where the unit is structured, and the type of equipment and supplies it requires. Focus also largely frames the IU's budget requests to the parent organization.

Investigative funding needs are often difficult to project because they can be drastically affected by one or a few major cases as well as new regulatory requirements or legislation. Therefore, justifying investigative budget requests is a daunting task.

One of the best ways to help achieve a favorable budget request is to show value to the organization or to demonstrate that the unit pays for itself. Support for budget justifications can be bolstered by any or all of the following:

- proper investigative focus to support the organizational mission as well as strategic and business goals
- accurate and detailed tracking of investigative costs
- effective implementation of cost management and efficiency measures
- demonstration of restitution and recovery benefits
- quantitative estimation of risk avoidance in monetary terms

Carefully tracking and managing operational and overhead costs can significantly improve the response to funding requests. Costs can be tracked by case type, location, business unit, or other variable. Additionally, recoveries and restitution figures should be tracked and reported to senior management to help demonstrate a financial benefit to the organization and support return on investment (ROI) arguments. Often, IUs can demonstrate ROI through civil recovery efforts, recovering not only the losses but also the related investigative costs.

Costs for personnel and outside services generally represent the largest budget items for an IU, while overhead costs are often the easiest to control. IU managers should leverage the use of liaison contacts and other organizational departments (such as IT, facilities, accounting and finance, legal, and risk management) to conserve financial resources.

1.3.6 UNIT MANAGEMENT

IU managers face a significant challenge in balancing the administrative and operational responsibilities of their positions. *Figure 1-4* shows the life cycle of the investigative process. It illustrates many of the functions that occur at the unit level and fall under the broad responsibilities of the IU manager. The chart is divided into four phases. The first shows various ways by which an investigation is initiated (e.g., incident report, audit, discrepancy report, or request for investigation). It includes both the reason for the investigation and the mechanism by which the case is opened. The second phase is the investigation itself, and the chart provides examples of case types for both incident/ allegation/situation investigations and level of trust investigations. The next phase deals with reporting the findings but also includes further use of the resultant information. Most investigative information is formally retained (often in an automated database) in specified field, summary, or full format. The final phase addresses the use of the resultant information on a case-specific basis (e.g., disciplinary action, referral to the law enforcement or judicial system, or adjudication) and also on an aggregate or follow-on basis. Examples of aggregate or follow-on use of the data include statistical analysis, program evaluation, strategic planning, and budgetary forecasting.

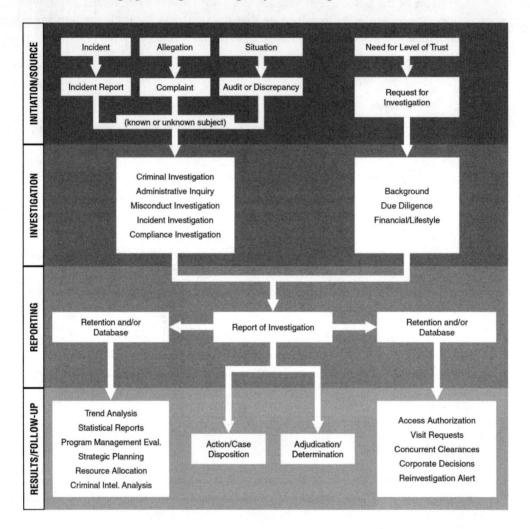

FIGURE 1-4

The Investigative Life Cycle

The IU manager is responsible for designing and implementing systems to manage the activity within each of the four phases of the investigative life cycle. Although it is easy to get bogged down in the day-to-day operations of the unit and specific investigative activity, it is important to keep up with unit management and administrative tasks.

Initiation

In the case initiation phase, an important issue in most settings is some sort of reporting mechanism whereby employees and others may conveniently provide information that they feel may warrant investigation or support an ongoing case.

Most credible information on losses, sexual harassment, and other problems comes from employee tips (which can also produce false, incorrect, or misinterpreted information) (Albrecht, 2004, p. 80). Dismissing anonymous complaints is contrary to best practices in any organization. The Federal Sentencing Guidelines and Sarbanes-Oxley Act of 2002 require, as an integral part of an effective compliance and ethics program, that publicly traded companies (in the case of Sarbanes-Oxley) and companies convicted of criminal activity (in the case of the Federal Sentencing Guidelines) have in place an internal reporting system that is non-retaliatory so employees to report suspected violations. Many corporations, organizations, and agencies have established hot lines for reporting fraud, waste, abuse, threats, security violations, and other potential adverse situations. It is also important to maintain an awareness program, which may include posters, payroll stuffers, wallet cards, and company communications documents such as newsletters. Companies are required to have a process in place to evaluate each communication and to investigate those deemed to require follow-up. Companies must make every effort to prevent any retaliation to the reporter, so it is prudent to make all calls anonymous. In some organizations, the hot line can be shared with departments that track reports of safety hazards, computer viruses, or discrimination complaints.

Investigation

Management responsibilities in the investigation phase include implementation of a case management system and appropriate administrative controls. The case management system may be manual or automated; most systems use computer software in today's environment. Such software aids both efficiency and data collection and retention. Modern software also often assists in the report writing effort. Although elaborate programs exist, most organizations choose a more straightforward and affordable package or create custom software designed for their company and the kind of investigation handled most often.

These programs can also assist with another critical task—case assignment and workload management—although the task is most often done manually. Case assignment in larger units (with several investigators) maybe based on caseload, experience, specialization, geography, or a combination of these factors. Regardless of which factors are used to make case assignments, the process should be done carefully and deliberately. Poor case assignment can quickly lead to investigator disenchantment and degrade the IU's effectiveness and its ability to resolve cases successfully. Some investigators could be overloaded while others have too light a caseload. Similarly, investigators with special expertise maybe working general cases while investigations requiring their special skills are assigned to others. Case assignment warrants close attention by the IU manager.

Oversight and administrative controls are essential in an IU. Managing an investigative assignment ledger falls under the function of the Controller or Manager. Aspects of each case, both operational and administrative (e.g., costs) require close scrutiny by the manager evaluated at least monthly. Checks and balances should be in place to ensure the following at a minimum:

- Requests for investigation are documented and responded to.

- Appropriate authorizations are in place to open a case.

- Investigators are given an appropriate number of cases to handle, and the right investigators are assigned to the right cases.

- Case status is briefed regularly (internally and externally as appropriate).

- Case leads are tracked as appropriate.

- Asset values (including estimated loss, recoveries, etc.) are properly recorded and updated.

- Liaison contacts are tracked and managed.

- Periodic written reporting occurs as prescribed.

- Case resolution and objectives are updated regularly.

- Case resources are tracked and managed.

- Post-case information (disposition, case files, etc.) is recorded.

The controls should operate so that all investigations have been authorized, all work assigned to a particular investigator can be identified, and the results and tasks remaining in any investigation can be determined quickly.

In the early days of a new IU, the need for formal controls may not be apparent. However, as the unit grows in size or activity and as personnel change, a formal system is required to derive maximum benefit from the accumulated investigative data. The system should attempt to answer such questions as how much a competent investigator should accomplish in a working day and how long it should take to complete an investigation.

Investigative production is affected by the temperament, competence, and working pace of the investigator; by the complexity of the case; and by the availability of informants and other sources of information. It is often impossible to predict what investigative steps can be accomplished on a given day. Therefore, the skilled investigator sets in motion as many leads or inquiry paths as can be managed simultaneously. The objective is to create information inputs that can be exploited as the opportunity arises and in the least amount of time.

One measure of effectiveness is the time it takes to complete a case. Although this figure varies drastically, statistical data can be used to derive average time requirements for particular types of leads or cases. The case average is then factored into the scheduling, budgeting, and case assignment routines. This approach may not work well in every environment or setting, but it can be useful in some organizations and can be applied to both case management and strategic planning efforts.

Reporting

The reporting phase is addressed here, as well as in the following subsection (*1.3.7 Case Management*) and in *Section 1.7 Investigative Documentation*. Reporting formats, frequency, distribution, and other requirements should become a part of the unit's policy and procedures and be followed carefully. Formal documentation activities are often among the first items to become neglected when caseloads increase and time pressure is experienced. However, lack of adequate and effective documentation along with sloppy record keeping can lead to failure quickly. Documentation and record keeping are tedious but important aspects of investigative management responsibility.

Follow-up

Executive leadership and IU managers must recognize that the results or follow-up phase goes beyond simply determining disciplinary, administrative, or judicial action. For example, investigative conclusions occasionally point not only to individual culpability but also to systemic features or business practices that represent significant causal factors (sometimes including security vulnerabilities) and clearly warrant corrective measures. Synergy is created by using the investigative results not only to resolve the issue at hand but also to correct conditions that allowed the incident to occur in the first place.

Investigative results should also be retained in files or databases for statistical purposes and trend analyses according to the unit's record retention policy. This information can be used to evaluate the effectiveness of the investigative and security or assets protection programs, support resource allocation decisions, and refine pertinent policy and procedures. It also represents valuable input to criminal intelligence analysis that may be employed in general terms or applied to specific future cases involving the same individuals, organizations, departments, locations, or modus operandi.

Three remaining key issues in managing the IU are setting objectives, motivating the investigative staff, and training. Setting objectives and monitoring progress toward them is a responsibility that is often neglected but is important for effective operation of the unit as well as demonstrating value to the organization. Objectives must be specific and measurable. They should also be established for different aspects of the unit, such as financial management, case resolution, overall unit performance, information flow, inquiries/complaints/leads handled, etc. In addition, they should be measured, docu-mented, and updated periodically—annually at least.

Motivating the investigative staff is a key task. The following issues investigators face can affect their self-image and attitudes:

- Testifying in court and administrative proceedings often subjects investigators to intense questioning, berating, and second-guessing by attorneys or other officials.

- Investigators may commit extensive time and effort on cases that are later shown to be based on false allegations, reports, or information, thereby making them feel their effort was wasted.

- Investigations—some of which require a great deal of investigative effort—may not be resolved, may be terminated prior to resolution, or may result in what the investigator perceives as an inappropriate disposition.

- Some investigations (e.g., fraud and white-collar crime) may stretch out for a long time—in some cases, for years—causing investigators to feel they are not making enough progress.

- Investigators may be subject to ethical temptations (e.g., dealing with unethical people who may be financially very successful due to their wrongdoing, the possibility of being offered bribes, using privileged information for personal gain, abusing their authority, using improper or illegal investigative techniques, etc.)

- Witnesses, interviewees, and liaison contacts may be uncooperative or frustrating to deal with.

- Executive management decisions not to pursue a matter (either before or after an investigation) may frustrate investigators who believe that significant case potential exists.

- Reluctance on the part of law enforcement officials or a government prosecutor to accept a case after significant effort has been put forth can prove frustrating.

- Investigators may become cynical, letting work pressures or issues carry over into their personal lives.

Without attempting to act as armchair psychologists, IU managers must be alert for signs of those frustrations. Some measures that may assist in motivating investigators and keeping them at peak performance are requiring periodic breaks or vacation time; sending investigators to training courses to give them time away from case work; conducting office social events; teaming investigators so they can motivate each other; recognizing both personal and professional achievements; supporting participation in professional and community organizations; and employing a participative management style.

Training can be used to benefit both the unit and the individual investigator. Although it takes time and money away from other investigative priorities, training is an essential part of maintaining a professionally staffed unit. Periodically, time should be set aside for internal training sessions to review policies, procedures, protocols, and issues affecting the employing organization. In addition, investigators should be given the opportunity to attend outside training courses and seminars both on specialty topics and advanced general investigative techniques. Specialty topics should be related to the individual's job function or the pertinent industry and may include the following subjects:

- computer investigations
- evidence handling
- white-collar crime
- forensic auditing
- criminal intelligence analysis
- environmental investigations
- safety investigations
- accident investigations

- sexual harassment
- workplace violence
- insurance fraud
- interviewing and interrogation
- general management
- communications
- self-improvement

1.3.7 CASE MANAGEMENT

The previous section discussed setting and monitoring objectives for the IU. However, objectives need to be set for individual cases as well. Even when the investigative objective is obvious, it is useful to deliberately identify and document the case predication and a primary objective and usually secondary objectives for a case (Webster University, 2004). This can assist greatly in keeping the investigative activity focused and directing the investigative steps. In more involved (complex or non-routine) investigations and all proactive investigations, a detailed investigative plan should be prepared, coordinated with all relevant parties, and approved by the IU manager or higher authority. Investigators should recognize that the primary and secondary objectives may change during the course of an investigation, and all such changes should be documented.

Case Files. At the outset of each investigation and upon the approval of the IU manager, a case file should be established. The case file contains the original complaint form or other initiation mechanism, the assigned case or file number, the name of any investigators assigned, complaint or subject information, initial leads, and documentation of management approval. Opening the case file should set in motion the following steps:

- assignment of a case or file number
- entry into the case management system (and other databases as appropriate)
- notification of management and others as appropriate
- staff coordination as appropriate
- efforts to corroborate the initial information

Administratively, the case file should include the following information, which may be tracked manually or via an automated case management system:

- case type or category

- case title or subject (if subject is known)

- file number

- location of the precipitating incident, if any

- value of assets lost or stolen

- assigned investigators

- date opened (and location opened if applicable)

- due date for a report or other action

- dates of any interim reports

- date of the final or closing report

- value of assets recovered

Following the Progress of a Case. An automated system can generally provide open case reports in order of due date, assigned investigator, or other factor. The IU manager can use the system to review the status of all open (or other) cases at any time. Interim reports can be reviewed electronically or in hard copy. Periodic oral case status briefings are also recommended in most environments. Larger IUs might have an operations coordinator who reviews cases, provides guidance, and makes recommendations on investigative steps. Whether investigators are working individually or in teams, it is a good idea to use supervisors and other investigators in the unit as sounding boards or for brainstorming. Investigation is, in part, a creative process, and the best ideas and approaches often result from collaboration.

Case file management can present difficulties if a formal system is not in place, even in a small IU or security department. Hard copy case files should be stored in a secured container (such as a safe or a file cabinet with a lock or lock bar). One or more persons should be designated to take responsibility for the cabinet or safe. No one should be allowed to add or remove a file for any reason. A checkout card should be used (and inserted in place of the removed file) to indicate who removed the file and when. This way, the file can be located when it is needed by the IU manager or another investigative team member. Electronically stored versions of case files (both in-progress and post-investigation) must be carefully controlled with access permissions and audit trail management set by the systems administrator or another official designated by the IU manager. The use of an analysis diagram will link the details regarding persons, events, etc. during an investigation whereas a horizontal diagram is a comparison of the different periods of a company's financial statement that will be beneficial during a fraud investigation.

During the course of the investigation, the lead investigator must ensure that the following tasks are undertaken:

- Track liaison contacts and information provided.

- Maintain surveillance logs (physical and technical).

- Maintain evidence logs (along with receipts and chain-of-custody documents).

- File original written statements and documentary evidence.

- Where applicable, track investigative costs by case (in some instances the costs of an investigation can be billed to another corporate or outside account).

- Maintain the suspense log (a list of due dates for reports, status checks, investigative leads and other milestones in the investigation) and ensure that delegated tasks are accomplished as scheduled whenever possible.

- Report to regulatory agencies when required.

These steps help ensure not only the legal credibility of a case but also a higher probability of a successful investigative outcome and a higher degree of efficiency.

Case Reporting and Information. Typically, investigative results are conveyed in a formal report of investigation. A final report and series of interim reports may be prepared as well as periodic and final investigative summaries or synopses. If interim reports are provided, each should include the information contained in the prior interim report. This technique eliminates the need for the reader to constantly go back to prior reports for clarification and understanding of the whole investigation. It means the latest report contains all the information to date. During and upon completion of a case, a careful balance must be achieved between sharing relevant information with the people who need it in order to support the investigation or make decisions, and protecting the information to ensure its integrity and the privacy of individuals involved. Most IUs have specific policies on distribution of investigative information, but gray areas still arise. Investigators should carefully consider the release of any sensitive information and coordinate its release with the IU manager or appropriate authority. This recommendation is particularly important when the investigation has been initiated by legal counsel and attorney work product privilege is an issue. No information should be released unless the attorney directs the IU to do so.

Disseminated reports and other investigative information should include a cover sheet or memo that clearly identifies the level of sensitivity of the information and provides instructions for disposing of the material when it is no longer needed (e.g., cross-cut shred the information, return it to the originator, etc). Recipients should also be advised, when applicable, that they may not retransmit the information or share it with anyone else. A log should be maintained indicating the distribution of reports, including whom they were sent to and when. In some instances a suspense date may be established for return of the material to the IU. This can help contain sensitive information as well as track its distribution.

OTHER INVESTIGATIVE MANAGEMENT ISSUES

1.3.8 LEGAL ISSUES

The legal issues outlined in this section relate to investigations in the United States. Legal matters must be considered for two reasons: (1) to protect the company against liability and (2) to ensure that an appropriate conclusion can be reached if the case goes to court or another legal forum. Other legal considerations include the following:

- compliance with laws regarding the licensing of private investigators and conduct of private investigations

- the possibility of civil suits (in some cases, criminal complaints) based on allegations of defamation, false imprisonment, false arrest, retaliation, and harassment

- the possibility of subpoenas to testify, produce written records of investigation, or both

It is incumbent on the IU chief to ensure that the organization is familiar with all applicable laws and regulations, as well as corporate policies. This can become a significant task, especially if the company has locations in several different jurisdictions, even in other countries. The venue of a particular case may not necessarily be within the expected jurisdiction. A legal proceeding might be held where the corporate headquarters resides, where an incident actually occurred (which may not be on company property), where a complainant is located, or in some other geographic location connected to the incident. Applicable laws, regulations, and restrictions may vary across the different jurisdictions. Many organizations never consider involving legal representative in case management.

Local Licensing Requirements. Most jurisdictions require paid investigators to be licensed, and licensing requirements and procedures vary widely from state to state within the United States and province to province in Canada. These requirements should be carefully reviewed before investigators are hired and before investigators are assigned to conduct activity that may take them into other jurisdictions. In the case of outsourcing for the use of investigators, consultants, or experts, the licensing status of both the individual and the firm that employs him or her should be verified. Current and proper licensing status cannot be assumed when using outside services, and violations can result in significant legal liability, fines, and dismissal of an otherwise good case. For employers with operations in several jurisdictions, the law of each jurisdiction in which investigative activity is conducted should be reviewed.

1.3.9 LIAISON

Professional working relationships are invaluable in the operation of an effective IU. Ensuring that the proper liaison relationships are established, nurtured, and appropriately employed is a key management responsibility. These relationships include internal and external, formal and informal, and individual and organizational contacts. Some examples of generally useful liaison contacts for corporate IUs are listed in *Figure 1-5*. Additional information on liaison and its benefits is provided in *Section 1.6.2 Liaison in Investigations*.

	INTERNAL	EXTERNAL
FORMAL	• Executive management • Facilities • Human resources • Information technology • Legal counsel • Operations • Public relations • Purchasing • Safety/occupational health • Security (if separate dept.) • Labor relations	• Local law enforcement • Other first responders • Local FBI (including ANSIR and InfraGard representatives*) • Other federal or regional investigative agencies • Military • Expert consultants or firms • Crime laboratory services • Outside employee assistance program providers • Equipment or supply vendors
INFORMAL	• Employee councils • Department or division contacts within the company • Accounting and finance • Other informants	• Local Chamber of Commerce • Other business associations • Professional associations • Company suppliers and vendors • Local community contacts • Other informants

* Most FBI field offices have appointed representatives for the ANSIR (Awareness of National Security Issues and Response) program. More information is available at www.fbi.gov/hq/ci/ansir/ansirhome.htm. Additional information on the InfraGard program is available at www.infragard.net. Related information can be found at www.fbi.gov.

FIGURE 1-5

Suggested Liaison Contacts

1.3.10 **CRIMINAL INTELLIGENCE ANALYSIS**

For organizations that require frequent, large, or more complex investigations, a criminal intelligence analysis function maybe advisable. According to Marilyn Peterson, past president of the International Association of Law Enforcement Intelligence Analysts, criminal analysis is "the application of particular analytical methods to data collected for…criminal investigation or criminal research" and is "practiced in law enforcement …and in private security organizations around the world" (M. Peterson, 1998, p. 1).

1.3.11 **PROTECTING INVESTIGATIVE INFORMATION**

An important aspect of investigative management, which often receives less attention than is warranted, particularly in the private sector, is that of protecting case-specific investigative information. Protecting such information is important because of the potential that its compromise could damage the future effectiveness of the investigators or IU involved, lead to potential civil liability against the organization, damage the reputations and careers of individuals (such as subjects, witnesses, interviewees, managers, coworkers, etc.), and damage important liaison relationships. In addition, improper handling of investigative information can energize the rumor mill, harming the investigation, stock prices, market share, and corporate reputation. In many jurisdictions, investigations involving electronic and other documented information require extraordinary protection and security. Organizations and investigators are subject to regulatory sanctions if appropriate measures are not taken to secure personal information obtained from investigations and surveillance. Investigations in most European countries, Australia, and Canada are subject to laws that strictly govern an individual's personal information privacy.

Particularly important applications for investigative information protection include the following:

- cases in which the subjects are senior executives or high-profile persons

- joint task forces

- major compliance or regulatory investigations

- cases involving sensitive issues, such as terrorism, child pornography, workplace violence, major fraud, or product safety

- cases involving information defined as protected, personal information that requires safeguards pursuant to privacy legislation (as in Canada, the United Kingdom, the European Union, and Australia)

It is particularly difficult to protect investigative information in joint task forces since each participating agency likely has different policies, definitions, perspectives, and attitudes toward what is sensitive and warrants protection (K. Peterson, 2002–2005).

In fact, protecting critical information is a key element of any investigation. This is even true in personnel BIs, as is evidenced by the well-known tenet that the investigator does not reveal derogatory information received from interviewees or other sources to subsequent interviewees.

Beside formal protocols (such as government classification systems), operational security and operations security represent effective means to identify and protect valuable investigative information. Operational security is the totality of all security and planning measures employed to ensure a successful outcome for a particular operation or activity as well as the safety of the investigators involved. It includes such measures as cover stories, backstopping (actions taken to support covers or contrived identities), communications protocols, agent infiltration plans, countersurveillance, covert meet security (measures to conceal a secret meeting), the use of carding (practice of keeping data about sources of information) and technical monitoring. In both the public and the private sector, operational security is generally applied to special activities, such as undercover or sting operations. This topic is examined in *Chapter 2. Undercover Investigations as a Protection Tool.*

By contrast, operations security (OPSEC) is a simple and systematic method of employing safeguards to protect critical information (Interagency OPSEC Support Staff, 2000). The OPSEC process includes five cyclical steps:

- Identify assets (critical information).
- Define the threat (collectors, capabilities, motivations).
- Assess vulnerabilities.
- Analyze the risk (impact, priority, existing countermeasures, etc.).
- Develop and implement countermeasures.

A key but often overlooked step is to realistically determine what information at each phase of the investigation or operation is sensitive and therefore warrants protection. This is the process of defining critical information. In the case of joint task force operations, for example, a deliberate process should be undertaken at the outset to define critical information and to reach an agreement among all participating agencies.

Defining the threat entails identifying, within reason, all potential information collectors or adversaries who may target an investigation or operation using legal or illegal means. The following are among likely candidates as potential adversaries:

- individuals or organizations with a stake in the outcome of the investigation
- friends or supporters of the subject of the investigation
- co-conspirators not yet identified (individuals or organizations)
- news media and simple public curiosity (especially in high-profile cases)
- potential copycats or others engaging in similar wrongdoing

An important rule of thumb is never to underestimate the lengths to which adversaries will go to get what they want. Many criminal elements (and others) apply the same surveillance and human collection techniques that law enforcement and legitimate investigators use (Interagency OPSEC Support Staff, 2000). They may monitor communications (radio, landline, cell phone, etc.), collect information from courtrooms and proceedings, conduct social engineering, exploit public affairs offices, use open sources (such as news sources and the Internet), gather information from trash, and target computers.

Vulnerabilities can be direct (such as physical or electronic interception of investigative information) or indirect (such as increased activity in the security department just prior to an important operation). Both should be carefully considered. Investigators should ask themselves whether they are exhibiting predictable patterns of behavior or doing anything that could be used by the adversary to block the success of their operation (Interagency OPSEC Support Staff, 2000).

A risk analysis—based on the nature of the critical information, the credible threats, the identified vulnerabilities, and the consequences of an information compromise—assigns levels or priorities to the information risks. These risks can then be addressed by appropriate countermeasures. Essentially, a countermeasure is anything that effectively negates or reduces an adversary's ability to exploit information or vulnerabilities (Townley, 2003). Typical countermeasures include the following:

- restricting conversations to face-to-face as much as possible
- limiting cell phone, radio, and wireless communications usage
- using encryption when possible
- avoiding conversations in public areas such as restaurants, airports, etc.
- carefully selecting surveillance vehicles, techniques, and participants
- coordinating closely with public relations offices of participating agencies and companies
- applying "need-to-know" procedures within the IU, agency, or company
- appropriately securing written information and office spaces
- immediately destroying trash that may contain sensitive information
- applying sound IT security procedures to systems containing sensitive information
- including information protection clauses in agreements and contracts for security or investigative support services

Figure 1-6 shows a generally applicable process flow chart outlining the steps for protecting investigative information.

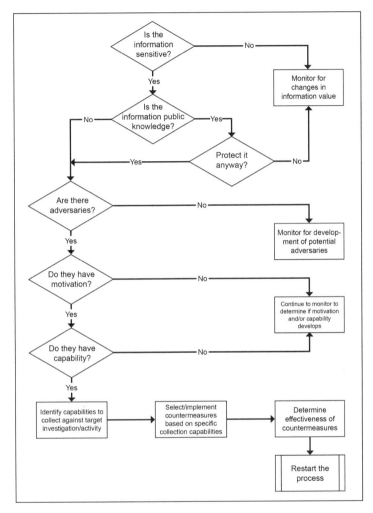

© 2004 Innovative Protection Solutions, LLC. Used With Permission.

FIGURE 1-6

Process Flow Chart for Protecting Investigative Information

Effective information protection measures should not hinder investigative operations but rather enhance them. Cost-effective countermeasures should be employed by all participants in an investigation or operation as well as anyone with access to related information (Townley, 2003). Such measures help to protect evidence, ensure successful investigative outcomes (including convictions), and protect individuals and organizations.

In summary, at the outset of an investigation or investigative operation, it is important to define the critical information; assess adversary capabilities and motivation to collect information against the activity; determine the adversary's likely (possible or probable) methods of collection; and then apply countermeasures to prevent, neutralize, or mitigate the collection effort.

1.3.12 WORKING IN MULTICULTURAL OR INTERNATIONAL ENVIRONMENTS

In the climate of globalization, both public and private sector investigators must be able to operate in a multicultural environment. Cultural issues can become a factor in an investigation in almost any type of company, industry, or organization. Examples include the following:

- a corporate investigation within a domestic firm where the investigation involves subjects or witnesses who are of a different ethnic background or are citizens of another country

- a corporate investigation that takes place (or follows leads) in another country

- a corporate investigation that involves partner firms, subsidiaries, joint ventures, vendors, or suppliers located or incorporated in another country

- due diligence investigations involving firms or individuals somehow affiliated with a foreign country

- an investigation involving international or multinational organizations

- a joint task force involving agencies from more than one country

According to a security professional who has worked in multinational environments at both the International Monetary Fund and the United Nations, differences in multinational and international investigations fall into one or more of three categories: laws, liaison, and approach (Nebo, 1999, p. 4).

Laws. Laws vary not only from country to country but also between jurisdictions within a country. They may also be affected by agreements and regulations within regional entities, such as the European Union, North American Free Trade Zone, or Association of South East Asian Nations. Investigators must be well informed of and sensitive to the pertinent laws and regulations—as well as customs—within the international arenas in which they operate.

Liaison. Like other investigative functions, liaison must be approached with specific cultural factors in mind. When operating in foreign nations, liaison with local law enforcement, security, and intelligence agencies is commonplace and often a necessity. Relationships with such agencies can range from very close and trusting to extremely tenuous. Regardless, working with these agencies in general and on specific cases is usually advisable. In most cases, a close working relationship with foreign counterpart or supporting agencies can have immense benefits and greatly expedite successful resolution. However, before a decision is taken to consult with agencies in foreign countries, discreet research on the reputation and practices of those agencies is critical.

Internal team liaison is also essential when working with multinational joint task forces. Understanding one another's investigative tactics, legal constraints, and culture contributes greatly to task force effectiveness and reduces both wasted effort and duplication of effort. Additional information on liaison as an investigative force multiplier is provided in *Section 1.6.2 Liaison in Investigations*.

Approaches. Particular investigative techniques as well as overall approaches and strategies are more appropriate in some countries and cultures than others. For example, offering money for information may be an insult in some cultures, while it is virtually a necessity in others. Legal counsel should be consulted before payments are offered for information. Interview techniques, the relevance of certain types of evidence, surveillance operations, and technical surveillance all may have significant culture-dependent ramifications as well.

Nations differ drastically in how they interpret crime and technology issues. For example, not all countries recognize computer crimes as a serious threat. In addition, the rules of evidence and the technical capabilities of law enforcement agencies can vary greatly, thereby affecting agencies' ability and willingness to assist in technology-related investigations (Nebo, 1999, p. 7).

Another factor is one nation's relationship with another in political, diplomatic, or economic matters. If relations between governments are less than cordial, those countries and their representatives may be discouraged from cooperating in the investigation or prosecution of cross-jurisdictional criminals.

Cultural differences are the most challenging problem in international investigations. Therefore, the investigator tasked with supporting investigative activity in multinational or international environments must understand cultural diversity in general as well as specific cultural and legal issues relevant to the country or ethnicity involved (Nebo, 1999, p. 13).

1.3.13 ENSURING AN APPROPRIATE CASE CONCLUSION

The overall objective is a successful investigative outcome or resolution of a case (whether an identified suspect is implicated or exonerated). The best way to help ensure an appropriate case conclusion is to focus on the basic qualities of an investigation: objectivity, thoroughness, relevance, accuracy, and timeliness. Investigative managers must also focus attention on legal issues, such as licensing and liability; technical issues, such as appropriate investigative techniques and the protection of investigative infor-mation; and management issues, such as effective coordination, documentation, and case presentation. By carefully and effectively balancing these key issues, management can help ensure successful case resolution and protection of organizational assets.

1.4 **TYPES OF INVESTIGATIONS**

As mentioned in *Section 1.3*, most IUs emphasize one or a few particular case types, which represent their most prevalent matters or the bulk of their caseload. Typical case types for the corporate and organizational environment are listed in that section. Some case types, however, warrant specific discussion. For example, background investigations deserve detailed discussion as they represent a distinct investigative function in terms of approach, resources, reporting, case disposition, and associated legal issues. In every case effective and reliable investigations are timely and accurate. Although some discussions are more detailed than others, each of the following subsections discusses how the case type is distinct, which special techniques might be applied, and associated issues of which investigators and IU managers should be aware.

1.4.1 **INCIDENT INVESTIGATIONS**

The initiation event in a private sector incident investigation is generally a security force incident report. *Appendix A* at the end of this chapter shows two examples of incident report formats commonly used by security forces in commercial and government facilities. Other initiation events for incident investigations include direct complaints, hot line calls, and security audits or assessments. For this reason, they are sometimes referred to as complaint investigations.

This is the most common type of investigation in many business and organizational settings. In fact, incident investigations are needed in almost all organizations, many of which do not maintain formal investigative units or capabilities. Thus, this type of inquiry is often performed by a security supervisor or the security director rather than a full-time, professional investigator.

Detailed, direct procedural guidance is recommended for incident investigations. Checklists, forms, and an incident investigation manual should be tailored to the organization and setting so that they meet the particular needs of the entity, are consistent with the culture of the organization, and satisfy applicable legal factors.

Like BIs, incident investigations require a particularly methodical and systematic approach, whereas other types of investigations often call for a more creative problem-solving strategy or a flexible, situation-based approach. Firms and organizations, especially those without an IU or full-time investigator, should develop straightforward procedures (protocols) for conducting and reporting on incident investigations. Those with an IU might consider establishing guidelines (or including guidelines in their investigative policy statement) to delineate responsibilities for such inquiries. The following is a sample guideline:

The following incidents will be investigated by or under the auspices of the senior security supervisor:

Theft (estimated loss ≤ $1000)

Unknown loss (estimated loss ≤ $1000)

Simple assault

Safety hazard

Vehicle accident

Property damage or vandalism (estimated loss ≤ $1000)

Unsecured area

The following situations will be referred to the Investigative Unit for action:

Theft (estimated loss > $1000)

Unknown loss (estimated loss > $1000)

Aggravated assault

Property damage or vandalism (estimated loss > $1000)

Employee misconduct Executive misconduct

Workplace violence (actual or potential)

Sexual harassment Sexual assault

Proprietary information loss

Fraud and economic crime

Contract irregularities

Unsecured area or forced entry

The preceding thresholds may also apply to law enforcement or legal referral. Even if there is law enforcement interest, it may take considerable effort to establish the existence of a specific crime or actually initiate a criminal investigation. This situation varies from one jurisdiction to the next and may depend on such factors as local law enforcement emphasis, capabilities, caseload, and past experience. In many jurisdictions, the police IUs are overworked and often will not undertake an inquiry unless it involves a clear threat to public order or a loss above a certain threshold. Each enterprise should establish its own loss thresholds to determine whether an investigation is warranted and, if so, what its parameters should be.

The same facts that establish a crime can also establish a tort or other actionable civil misconduct. A for-profit entity maybe as interested in civil remedies as in criminal convictions. In either case—criminal or civil—a thorough and accurate investigation is necessary. For example, during an embezzlement investigation, cash disbursements are the most common form of workplace embezzlement. Therefore, the accounts payable ledger reflecting dates and amounts paid to company suppliers should be reviewed. In addition, investigative results can be crucial in any administrative or personnel proceedings. The investigative unit can work with the departments to ensure that there is a separation of duties so that an accounts payable clerk doesn't have access to add or delete names to the master vendor file.

Investigative Process for Incident Investigations

Investigative protocols should be approved by executive management in order to lend credibility and authority to the process, regardless of whether the organization has a separate IU or full-time investigator. A protocol should generally include a decision logic matrix to quickly identify who has responsibility for the inquiry, who should be notified, and whether immediate referral to law enforcement or the legal department is appropriate. The protocol should then outline the prescribed investigative steps.

The following sample provides a general idea of recommended contents for a protocol:

- Assess the credibility of the source of the information and the information itself.

- Determine whether physical evidence is present and warrants collection (i.e., is there a scene to be processed?).

- Conduct initial witness interviews.
  - Give priority to those who were directly involved in the incident or may have perishable information.
  - Give priority to those individuals who may not be available later for interview (e.g., visitors, employees scheduled for a trip or reassignment, informants only temporarily in the area, etc.).
  - Get recommendations for follow-on interviewees (i.e., find out who else should be interviewed and obtain identifying or contact information for them).

- Document individuals (witnesses, bystanders, etc.) who declined to be interviewed or who were not available for interview.

- Document other potentially relevant situational or environmental conditions.

- List all security, corporate staff, and other officials who were involved in the initial response, assessment, and investigative steps.

- Conduct third-party interviews (of individuals or agencies that did not witness the incident or were not present but may have relevant information).

- Check security and investigations indices or databases for relevant information.

- Make and document all notifications regarding the incident.

- Determine information gaps, and identify sources or methods to fill the gaps (via interviews, evidence collection, surveillance, observation, investigative research, records checks, etc.).

- Recommend follow-on action or referral.

- Complete appropriate documentation and database entry.

Security officers and staff should receive training on applicable investigative protocols, including the need to protect investigative information (ASIS International, 2004, pp.18-19). Particular care should be taken with hot line or complaint calls. Callers should be made to feel that the information they provided is important and appreciated and that the matter will be looked into. Failure to do so may discourage future reporting of valuable information. At the same time, potentially sensitive information must not be provided to complainants or others because complaints may lead to the initiation of undercover operations or other investigative activities that must be kept confidential.

The report of investigation for this type of inquiry is often a standardized form. It is particularly important that reports be properly filed or entered in a database so the information they contain is retrievable later. The report should note whether a follow-up is required or recommended and whether referral to the IU or an outside investigative services firm or law enforcement agency is advisable or required.

1.4.2 MISCONDUCT INVESTIGATIONS

An important subcategory of constructive incident investigations is the misconduct investigation. This is generally an internal investigation conducted when an employee or other individual closely affiliated with the organization is suspected of violating a written corporate policy, a directive, terms of employment, or a federal, state, or local law.

An important characteristic of workplace misconduct investigations is that they leave the employer particularly open to legal action by employees or former employees who feel they have been treated unfairly. Among the alleged causes for legal action are discrimination, wrongful termination, sexual harassment, defamation, and false arrest. The best way to prepare for such investigations is to coordinate the matter as soon as possible with the human resources director and corporate legal counsel (or equivalent officials). This recommendation pertains to most types of private sector investigations but is particularly important in employee misconduct cases.

Investigative Techniques and Issues in Misconduct Cases

In general, those involved in a misconduct investigation should consider the differing perspectives of the parties on both sides—complainant and subject. From the employer's perspective, the issue is a routine policy or disciplinary matter. From the subject's perspective, it may be traumatic situation. Subjects may feel their career, livelihood, and reputation are at risk.

Experienced corporate investigators do not use techniques that may induce an innocent person to confess to guilt. The use of coercive interview techniques can significantly impair the reputation of fairness in a corporate setting—and thus damage the credibility of and confidence in the IU and individual investigator. Some individuals are easily intimidated and, although innocent, may confess to crimes and wrongdoing when confronted with unfounded promises of leniency or fabricated and supposedly overwhelming evidence. The use of inappropriate techniques and failure to protect personal or confidential information during the investigation can lead to embarrassment for the corporation, erroneous investigative conclusions, and lawsuits against the enterprise.

Suggested practices in misconduct investigations include the following:

- Determine the proposed outcome or disciplinary action (should the allegation be proven) at the outset of the investigation. This helps prevent claims of personal discrimination or the appearance that the intended action was modified during the course of the investigation based on what or who was shown to be involved.

- Use information sources both internal and external to the organization to help prove or disprove allegations. Relying solely on internal sources may limit the scope of the information collected and may conceal critical facts or data points.

- Gather relevant information from previous employers of the individual in question. The information may show patterns of behavior and reveal significant data that can be used to direct the investigative efforts, strengthen the case, explain existing known facts, and provide additional leads. High turnover rates, common today, make it even more important to conduct thorough background checks and consider interviewing past coworkers, supervisors, colleagues, and other associates.

- Even in cases not involving IT system abuse, consider collecting electronic evidence, such as e-mail records, access requests, logons, file downloads, and remote access sessions. These sometimes overlooked sources can provide valuable information.

Finally, the potential side effects of a misconduct investigation and the way in which it is conducted must be considered. For example, when deciding to use surveillance (covert monitoring to gather intelligence) it is important to remember that it is difficult and vulnerable to discovery if conducted while moving. However, an overt surveillance, whose main goal is to prevent crime or misconduct, may be effective. Effects may include diminished workforce productivity, strained interoffice relationships, and threats and intimidation. An internal investigation (or even a rumor of one) may turn coworker against coworker, create other frictions in the office, and have a short- or long-term impact on workplace comfort level and trust relationships. Although the potential for side effects cannot be allowed to dictate the aggressiveness or outcome of an internal investigation, it should be considered in terms of the overall investigative strategy, information dissemination, treatment of individuals, and professional demeanor of those involved in the case.

Examples of Misconduct Case Types

Misconduct investigations often focus on conflict of interest, corporate resource abuse, employee theft, workplace violence, and substance abuse. For each issue, the existence of an attitude toward a specific corporate policy is critical to effective detection, successful investigative outcomes, and legal sufficiency.

Several features of corporate policy can help protect the assets of the enterprise as well as the rights of individuals who may be accused or implicated in wrongdoing. According to one commentator (Rudewicz, 2004, pp. 46–49), it is important that management make corporate policy clear and "ensure that no employee or manager can plausibly claim not to have been well informed of its meaning and consequences." In addition, such policies should "encourage or require employees to help the company detect early warning signs from other workers, vendors or customers by reporting suspicious threatening or inappropriate behavior" and should "state that the employee is obligated to cooperate" in any investigation, including cases of alleged misconduct.

Besides sound, clearly communicated policy, the investigative process itself is also critical to deterring, detecting, and resolving misconduct. In fact, "while some types of investigations are prohibited by law, others are mandated. For example, harassment charges must be investigated" (Goemaat, 2004, p. 54). The IU manager must be familiar with investigative prohibitions and requirements at the international, federal, and local levels. In addition, "prior to conducting an investigation of employee conduct, an employer should determine whether the conduct is a legitimate subject of discipline and inquiry under state and federal laws" (Goemaat, 2004, p. 57). Some factors in making that determination include whether an incident occurred on or off the employer's property, whether an employee's conduct was during duty hours or after hours, and whether the offender represented himself or herself as a representative of the organization.

Once an investigation has been initiated, the company must make several decisions. These decisions include whether any offense or infraction actually occurred, whether reporting to law enforcement is required or appropriate, and how the employee will be notified of the findings and action to be taken (Ray, 2003, p. 58). Such decisions are generally made as the investigation proceeds and should be reached in close coordination with legal counsel and other organizational officials.

Conflict of Interest. The definition of this case type can vary widely and be influenced by the organization's mission, structure, and culture. Generally, conflict of interest (CoI) issues are clearly defined in corporate policy and employee materials. From a legal perspective, it is essential that all employees and affiliates (consultants, contractors, subcontractors, vendors, etc.) be made fully aware of CoI definitions, policies, and consequences. In instances where an investigator has a conflict of interest, this must be disclosed to the client, and the investigator should not be associated with this assignment in any way.

Corporate Resource Abuse and Employee Theft. This phenomenon represents a significant loss and is therefore significant from a corporate investigative perspective. The following are among the issues that may be addressed as abuse or misuse of corporate resources:

- personal use of telephone or IT systems

- inappropriate use of IT systems (e.g., downloading pornography, accessing unauthorized information, spamming, phishing, etc.)

- personal use of company vehicles

- unauthorized or inappropriate use of company information

- inappropriate use of company aircraft

Principal characteristics of internal theft include diversion, conversion, disguise and divergence. Additionally, motivated by economic conditions, internal theft remains a significant source of loss worldwide. According to the 2002 National Retail Security Survey, retail security managers attributed more than 48.5 percent of their losses to employee theft, up from 46 percent the prior year. Further, internal theft by employees cost retailers a record $15 billion (University of Florida, 2002).

Workplace Violence. Investigations should be considered one component of an overall prevention/response/recovery program for workplace violence. Like most other misconduct issues, workplace violence incidents are usually preceded by indicators or warning signs (which are, unfortunately, often recognized only after the fact). The best prevention of exposure to workplace violence is a preemployment background investigation program. Lacking that as a preventative measure, investigations should be initiated as soon as possible when warning signs are reported. Depending on the level of the threat and other factors, it may be appropriate to simultaneously suspend the subject of the investigation (Rudewicz, 2004, p. 49).

Substance Abuse. According to U.S. government sources, on-the-job substance abuse costs American businesses $81 billion to $100 billion annually. These costs include absenteeism, reduced productivity, accidents, theft, and increased healthcare costs. Substance abuse in the workplace can also represent a threat to public safety and worksite security, cause friction among coworkers, and lead to drug trafficking on the job (U.S. Department of Labor, 2005) (Drug Enforcement Administration, 2003).

Some sources also suggest that although employees should be encouraged to make use of a corporate employee assistance program (EAP), the initiation of discipline following a drug or alcohol infraction should not be postponed during the employee's involvement in the program (Drug Enforcement Administration, 2003). In Canada, an employee with substance abuse issues is deemed to have a physical disability and the employer must be aware of the legal requirements for providing reasonable accommodation (e.g., EAP and time for recovery) to the employee.

In all types of investigations, false allegations represent a significant nuisance to the IU and consume valuable investigative resources. In addition, they can damage individuals' reputations, cause mistrust within an organization, and affect investigators' morale.

False allegations may be unintentional, resulting from an observer's misinterpretation of certain actions as a crime where, in fact, no actual crime or infraction was committed. The false reports can also be intentional, resulting from a disturbed complainant's attempt to get attention, gain revenge, or cover up his or her own wrongdoing (by diverting attention to another individual to avoid detection or adverse action).

Investigators must follow all reasonable investigative leads to resolve a matter, whether or not they believe a false allegation might be involved. However, security and investigative professionals should remain alert to the possibility of false allegations and be prepared to take appropriate action in response.

1.4.3 **COMPLIANCE INVESTIGATIONS**

Compliance investigations share many characteristics with incident and misconduct investigations and can, in fact, fall into either of those categories as well. Compliance issues are increasingly significant to organizations as well as the individuals who run them.

In light of recent corporate scandals and increasing government regulation, companies are taking a more proactive approach to identifying and responding to wrongdoing. According to a privacy and compliance professional at a major U.S. telecommunications firm, it makes good business sense to have an internal capability to investigate compliance issues. Team members should be trained on current regulatory issues and investigative methods and have a strong understanding of business practices and procedures in their industry and in business generally. Increasingly, even small and medium-sized companies are turning to formal compliance programs and internal IUs to limit their risk of exposure to government investigations (Garcia, 2000, pp. 2 and 7).

With new, post-Enron legislation such as the Sarbanes-Oxley Act and the recently enhanced U.S. Federal Sentencing Guidelines for Organizational Crime, corporate compliance programs take on even greater emphasis and executive visibility. The purpose of a corporate compliance program is to protect the organization against violations of law, lapses in business ethics, and concomitant legal sanctions. An effective program encourages enforcement, monitoring, and employee training (Garcia, 2000, p. 11).

Like other investigative issues, a compliance program should be built on a clear corporate policy, often couched in a comprehensive code of conduct. The following are some policy issues that may be covered under an organization's compliance code of conduct:

- equal employment opportunity
- harassment
- workplace safety
- confidential and proprietary information
- copyright, patent, and trademark
- company property and records
- computing systems, information access, and authorized uses
- conflict of interest
- government entities
- antitrust violations
- political activities and lobbying
- securities requirements from various jurisdictions
- regulatory violations

Since compliance issues may harm the company's bottom line, it is importance that employees be trained and be familiar with code violations so they can immediately identify when a violation has occurred and know to whom to report the issue (Garcia, 2000, p. 6).

A key element of any compliance program is an effective reporting mechanism. As Garcia observes, "[T]he biggest challenge in investigating compliance issues is getting employees to come forward and report wrongdoing at any level of the organization... There must be a way to report violations and have a mechanism for investigating these allegations" (Garcia, 2000, p. 5). Many organizations have an employee hot line, but that has pitfalls. Multiple hot lines can be confusing, and lack of reaction or follow-up can discourage people from reporting. (Some companies have separate hot lines for regulatory violations; fraud, waste, and abuse; security violations; safety hazards; and management issues.) A consolidated hot line with well-trained and professional operators, when combined with an effective system for distribution and follow-up, will generally result in high-quality, valid, and useful reporting. This hot line can be administered internally or by an outside firm (often more cost effectively). An advantage of using an outside firm is that employees can be more confident their voices will not be recognized. An effective hot line can significantly reduce losses in most corporate and organizational environments. The efficacy of the hot line can be enhanced greatly through an ongoing awareness program that communicates with all employee groups by means of wallet cards, payroll stuffers, notices on payroll stubs, and signage in the work areas and break rooms.

An article in the *National Law Journal* notes that an effective reporting avenue, such as a hot line, not only demonstrates the importance an enterprise places on compliance but also provides the company with information that can be used to prevent future losses (Ackerman, 2004).

Once credible information indicating that a violation has occurred is brought to light, a thorough investigation gathers and correlates the facts of the case. Investigations generated internally in the corporate arena tend to be broader in scope than law enforcement and government regulatory investigations, according to Garcia. Cases involving violations of internal policies or procedures do not typically face the judicial scrutiny of a criminal investigation and can address wide-ranging issues involving the business practices of the enterprise. On the other hand, cases brought forward because of a government violation (like insider trading or Federal Communications Commission violations) tend to be narrow in scope because of legal constraints, although they may involve severe criminal sanctions (Garcia, 2000, p. 8).

Corporate entities should not only provide for internal investigative capabilities but also be prepared to cooperate with investigations conducted by law enforcement or government regulatory agencies. This is even more important in light of the revised Federal Criminal Sentencing Guidelines. Under those guidelines, an organization's culpability in the event of criminal wrongdoing is lessened by having an effective program to detect and prevent violations (RSA Security, 2000, p. 4). In fact, "the sentencing guidelines have become the universally accepted standard for corporate compliance programs" (Ackerman, 2004).

The guidelines allow a reasonable period to conduct an internal investigation and assume that the company's cooperation will be timely and thorough (United States Sentencing Commission, 2002). However, the guidelines also state the following (United States Sentencing Commission, 2004, p. 1):

> Failure to follow applicable government regulations and industry standards and recurrence of similar misconduct undermine an organization's eligibility for compliance credit...The guidelines mandate high fines for organizations that have no meaningful programs to prevent and detect criminal conduct or in which management was involved in the crime.

Figure 1-7 provides agencies at the international and U.S. federal, state, and local levels that may have an interest, role, or enforcement mission in compliance investigations in the corporate arena.

International
• International Atomic Energy Agency (IAEA)
• European Union Network of Environmental Enforcement Authorities
• International Network for Environmental Compliance and Enforcement (INECE)
• Compliance and Enforcement Unit, UN Environmental Programme (UNEP)
• Secretariat for the Convention on Biological Diversity (CBD)
• International Civil Aviation Organization (ICAO)

U. S. Federal	
• Nuclear Regulatory Commission	• United States Coast Guard
• Federal Communications Commission	• Federal Trade Commission
• Federal Aviation Administration	• Securities and Exchange Commission
• Occupational Safety and Health Administration	• Internal Revenue Service
• Environmental Protection Agency	• Animal and Plant Health Inspection Service
• Department of Justice (various offices)	• Biotechnology Regulatory Services
• Bureau of Alcohol, Tobacco, Firearms and Explosives	• Immigration and Customs Enforcement
• National Labor Relations Board	• Federal Energy Regulatory Commission
• Equal Employment Opportunity Commission	• U.S. Consumer Product Safety Commission
• Food and Drug Administration	• National Indian Gaming Commission
• Bureau of Industry and Security	• U.S. Postal Inspection Service
• Department of Transportation	• International Trade Commission

U.S. State and Local	
• Health Department	• Zoning Board
• Department of Motor Vehicles	• Gaming Commission
• Department of Transportation	• Licensing Board
• Department of Criminal Justice	• Food Services Agency
• Alcohol Control Board	• Utilities Board
• Attorney General's Office	• Department of Education/School Board
• Construction Commission	• Animal Control Agency

FIGURE 1-7

Examples of Regulatory Agencies with Enforcement Authority

1.5 INVESTIGATIVE TECHNIQUES AND TOOLS

This section outlines the primary techniques and tools employed by investigators in the performance of their duties. It is meant to advise managers, unit chiefs, and security directors on general methods employed in investigations. Investigative techniques are subject to policies and regulations applicable to the particular IU and the jurisdiction in which it operates. Investigators should be thoroughly trained in basic investigations, any relevant specialty areas, and the legal constraints to which they are subject.

1.5.1 INTERVIEWING AND INTERROGATION

The success of an investigator is sometimes measured by his or her ability to interview or interrogate people. This topic is addressed in *Chapter 5. Interview and Interrogation.*

1.5.2 RECORDS AND DATABASE CHECKS

Records and database checks represent a key element of almost any investigation. An excellent reference for information on techniques and sources for record checks is Derek Hinton, *Criminal Records Manual—Criminal Records in America: A Complete Guide to the Legal, Ethical, and Public Policy Issues and Restrictions, Third Edition* (Tempe, Arizona: Facts on Demand Press, 2008). The book is available from the ASIS Bookstore and other vendors.

1.5.3 EVIDENCE COLLECTION AND HANDLING

The collection, handling, processing, and use of evidence is a key component of investigation. Proper procedures in gathering, protecting, examining, storing, and presenting evidence are crucial to the successful resolution of a case. Some cases are resolved quickly with an employment termination action, restitution, or both. Other cases may proceed through the judicial system, and some may not go to trial for years. Evidence tasks can be tedious and resource-intensive (including the possible consumption of a large amount of secure storage space). However, physical, technical, and other forms of evidence can be absolutely critical to case resolution and resultant action determinations (judicial, administrative, etc.) in all investigative settings. This topic will be addressed further in *Chapter 6. Evidence.*

1.5.4 SURVEILLANCE

The *Security Dictionary* defines surveillance, in part, as "observing the behavior of another, usually secretly" (Fay, 2000, p. 239). The primary purpose of surveillance is to obtain information about the identities or activities of those under investigation. It is essential that notes are taken during surveillance. A key investigative tool, surveillance can be broken down into three broad categories, physical (i.e., human observation or tracking), psychological (i.e., behavioral analysis), and data (e.g., technical or electronic). Surveillance is used extensively in both public and private investigations. Examples of effective methods are the ABC method in conducting foot surveillance and checkpoints in mobile surveillance.

1.5.5 COMPUTER FORENSICS

Electronic Crime Scene Investigation: A Guide for First Responders (National Institute of Justice, 2001, p. 2) describes electronic evidence as follows:

> Electronic evidence is information and data of investigative value that is stored on or transmitted by an electronic device. As such, electronic evidence is latent evidence in the same sense that fingerprints or DNA ... evidence are latent. In its natural state, we cannot "see" what is contained in the physical object that holds our evidence. Equipment and software are required to make the evidence visible.

Computer forensic science is the science of acquiring, preserving, retrieving, and presenting data that has been processed electronically and stored on computer media. It is different from most traditional forensic disciplines. Traditional forensic procedures are normally carried out in a laboratory environment. Computer forensic examinations are conducted in forensic laboratories, data processing departments, and in some cases virtually any physical location. Traditional forensic science relies on the ability of the scientists to produce a report based on the objective results of a scientific examination. Computer forensic science, by comparison, extracts or produces information.

Forensic science generally does not need specific details from the investigation. For example, a DNA examination can be conducted without knowledge of the victim's name, the subject, or other specific information. Conversely, computer forensic science, to be effective, must be driven by information uncovered during the investigation. As a practical matter, the computer forensic examiner cannot examine every file stored on a computer system. Personal computers are currently available with a data storage capacity of hundreds of gigabytes. The storage capacity of a large hard drive or a central server makes the task of reading every file in detail essentially impossible in the time available for the examination. Thus, the investigator must provide the forensic examiner with the details of the investigation. The examiner can then create a list of key words or phrases to search for. To be effective, the examination must be a coordinated effort between the investigator and the examiner.

1.6 **INVESTIGATIVE FORCE MULTIPLIERS**

The term *force multiplier* originated in the military arena and applies to such activities as electronic warfare, intelligence operations, and perception management. The official Department of Defense definition is as follows (U.S. Department of Defense, 2005):

> A capability that, when added to and employed by a combat force, significantly increases the combat potential of that force and thus enhances the probability of successful mission accomplishment.

For present purposes, a force multiplier is any activity, capability, or resource that enhances the effectiveness or efficiency of the investigative function. Two examples illustrate the importance of force multipliers in the investigations field:

- A U.S. Air Force initiative dubbed the Eagle Eyes program was implemented in the wake of the September 11, 2001, terrorist attacks. The program is focused on enlisting the aid of citizens (including military personnel, family members, retirees, local residents, and law enforcement colleagues) to serve as eyes and ears and report any suspicious activity that maybe related to terrorism or other threats. The program combines training, awareness, marketing, and establishment of new reporting channels. Information on best practices in Eagle Eyes is compiled from installations nationwide and shared with other IUs and counterpart agencies. The commander of the Air Force Office of Special Investigations has stated, "I'm reluctant to use the term 'force multiplier,'... but if ever a program was a perfect match for the term, it's 'Eagle Eyes'" (Patterson, 2002).

- Joint efforts such as the FBI's Safe Streets Violent Crime Initiative bring together federal law enforcement, local law enforcement investigators, and prosecutors to focus on specific high-profile issues. Such collaboration conserves valuable resources, encourages information sharing, eliminates duplication of effort, and effectively reduces crime. This type of effort is considered a true force multiplier in the investigative arena (Ashley, 2003).

Three important force multipliers in investigations are online information sources, liaison, and intelligence information. Each can contribute significantly to successful and expedient investigative outcomes. Nevertheless, they have costs and thus represent an investment in the investigative function of an organization or company. This must be clearly understood by both investigative managers and executive decision makers (i.e., the front office).

The following subsections describe these three force multipliers. Some sources also consider technology a force multiplier in investigations since it can contribute to faster analysis and data fusion, better knowledge management, a more predictive approach, and more efficient information dissemination (Parsons, 2000).

1.6.1 ONLINE INFORMATION SOURCES

The core of any investigation is information. Anything that significantly improves the speed and efficiency of information gathering, collation, analysis, or organization is an important force multiplier. Online resources are such a tool and are expanding at a rapid pace. The following are examples of such resources:

- databases

- collaboration tools

- automated analysis tools

- information on vendors (experts, laboratories, etc.)

Online research can represent both an outstanding source of information and a cost-saving measure for a typical IU. Although specific training in online research—and in some cases a dedicated individual or team—is recommended, the following references can provide an initial overview of the technique. They contain valuable information on research techniques, suggested strategies, and sources:

- *Find It Online: The Complete Guide to Online Research*, 3rd Edition, by Alan M. Schlein, published by Facts On Demand Press, Tempe, Arizona, 2002.

- *Public Records Online: The National Guide to Private & Government Online Sources of Public Records*, 4th Edition, edited by Michael L. Sankey and Peter J. Weber, published by Facts On Demand Press, Tempe, Arizona, 2002.

In general, IU managers should evaluate their research needs and determine the most mission- and cost-effective approach to meeting them. Some units maintain a full-time individual or staff for investigative research. Others assign team members to the function as an additional duty or outsource the function. In some organizations, a research function or department may already exist—perhaps to conduct legal research or contract research. It may be most efficient to recruit and vet a member of that department to assist the IU on an as-needed basis (keeping in mind the need for confidentiality).

Training courses are widely available in both general online research and specific investigative research techniques. Such courses are recommended and should be included in the IU's budget. Periodic retraining or advanced courses are advisable since techniques, technologies, and legal ramifications change rapidly.

In general, sources for online research include the following:

- Internet search engines and web resources
- library resources
- internal databases (including the organization's investigative or security data management system)

- industry and professional association resources
- commercial databases
- law enforcement databases

All these potential sources should be considered when searching for information to support investigations.

Three major cautions must be stated, however. First, investigators and staff members may go off on a tangent, spending a great deal of time inefficiently by searching online for the sake of searching online. This is a common temptation, especially as the typical person becomes more and more familiar with working online. In some cases, guidelines may need to be established regarding this issue, such as an appropriate-use policy for IT systems or databases.

Second, there is a natural tendency to assume that information extracted from databases or online sources is credible (in terms of accuracy, relevance, timeliness, and source reliability). Team members should be reminded periodically to employ the standard investigative techniques of corroborating sources and verifying information to the greatest degree possible. Online databases are updated at different intervals, and many do not independently verify the information they accept. Investigators should look into those issues before relying on data derived from online sources.

Third, while most investigators enjoy searching the Internet, that may not be the best use of their time. In some cases it may be faster and cost-effective to use an experienced research contractor.

Commercial Databases

Many research tools and services are available, particularly in employee screening services. Some of them offer comprehensive search capabilities for different types of investigations at a single source.

Among the uses of commercial databases are prescreening and background investigations, general corporate investigations, legal research, business research, due diligence research, and investigative planning. Some databases operate solely on a subscription basis, while others allow one-time, fee-based access as needed.

In addition, some services have interconnected or related systems that flag individuals who provide information that contradicts data on file by returning names, addresses, and social security numbers based on input information. Some can find the current and previous addresses of any person on file identified by his or her social security number.

Commercial databases may require prior agreement by a user of their services that neither the commercial network provider nor the information provider is liable for the use or misuse of the service. The agreement for one commercial site states, in part,

"Neither the provider nor any database supplier makes any representation or warranties regarding the performance of the network or the accuracy of any indexing, data entry or information included in the network."

Law Enforcement Databases

Various databases have been established to support the specific needs of law enforcement agencies, particularly on the federal level in the United States and various levels in Canada. Many of these databases are available to state and local law enforcement agencies and in some cases international agencies.

Although the information contained in these databases is generally limited to the law enforcement community, it may be available to corporate investigators in some instances, particularly when a joint internal/law enforcement investigation is underway. Access to specific databases may be coordinated on a case-by-case basis with law enforcement counterparts.

Summary of Online Sources

The proliferation of available information, ease of access, and ongoing budget restrictions dictate that the modern assets protection department use online investigative techniques. Every day, new Web sites and databases become available while others become obsolete.

1.6.2 LIAISON IN INVESTIGATIONS

One of the most significant force multipliers in the investigative function is liaison. Liaison comes in many forms: internal and external, formal and informal, and individual and organizational. In all its forms, it allows IUs and individual investigators to leverage the resources of others; share best practices and lessons learned; collaborate on specific cases; more effectively address common issues; and share information, equipment, and facilities—in short, to do more with less. In addition, effective liaison allows IUs to be more proactive in their focus, thus making them a greater value-added asset to the organization (K. Peterson, 1998, p. 1).

Investigators should be allowed, in fact encouraged, to develop and maintain their own formal and informal liaison contacts. Large law enforcement agencies may have agents stationed worldwide with high-level access to officials and information. Investigators and security directors in the corporate arena usually do not have that luxury. Therefore, to be effective in assessing threats, gathering information, and conducting investigations, IUs and individual investigators must establish professional relationships in the community. These relationships should include law enforcement agencies, government services, security colleagues, and associations. Effective relationships provide resources that can either produce investigative results or provide the facts, evidence, and witnesses that lead to such results (Hudak, 2005). Even when an organization has an active, large-scale network in place, liaison can expand that network and help it operate more efficiently.

Another reason to maintain liaison contacts is highlighted in a *Security Management* article titled "Guilt by Investigation and Other Pitfalls." According to the authors, certain violations or issues may arise in an organization very infrequently, so investigators and other corporate players will not be accustomed to dealing with them (Albrecht, 2004, p. 78). Such issues may include large-scale fraud, cyber attacks, workplace violence, or executive misconduct. Early and close coordination with internal liaison contacts such as the general counsel and human resources director is critical in these cases. Calling on outside contacts, such as functional experts or consultants, may also be useful to ensure that appropriate and up-to-date investigative protocols are employed.

IUs strive to be as proactive as possible. This enhances their effectiveness and credibility and demonstrates their value to the enterprise or community they serve. Although it is possible for liaison to occur in a reactive environment (e.g., during a crisis or emergency), it is primarily a proactive medium. In fact, many consider it an essential tool in fighting pervasive societal problems, such as illicit drugs, street violence, workplace violence, and fraud. By working together, law enforcement agencies, corporate staff, security professionals, and the legal community can be more effective in protecting assets, resolving incidents of wrongdoing, and preventing future losses (K. Peterson, 1998, p. 10).

Finally, a more philosophical reason for liaison is simply professionalism. Most true professionals are eager to share their expertise and learn from others. This mutually beneficial exchange contributes to the profession in general and at the same time helps individuals hone their personal and organizational body of knowledge.

How to Establish Liaison

Professional relationships are established through introductions, references, contacts (both formal and social), and mutual assistance. An excellent opportunity for establishing liaison contacts is through professional and civic associations. Security directors, IU managers, and investigators should be encouraged to join organizations—professional, athletic, service, community, and social (Hudak, 2005).

Emergency planning exercises can also be an excellent venue for meeting colleagues and developing liaison contacts. It makes good sense to get to know the individuals and agencies that will support the organization in an emergency. They can be of great assistance not only in times of crisis but also in reviewing plans, providing awareness training, gaining facility familiarity, and exchanging general information.

Participation in multilateral forums should be encouraged. Examples of such forums include the following:

- local business and community security associations

- industry security associations (e.g., healthcare, utilities, retail, etc.)

- local InfraGard chapters[2] or similar organizations

In some cases, it may be necessary to justify such participation to senior management. That is not usually difficult. It may be advisable to invite a senior representative of the particular forum to meet (or help educate) corporate executives or staff.

Professional associations are an important part of public–private partnership between law enforcement and corporate security professionals. The director of the Bureau of Alcohol, Tobacco, Firearms and Explosives stressed that point when he said, "Professional societies such as ASIS play a key role in fostering these critical relationships" (Magaw, 1998). Training and professional development courses are also excellent places to meet people who will add to an investigator's network. Additional advice on establishing liaison contacts comes from a seasoned security and investigations professional (Hudak, 2005):

> Establish relationships with professionals at different levels of organizations. When first entering the community, make a courtesy visit to the highest official in the agency you can manage. Later, you can use that meeting as a reference to others in that organization. Do not limit your contacts to law enforcement—expand the courtesy visits to the fire department, emergency services, utilities, Mayor's Office, Postal Inspectors office, hospital security directors, any organization that could be of service to your company.

Internally, it is wise to develop close working relationships with key people within the enterprise by making an introductory visit and periodic follow-up visits and by exchanging information and favors. A crisis or major investigation is not the best moment to meet colleagues for the first time! Suggested internal contacts include the following:

- executive assistant and front office staff

- general counsel

- contracting or procurement officer

- human resources director

- facilities manager

- public relations or information officer or equivalent

- accounting and finance director or chief financial officer

- operations manager

---

[2] InfraGard is an FBI initiative to facilitate public/private partnerships with businesses associated with the nation's critical infrastructure. InfraGard chapters have been established near each FBI field office and meet on a regular basis for information sharing, networking, and education.

- information technology manager or chief information officer

- security or safety director

- occupational health staff

- leaders of the union or collective bargaining unit

Depending on the size of the enterprise, it is advisable to develop internal liaison contacts at different levels within each of the preceding functions.

In the global business environment, liaison relationships are critical to effective investigations. The intricacies of culture, host nation laws and regulations, local law enforcement policies and procedures, language differences, and local familiarity can have a tremendous bearing on investigations in foreign countries. Local liaison contacts can make all the difference in successful investigative outcomes and in the ability of investigative team members to avoid trouble and keep a low profile.

Whenever possible, international liaison relationships—with agencies and individuals—should be established well in advance of a crisis or investigation. Many foreign security and law enforcement agencies have special units in topics such as counterterrorism, cyber crime, financial crimes, import/export issues, and organized crime. Investigators should establish liaison, to the greatest extent possible, with their direct counterparts and exchange correspondence periodically. When visiting corporate facilities in other countries, it is useful to meet with counterpart investigators and become familiar with their policies, procedures, and concerns. This will make subsequent interactions much smoother and more effective for both parties (K. Peterson, 1998, p. 5).

How to Maintain Liaison

Once established, liaison relationships require maintenance. Liaison is based on a professional trust relationship and requires periodic exchange as well as mutual benefit. The following suggestions support strong, sustainable liaison relationships:

- Make sure each party derives some benefit without unduly taking advantage of the other. Liaison relationships must be mutual in nature, though not necessarily quid pro quo.

- To avoid disciplinary action and harm to the liaison relationship, follow legal limits and agency regulations on the maximum value of liaison gifts.

- Never violate the trust of a liaison contact. Doing so will generally terminate the relationship and brand the offending investigator and his or her agency for a long time. A key asset of any investigator or IU is a good reputation.

- Maintain contact periodically, even when there is no specific information to exchange. Doing so demonstrates that the relationship is important and helps maintain familiarity with individuals and their organizations.

Joint Task Forces

One highly structured form of liaison is the task force. Complex, often multijurisdictional issues such as terrorism, cyber crime, and major procurement fraud are frequently addressed by joint task forces (JTFs). JTFs may be case-specific (e.g., the 2002 National Capital Area Sniper Case and the Unabomber Task Force) or longstanding (e.g., the President's Corporate Fraud Task Force and the National Joint Terrorism Task Force). *Figure 1-8* shows some of the resources and activities of JTFs.

JTFs often feature special expertise and cross-jurisdictional boundaries. They may incorporate multiple international, federal, and local law enforcement agencies as well as industry resources, auditors, analysts, consultants, prosecutors, and others. The diversity of members in a task force introduces many benefits, but it can also lead to misunderstanding, conflict, and inefficiencies. The JTF should be managed in a way that compensates for any adverse affects while capitalizing on the strengths of diversity.

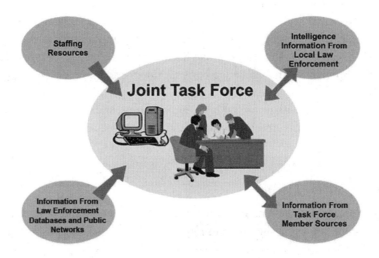

Source: *Applying Security Practices to Justice Information Sharing*, Office of Justice Programs, U.S. Department of Justice.

FIGURE 1-8

Joint Task Force Resources and Activities

When operating within or managing a JTF, investigators must be alert for a number of other important issues, including parochialism, protection of sensitive information, data management, and reporting chains. Parochialism can occur when JTF members arrive with varying agendas, either individual or organizational. This inevitably causes conflict, whether explicit or subtle, and can seriously detract from the effectiveness of the unit. Besides limiting investigative or prosecutorial results, this behavior can erode the public's or corporate executives' confidence in the task force.

Information protection in a JTF environment presents several challenges. Members may have different perspectives on what information is sensitive (or over what time particular information is sensitive). In addition, most members are dealing with multiple reporting chains, varying departmental policies, pressure to inform different constituencies, and different secure communications capabilities. To minimize these challenges, JTFs should have a tailored operations security (OPSEC) plan for the protection of information in both physical and electronic formats (ASIS International, 2002–2005).

Reporting chains can be confusing in the JTF environment. Such confusion can lead to the dissemination of fragmented and apparently contradictory information regarding task force progress, successes, needs, and relationships. Well-defined reporting chains involving both the task force itself and member departments will go a long way toward minimizing the confusion and apparent miscommunication.

The preceding advice regarding JTFs can also be valuable in the corporate arena. For example, it can be applied to multidisciplinary or integrated product teams within an organization or to multi-organization collaborative efforts.[3] These entities operate like JTFs and face many of the same issues.

In summary, liaison comes in many shapes and sizes, ranging from informal face-to-face conversations to detailed international agreements (K. Peterson, 1998, p. 11). Regardless of the form it takes or level at which it occurs, liaison is a significant force multiplier for any IU. In the words of a former Special Agent in Charge of the largest U.S. Air Force Central Systems Fraud Detachment, "The establishment of good liaison is much like a good informant program...Without it you simply can't be proactive or establish a proactive posture" (Smith, 1997).

1.6.3 INTELLIGENCE INFORMATION

Although intelligence information is a key force multiplier for IUs in almost any setting, an organized approach to managing it is frequently lacking in the corporate arena. IU managers should establish a formal intelligence management program that includes policies, procedures, and systems for the following:

- defining general and specific objectives
- gathering intelligence information

---

[3] Examples of such efforts include the Identity Theft Assistance Center, established in 2004 as an initiative of the Financial Services Roundtable (www.fsround.org), a group of representatives of major financial institutions; and the initiative by Internet service providers AOL, Earthlink, MSN, and Yahoo known as the Anti-Spam Technical Alliance.

- integrating and analyzing information

- organizing and storing information (in physical or electronic format)

- sharing information internally and externally as appropriate

- retrieving information

- controlling access to the data itself

- controlling access to information on methods and sources

- periodically evaluating and enhancing the program

As part of the program, the unit should set both general and specific intelligence objectives, including the topics that must be emphasized. In addition, strategies for collecting and using the information should be developed, and in some cases intelligence requirements should be assigned to specific investigators or locations.

Potential sources of information are defined by the type of inquiry being conducted and the functional focus of the IU. Of course, skilled and experienced investigators are generally better able than novices to quickly recognize and exploit intelligence sources. These skills are taught in almost all basic and advanced investigations courses, and even the newest investigators, if properly trained, should have a basic understanding of the intelligence function.

A basic maxim of investigations is to "check your own files first." It is not uncommon for valuable sources of information within the organization to be overlooked. This is particularly true in large, complex, or multilocation enterprises. Case management software that accommodates exhibits and photographs and allow link analysis is extremely helpful—especially if it is stored on the organization's network and can be accessed by all IU personnel. Using off-the-shelf programs, many of which allow customization, is more cost-effective than building programs from scratch.

The most significant sources may be those recognized and used because of their specific and perhaps unique relevance to the particular investigation. Possibly used only once, such sources can provide critical data for resolving the case.

Long-term continuous information sources are also of tremendous value. They may include liaison contacts, controlled informants who have the greatest potential to deliver, and confidential sources. In addition, each investigator develops personal sources that can provide certain kinds of information on a regular basis. Whenever possible, these sources should be shared with the IU; however, contact should be coordinated through the originating investigator.

A key element in any intelligence program is protecting information about methods and sources, some of which may be extremely sensitive. (Of course, only legal methods and sources should be used.) A mechanism for code names or numbers should be established where appropriate to conceal the identities of individuals, organizations, or technical sources of information. The confidentiality mechanism should strive to minimize the possibility of compromise via inadvertent disclosure and through legal processes such as discovery, particularly when compromise of the source would represent a significant embarrassment or cause a physical threat to individuals or organizations.

Intelligence sources vary widely and often depend on the functional focus of the IU, the geographic location, or the industry involved. The following are some common intelligence sources:

- news media
- Internet sources
- internal files and historical records
- local (province, state, county, city) court filings and records
- criminal justice agency files
- IT department records and audit trails
- contracting and procurement records
- accounts payable and accounts receivable records
- operations and production records
- regulatory filings and agencies
- tax filings
- motor vehicle records
- insurance carriers and claims histories
- safety and incident records
- inventory management systems
- human resources data
- personnel evaluations, awards, and disciplinary files
- payroll and travel records
- medical and financial records (Various federal and state regulations protect these records; much care must be taken to ensure they are not accessed illegally. If they are, the information is useless and the source, investigator, and company can be prosecuted criminally.)
- security files
- licensing or permit and other county, municipal, or state records

1.7 INVESTIGATIVE DOCUMENTATION

1.7.1 REPORT WRITING

An investigative report is a written document in which the investigator records the activity in the investigation and the evidence gathered. If it is not the final report of the investigation, it may still provide leads for other investigators to pursue. The report also serves as the basis for post-investigation administrative action, such as prosecution or disciplinary action. A report should enable the reader to understand readily what the investigator did, why it was done, and what resulted. The most diligent and professionally conducted investigation loses its value if the effort is not properly reported. The five basic steps of report writing are to gather the facts, record the facts immediately, organize the facts, write the report and evaluate/edit the report if necessary.

Types of Reports

Although the exact nature of the reporting process varies, the following types of investigative reports are typical:

- *Initial report.* The initial report is filed a few days after the investigation is opened. It describes the progress of the investigation and details the leads, if any, that remain to be followed. In a simple case, the initial report may be the final or closing report.

- *Progress report.* An investigation can last for months in the private sector; public sector cases may remain open and under investigation for years. Progress or interim reports of the case status are submitted at fixed intervals to detail the progress of the investigation and any leads that remain to be followed. In the private sector, the normal interval for progress report submission is 30 days.

- *Special report.* The special report documents an action other than normal in the course of the investigation. The special report can be a supplement to a progress report, but it must be able to stand separately from the progress report. An example of a special report would be a report of surveillance conducted in an undercover investigation.

- *Final report.* It is most important that a final report is logical and submitted under these circumstances: when the investigation is successfully brought to a close; when all investigative leads have been followed without success and further investigative action is deemed to be unproductive; or as directed by the person or office that authorized the opening of the case.

Elements of the Report

The format of the investigative report varies widely among organizations. One method is to separate the report into various topics such as statements, surveillance logs, etc. Hard copy reports are required in many enterprises; however, the electronic filing of reports to a master file and centralized database is becoming common. Regardless of the report's form, it should contain relevant information obtained during the investigation as well as administrative information, a summary, a narrative, conclusions, and enclosures.

Administrative Information. The report must be complete and readily understood without reference to other reports. Therefore, it must include the following administrative information:

- name of the subject of the case
- case or file number
- type of case (if not identified by the case or file number)
- status of the case (open or closed)
- reporting investigator
- date of the report

Summary. A summary or synopsis of the report, given at the beginning, permits a quick assessment by readers. The general rule is that every major point covered by the report requires at least one sentence in the synopsis. Supporting facts are not cited in the synopsis. Conclusions are permissible if they fairly represent the detailed information in the body of the document.

Narrative. The narrative segment of the report contains the details of the investigative effort. It provides an easily understood recitation of the chronology of the investigative process and the facts of the matter. Each step in the investigation should be covered in a separate paragraph. It should be clear, simple, and brief. The vocabulary should be easily understood. Technical terms should be avoided or at least defined. The narrative portion of an undercover operative's report should be written in the first person so that his activity is easily understood.

Conclusions. Some organizations request that the investigator's conclusions and recommendations be provided as part of the investigative report. For example, after a successful fraud investigation, an investigator may recommend corrective action (such as control enhancements) or after a burglary investigation the investigator may recommend enhanced physical security measures (such as surveys, alarms, guards and closed-circuit television). However, the investigator is primarily a collector of relevant evidence, and the appropriate authority in the organization should decide any judicial or administrative actions to be taken.

Enclosures. Enclosures to the report should include at least the following:

- the initial complaint
- complainant and witness statements
- other interviewees' written statements
- evidence documentation and reports of analysis results (including physical, documentary, electronic, and technical evidence)
- surveillance logs (if appropriate)
- photographs, audio recordings, videotapes, or DVDs

Distribution and Protection of Investigative Reports

Investigative reports may be subject to disclosure during the judicial process of discovery. Through this process, an investigative agency or unit can be compelled to release its report and other files to the opposing party in a legal action. For that reason, it is important to keep the report clear of extraneous and irrelevant material, particularly the names of people and places not relevant to the inquiry. The report should be delivered to and retained by the company's attorney of record only. It will then likely be classed as attorney work product and be protected from subpoena. This technique is not foolproof, but at least discovery of the report will generally require a court order after argument at a hearing.

Generally, properly controlled investigative reports will be granted qualified privilege and hence not be actionable for defamation, even when they contain false data (unless it can be shown that the false information was placed there with malice). Even so, care should be taken not to include opinions and conclusions by the investigator. The items in the report should be the statements of others or the personal observations of the reporting investigator and should be clearly identified as such.

The final process in the investigative report is distribution. Distribution should be restricted to those with a genuine need to know. The report could contain damaging information about or statements from employees or other people. Copies of the report should be controlled closely. Finally, any person receiving a copy or retaining a file should have the appropriate security protection and be advised of the sensitive nature of the document and relevant handling instructions.

The requirement for dissemination on a need-to-know basis also affects the qualified privilege accorded an investigative report. Later, if the report is found to contain inaccurate and damaging material, the privilege can be lost due to unnecessarily wide distribution. Again, many organizations distribute investigative reports only through in-house or contract legal counsel to ensure that attorney-client privilege protects the reports.

1.7.2 **OTHER REPORTING FORMATS**

Other formats may be used for specific purposes or for certain types of investigations. Forexample, a simple incident investigation conducted by a security supervisor may be documented on the incident report itself and filed either in hardcopy or electronically (e.g., in anautomated incident management system).

Preemployment and background investigations may also use slightly different formats as designated by the organization or requesting authority.

1.7.3 **TESTIFYING AND DEPOSITIONS**

Investigators in most fields are often called to testify in judicial or administrative proceedings. Further reading of this subject matter is presented in *Chapter 8. Testimony*.

1.8 **PROJECTIONS**

A number of themes pertinent to the future of investigations can be drawn from the historical perspectives presented at the beginning of this book. First, the distinction between public and private investigating is becoming blurred, as is evident in the experience of Pinkerton and Burns and in fact throughout history. This same situation is present today in the early 21st century (Bayley, 2001, p. 39).

Second, history shows a consistent and strong correlation between security and investigative functions (Webster University, 2004). Examples include the deterrent (security) value of investigations, the assignment of the investigative function to the security department in many modern corporate structures, and the fact that many private companies (including Pinkerton, Burns, Wackenhut, and Wells Fargo) throughout history have offered both security and investigative services.

Third, allegations of corruption in private investigations firms as well as police departments have been commonplace. It is important to work hard today and in the future to maintain the reality and the image of high ethical standards. Such standards have a direct impact on the credibility of investigators and IUs, and that credibility has a direct impact on their effectiveness.

Finally, contemporary issues in the 21st century global environment have, in fact, been a concern throughout history. A few examples of these issues, which often mold the direction and focus of the investigative function, are as follows:

- terrorism concerns (e.g., England in the 1800s)
- burglaries and street crime
- violent crimes
- executive protection needs
- economic and white-collar crimes
- corporate assets protection needs
- international and cross-border crime
- large-scale thefts and cargo or in-transit crimes
- organized crime rings
- information theft and business intelligence
- corporate compliance (Sarbanes-Oxley)
- competitive intelligence and espionage

Of course, advances in science, technology, legal theory, and international affairs will continue to affect the investigative function. Regardless of an IU's focus, new scientific developments will offer advancements in investigative tools, evidence collection and analysis techniques, surveillance capabilities, database and knowledge management, and information sharing mechanisms. Closely related to those advancements is the continually growing reliance on IT in every facet of life. This will place greater demands on IUs to develop increasingly sophisticated IT savvy and computer forensics capabilities (whether internal or outsourced).

In addition, there is a trend toward increasing self-reliance on the part of corporate entities, organizations, and communities in terms of satisfying their security and investigative needs. According to the International Foundation of Protection Officers, due to budget and other constraints, public law enforcement and society in general will increasingly place greater expectations on businesses to provide their own internal investigations of white-collar crime (Davies, 1999, p. 14). This position is echoed by the National Institute of Justice in *The New Structure of Policing* (Bayley, 2001, pp. vii and 1):

> Gradually...policing has been "multilateralized": a host of nongovernmental groups have assumed responsibility for their own protection, and a host of nongovernmental agencies have undertaken to provide security services...We believe that the current restructuring is worldwide...In most countries, private police outnumber public police. In these same countries, people spend more time in their daily lives in places where visible crime prevention and control are provided by nongovernmental groups rather than by governmental police agencies.

The realm of homeland security also plays a significant role in today's government and corporate investigative environment. Cooperation and information sharing not only among federal, state, local, and international law enforcement agencies but also between the government and private sectors has become paramount in protecting assets. For example, a major step toward closer ties and information sharing between federal agencies and the business community grew out of the Critical Infrastructure Protection efforts in the late 1990s (President's Commission on Critical Infrastructure Protection, 1997). These efforts expanded into semiformal Information Sharing and Analysis Centers within key industry sectors and have now forged even more productive relationships under the domain of homeland security. These relationships and the trust on which they are founded must continue to expand and evolve (General Accounting Office, 2004, pp. 3–4). As indicated on the Web site of the Homeland Security Information Network, "Homeland security is no longer solely law enforcement's responsibility, but necessitates a collaborative effort among citizens, corporations and the government" (Southwest Emergency Response Network, 2004).

In summary, the 21st century will likely see a continuation of several historical trends in investigations. These include an expansion of private sector investigative responsibilities and capabilities; a close relationship between the investigative function and the security or assets protection function; and an emphasis on high ethical standards and professionalism in the corporate or organizational investigations arena (including the professional investigative services industry). New scientific advances will be incorporated into the investigative process rapidly, and information sciences such as database or knowledge management and technology-based information sharing mechanisms will play an increasingly integral role in the field.

To some degree, these developments will affect the necessary background, training, qualifications, and use of investigative personnel in the future, as well as the use of outside expertise. Still, there will continue to be heavy reliance on traditional investigative techniques and processes, such as interviewing, interrogation, use of human sources, physical surveillance, and report writing.

APPENDIX A

Security Incident Reports

The two sample formats that follow are representative of those used by government and commercial environments. Incident reports frequently comprise the initial complaint that is used to initiate an investigation. The formats are provided courtesy of MVM Security, Incorporated, of Vienna, Virginia.

Security Incident Report—Sample 1

1. Date of Report	2. Date and Time of Incident	3. Report No.
4. Type of Incident (see #43)	5. Person Reporting Incident	6. Time Reported
7. Location Description/Building Address		
8. Tenant		

Complaint/Incident Information

9. Name: Ms. ▢ Mr. ▢	10. Emergency Contact Person	
11. Home Address		12. Home Phone
13. Work Address		14. Work Phone
15. Injury Sustained		
16. Cause of Injury (please check appropriate box) Falling Object ▢ Tripped ▢ Slipped ▢ 16a. Type of Shoe Fell ▢ Other ▢		
17. Condition of Area (please check appropriate box) Liquid Spill ▢ Food Spill ▢ Dark Area ▢ Uneven Surface ▢ No Adverse Conditions ▢ Other ▢		
18. Medical Services Contacted? Yes ▢ No ▢ If no, why not?	19. Responding Unit	20. Transported to:
21. Property Description (if necessary, include additional property in narrative)		
22. Property (please check appropriate box) Stolen ▢ Missing ▢ Damaged ▢ Serial # _____ Value $ _____ Recovered ▢ Other ▢		

Suspect Information

23. Name: Ms. ▢ Mr. ▢	
24. Barring Notice Yes ▢ No ▢	25. Sex
26. Home Address	27. Home Phone
28. Work Address	29. Work Phone
30. Physical Description	
31. Additional Information	

Rev. (date)	*Page 1 of 2*	*Form No.* _____

Report No._____

Witness Information

32. Name: Ms. ▮ Mr. ▮

33. Written Statement Requested?
Yes ▮ No ▮ If no, why not?

34. Home Address	35. Home Phone
36. Work Address	37. Work Phone

38. Print Name of Reporting Security Officer	38a. Signature	
39. Supervisor	40. Police Officer	41. Badge No.

42. Narrative

a) Incident Description

_____

_____

_____

b) Action Taken

_____

_____

_____

c) Notifications Made

_____

_____

_____

43. Examples of Incidents

a) access denial
b) accidents/damage auto
c) assaults, physical/Verbal
d) bomb threats
e) disorderly conduct
f) alarm perimeter (door)
g) illegal weapon (concealed)

h) facility/structural damage
i) fire alarm
j) medical emergencies
k) personal injuries
l) sexual assaults (exposure)
m) suspicious activities
n) stuck elevator

o) thefts
p) trespassing
q) unauthorized entry
r) unleashed animals
s) vandalism
t) domestic
u) other

Security Incident Report—Sample 2

OPERATIONS DIVISION

UNIFORMED PROTECTIVE SERVICES BRANCH
GENERAL INFORMATION/INCIDENT REPORT

DATE OF REPORT _____

TO: Director of Operations
Manager, Uniformed Protective Services
Senior Field Supervisor

Other: _____

_____

_____

FROM: _____

Client _____ Type of Special Services _____

Day and Date of Information/Incident _____ Time _____

General Nature of Information or Incident _____

Details (Who was involved? What happened? Where? Actions taken/other information)

Retain original in client's Information/Incident Report File   Page ____ of ____ pages

---

REFERENCES

Ackerman, N. (2004, July 5). New guidelines' impact. *National Law Journal.*

Albrecht, W. S., Albrecht, C., Albrecht, C., & Williams, T. L., CPP (2004, November). Guilt by investigation and other pitfalls. *Security Management.*

Ashley, G. D. (2003, September 17). Assistant director, Criminal Investigative Division, Federal Bureau of Investigation. Testimony before the Senate Judiciary Committee.

Anderson, T. (2004, December). The earnings factor. *Security Management*, p. 36.

Anderson, T. (2004, December). The earnings factor. *Security Management*, [Online]. Available: http://www.securitymanagement.com [2009, December 22].

ASIS International, Commission on Guidelines (2004). *Private security officer selection and training guideline.* Alexandria, VA: ASIS International.

ASIS International, Commission on Guidelines (2004). *Private security officer selection and training guideline.* Alexandria, VA: ASIS International, [Online].
Available: http://www.abdi-secure-ecommerce.com/asis/ps-74-30-1586.aspx [2009, December 22]

ASIS International (2006). *Security industry buyers guide,* Alexandria, VA: Author, [Online]. Available: http://www.sibgonline.com [2009, December 22].

Bayley, D. H., & Shearing, C. D. (2001). *The new structure of policing* (NCJ 187083). Washington, DC: National Institute of Justice, U.S. Department of Justice.

Brown, M. F. (2001). *Criminal investigation: Law and practice* (2nd ed.). Woburn, MA: Butterworth-Heinemann.

Cassel, E. (2000, February). Behavioral science research leads to Department of Justice guidelines for eyewitness evidence. *Virginia Lawyer.*

Davies, S. J., & Minion, R. R. (Eds.). (1999). *Security supervision: Theory and practice of asset protection* (2nd ed.). Woburn, MA: Butterworth-Heinemann.

Dempsey, J. S. (1996). *An introduction to public and private investigations.* St. Paul, MN: West Publishing Company.

Drug Enforcement Administration. (2003). *Guidelines for a drug-free workplace* (4th Ed.), [Online].
Available: http://www.usdoj.gov/dea/demand/dfmanual/index.html [2006, February 22].

Eco, U. (1983). *The name of the rose.* New York: Harcourt.

Fay, J. J., CPP. (2000). *Security dictionary.* Alexandria, VA: ASIS International.

Federal Bureau of Investigation. (2002). *Handbook of forensic services*, Chapter 16, Crime-scene search tips, [Online].
Available: http://www.fbi.gov/hq/lab/handbook/forensics.pdf [2009, December 22].

Garcia, R. (2002). *Conducting corporate compliance investigations*. Washington, DC: Webster University.

General Accounting Office. (2004). *Critical infrastructure protection: Improving information sharing with infrastructure sectors*. Washington, DC: Author.

General Accounting Office, Office of Special Investigations. (1997). *Investigator's guide to sources of information* (Report Number GAO/OSI-97-2), [Online].
Available: http://www.gao.gov/special.pubs/soi.htm [2009, December 22].

Gifis, S. H. (1975). *Law dictionary*. Woodbury, NY: Barron's Educational Series.

Goemaat, J. (2004, May). A case of good judgment. *Security Management*, p. 53.

Goemaat, J. (2004, May). A case of good judgment. *Security Management*, [Online].
Available: http://www.securitymanagement.com [2009, December 22].

Hinton, D. (2002*). Criminal records book: The complete guide to the legal use of criminal records*. Tempe, AZ: Facts on Demand Press.

Hudak, R. (2005). Former FBI, Adjunct Professor at John Jay College, and Director of Corporate Security for Loews Corporation. Unpublished document.

Interagency OPSEC Support Staff (Producer). (2000). *Applying OPSEC to criminal investigations* [Motion picture]. (Available from Interagency OPSEC Support Staff, 6411 Ivy Lane, Suite 400, Greenbelt, MD 20770)

Interpol. (no date). *Criminal intelligence analysis*, [Online].
Available: http://www.interpol.int/public/cia/default.asp [2009, December 22].

Jackson, G. (1999). *Golden nuggets for investigators*. U.S. Air Force Office of Special Investigations.

Magaw, J. W. (1998, March). Comments of the director of the Bureau of Alcohol, Tobacco and Firearms at the ASIS Washington, DC, Chapter Leadership Awards Luncheon.

Merriam-Webster. (2009). "Management" entry, [Online].
Available: http://www.merriam-webster.com/dictionary/management [2009, December 16].

National Institute of Justice, Office of Justice Programs. (2001). *Electronic crime scene investigation: A guide for first responders*. Washington, DC: Author.

National Institute of Justice, Office of Justice Programs. (2000). *Crime scene investigation: A guide for law enforcement*. Washington, DC: U.S. Department of Justice.

National Institute of Justice, Office of Justice Programs. (2000). *Fire and arson scene evidence: A guide for public safety personnel.* Washington, DC: U.S. Department of Justice.

Nebo, P., CPP. (1999). *Multinational and international investigations: Cultural analysis.* Washington, DC: Webster University.

Office of Justice Programs. (2003). *Applying Security Practices to Justice Information Sharing.* Washington, DC: U.S. Department of Justice.

Panaro, G. P. (2004). Attorney at Howe & Hutton, Ltd. Unpublished document.

Parsons, M. (2000). *Computer investigations and operations update.* Washington, DC: Naval Criminal Investigative Service.

Patterson, E., Brigadier General, Commander, Air Force Office of Special Investigations. (2002, May/June). Eagle eyes up and running around Air Force. *Global Reliance.*

Peterson, K. E., CPP. (1998). *The liaison advantage.* Herndon, VA: Innovative Protection Solutions.

Peterson, K. E., CPP. (2002–2005). *National Operations Security Program.* Presentation to the Federal Protective Service Physical Security Academy.

Peterson, M. B. (1998). *Applications in criminal analysis: A sourcebook.* Westport, CT: Praeger Publishing Company.

President's Commission on Critical Infrastructure Protection. (1997). *Critical Foundations.* Washington, DC: Author.

Presley, L. (2004). Director of Criminalistics, National Medical Services. Interview. Willow Grove, PA.

Presley, L. (2002). *The use of forensic science in private and corporate investigations.* Presentation to the ASIS International Seminar & Exhibits.

Ray, D. (2003, February). Don't make a federal case out of it. *Security Management,* p. 56.

Repetto, T. A. (1978). *The blue parade.* New York: The Free Press.

RSA Security. (2000). A *guide to security policy: A primer for developing an effective policy.* Bedford, MA: Author.

Rudewicz, F. E., CPP. (2004, February). The road to rage. *Security Management,* p. 40.

Rudewicz, F. E., CPP. (2004, February). The road to rage. *Security Management,* [Online]. Available: http://www.securitymanagement.com [2009, December 22].

Securitas Security Services USA. (2004). *History,* [Online]. Available: http://www.pinkertons.com [2004, October].

Smith, R. (1997). Former Special Agent in Charge, Central Systems Fraud Detachment, Air Force Office of Special Investigations. Unpublished document.

SouthWest Emergency Response Network (SWERN). (2004). *Homeland security information network—Critical infrastructure*, [Online].
Available: https://www.swern.gov [2004, November].

Thompson, A. L. (2004). President, Applied Communications & Technology, Columbia, MD. Interview.

Townley, M., Chief, Office of Operations Security, U.S. Bureau of Alcohol, Tobacco and Firearms. (2003). *Protecting critical information.* Presentation to the National Operations Security Conference, Monterey, CA.

U.S. Department of Defense. (2005). *DOD dictionary*, [Online].
Available: http://www.dtic.mil/doctrine/dod_dictionary/ [2009, December 22].

U.S. Department of Justice, National Drug Intelligence Center. (2005). *National drug threat assessment for 2005*, [Online].
Available at http://www.justice.gov/ndic/pubs11/12620/12620p.pdf [2009, December 22].

U.S. Department of Labor, Office of the Assistant Secretary for Policy. (2005). *Working partners for an alcohol and drug-free workplace*, [Online].
Available: http://www.dol.gov/workingpartners [2009, December 22].

U.S. Sentencing Commission. (2002). *Federal sentencing guidelines, chapter 8: Sentencing of organizations*, [Online].
Available: http://www.ussc.gov/2002guid/tabconchapt8.htm [2009, December 22].

U.S. Sentencing Commission. (2004). *Sentencing Commission toughens requirements for corporate compliance and ethics programs.* News release, April 13, 2004.

University of Florida (2002). National retail security survey.

Webster University, Business and Organizational Security Management Program (2004). *Investigations management* (Graduate Course Material, SECR 5130). Washington, DC: Author.

U N D E R C O V E R
I N V E S T I G A T I O N S
AS A PROTECTION TOOL

2.1 THE NEED FOR UNDERCOVER INVESTIGATION

Undercover investigations, although complicated and difficult at times, can be of great value to the protection and preservation of corporate assets. However, undercover investigation should only be chosen as a preventive measure when no other alternatives are available and when the company can reasonably expect a significant return on the investment. Therefore, knowing when and how to employ undercover investigation is critical to its success.

The purpose and objectives of an undercover investigation must be clearly identified in advance. A qualified investigator from a reputable agency should be selected to conduct the fact-finding and drive the process. A project management team, consisting of representatives from both the company and the agency, should communicate frequently during the course of the investigation. Law enforcement agencies and personnel should only become involved when necessary. Following the investigation, proper communication with the workforce is critical.

Despite the best intentions, every undercover investigation encounters unique problems, and those participating in the investigation should anticipate difficulties and set up contingencies. With proper planning and the necessary resource allocation, many problems can be avoided.

The main potential problem in an undercover investigation is the possibility that the investigation will be exposed or compromised. Exposure of an undercover operation, to the workforce, customers, suppliers, or the general public either during or following the investigation, is usually undesirable If employees are made aware of an undercover investigation before its completion through some form of communication by management, for example, morale and productivity may be adversely affected. Customers or suppliers may feel resentful at having been part of the investigated activity and may choose to discontinue their relationship or patronage. Public exposure of a compromised investigation may spark further resentment and an onslaught of painful adverse publicity.

To prevent a compromise or unwanted exposure of an investigation, confidentiality must be maintained. Only those with an absolute need to know should be involved in or told of the investigation. To do otherwise may risk the organization's investment and put people (including the undercover investigator) at risk.

2.2 **THE HISTORY OF UNDERCOVER INVESTIGATIONS**

While an authoritative history on the development and use of undercover investigations in the United States does not exist, Alan Pinkerton appears to be the first to write about the practice. Pinkerton, a Scottish immigrant, formed one of America's first private detective agencies in Chicago during 1850. The Pinkerton Agency's operatives quickly established themselves as innovators and risk-takers.

Shortly after the start of the Civil War in 1861, Pinkerton became Union General George McClellan's Secret Service chief. In his book on the times, *The Spy of the Rebellion* (1883), Pinkerton details the inner workings of America's first organized spy network. With great admiration and affection, Pinkerton also reveals the exploits of his favorite undercover agent, Timothy Webster. Pinkerton writes, "No historian will ever relate the thousand perils through which [Webster] passed in the service of his country." Webster's career as a Pinkerton undercover investigator was not a long one however. He was arrested, quickly condemned as a spy, and put to death on April 13, 1862, in Richmond, Virginia, by order of Confederate President Jefferson Davis.

In his book, Pinkerton also identifies Mrs. Carrie Lawson as America's first female undercover agent. According to Pinkerton, the efforts of Mrs. Lawson and her butler, John Scobell (also a Pinkerton employee and undercover operative), provided McClellan's Secret Service with critical information that in no small measure aided the North and helped defeat the South.

Following the war, Pinkerton was sent to Washington, D.C., to form the United States Secret Service. Pinkerton's undercover operatives were also busy after the war. It was Pinkerton's James McParlan, for example, that ultimately lead to the ruin of the Molly Maguires, a secret organization of Irish-Americans operating in the mining districts of central and eastern Pennsylvania. Allegedly, the name immortalized a woman who had led an anti-landlord rebellion in Ireland during the 1840s.

Between 1865 and 1875, the Mollies and their movement rose up against oppressive labor practices in the coal mining industry and the squalid living conditions in their rural communities. Because the police and the criminal justice system were entirely controlled by the mine owners, the Mollies often resorted to murdering or intimidating law enforcement or government agents and company officials.

In an 1875 show of power, the Mollies established a union in a previously unorganized region of Pennsylvania and called a strike. Franklin Gowen, president of the Reading Railroad, which had extensive mining interests, hired Alan Pinkerton and his agency to infiltrate the union. Pinkerton inserted his best undercover agent, McParlan, into the organization and its unlawful union. Ultimately, ten Molly Maguires were hanged. For unknown reasons, McParlan died a wealthy man. Suspecting collusion, ancestors of those condemned pressed the U.S. Congress for release of McParlan's secret reports, but they were not released for study until 1947.

During the 1920s and 1930s, as revealed by actual operatives years later, Detroit's motor car companies used undercover agents to address employee theft and on-the-job alcohol use. Although, leading physical security companies such as Pinkertons, Wackenhut, and Burns offered an undercover service to their clients, it remained only a sideline. As a result, undercover investigations as a major factor in the protection of private industry did not surface again in written accounts until the 1980s.

In 1981, industry realized that substance abuse had begun to take a grip on America's workers. Through articles published in the mainstream media of the day, managers were forced to acknowledge that a social problem had become a workplace problem. By 1985, undercover became, and remains to this day, the preferred method of investigating substance abuse and criminal activity in the workplace.

2.3 WHAT IS UNDERCOVER INVESTIGATION?

Corporate undercover investigation is the surreptitious placement of a properly trained and skilled investigator, posing as an employee, into an unsuspecting workforce for the primary purpose of gathering information. They are, by nature, covert operations. Undercover investigations are complicated and are not suitable in all environments. As a result, undercover is the least understood and most underused form of investigation.

The chief distinction between undercover and other type of investigations is that the undercover investigator neither conceals his or her presence nor attempts to operate unnoticed. The sub-rosa aspects of the investigation center on the true identity of the investigator, called the operative, or the purpose of the study. Along with interviewing, undercover investigation is a form of interactive investigation. This unique quality allows the skilled operative to not only gather information concerning a workplace problem but also to learn the "how" and "why" behind the actions of those under investigation.

2.4 **WHEN SHOULD UNDERCOVER BE USED?**

Undercover investigation should be the exception, not the rule. The technique should only be contemplated when no other options are available. While the technique might appear deceivingly simple, in truth, it is complicated, demanding, and fraught with the potential for legal challenges and liability for both the employer and the investigator. Undercover practices also require an investment of time, patience, and resources by the company. It requires a highly structured process and flawlessly executed plan.

Because the undercover operative does more than periodically collect information and mingle with coworkers, he or she may need to interact socially as well as professionally with the target group or individual. Association with the target may be close and continuing, such as in daily work assignments, or periodic or coincidental, such as when the investigator occasionally meets the target at a recreational activity or takes the same public transportation. As a result, the professional pursuit of information can lead to entrapment and may collide with the personal need for safety, immunity, and privacy. This tangled web of considerations and complexities are among the reasons why undercover investigation is not for everyone or for every organization.

How an undercover investigation unfolds will be dictated by the nature of the information sought. The following situations are typical of those that lend themselves to the use of undercover:

- Consistent, reliable information suggests employee misconduct, conversion (term used for receiving money or property of another and fraudulently withholding or applying it to one's own use) or criminal activity but insufficient details hinder prevention efforts or the identification of those involved.

- Losses are known to be occurring in a specific sector of the company, as in the case of failing to record cash accepted from customers, but available information cannot pinpoint how they occur or who is responsible if it was a conspiracy (two or more individuals involved).

- Management strongly suspects that alcohol use, drug abuse, or drug dealing is occurring in the workplace, or actual indicators of these behaviors have been detected.

- Alcohol or drug abuse is impairing on-the-job performance, yet supervisors are unresponsive or incapable of intervening.

- Actual work practices need to be compared with required or stated policies, and routine auditing is not possible.

- Management believes embedding operatives will produce significant results, and all other reasonable options have been ruled out.

2.5 **WHEN UNDERCOVER OPERATIONS
ARE NOT APPROPRIATE**

Clearly, undercover investigations should not be used to gather or collect information of a personal or confidential nature or to offensively intrude into the private life of anyone where a reasonable expectation of privacy exists. Such efforts are actionable and may give rise to legal claims against the employer and its investigators. Specifically, the option should not be considered in the following circumstances:

- To investigate any activity permitted or protected by any governmental statute, rule, or regulation.

- To replace some other form of investigation or fact-finding that will likely produce the same results while consuming less time and resources.

- To investigate protected union activities. Federal law prohibits surveillance or investigation of union activities.

The use of undercover should not automatically be ruled out simply because a workforce is unionized. It is permissible for an employer to use undercover and even place undercover investigators into a unionized workforce as long as the investigation does not impinge upon the lawful and protected activities of that union or its membership. However, an employer should not use existing union employees in an undercover role.

2.6 THE FIVE PHASES OF THE INVESTIGATION

No organization should be afraid to use undercover investigation when the situation warrants this action. While the practice can be complex and expensive, the operation can be managed effectively with a well-thought-out plan. Successful workplace undercover investigations unfold in five distinct phases: planning and preparation, information gathering, verification and analysis, disciplinary and corrective action, and prevention and education.

2.6.1 PHASE ONE: PLANNING AND PREPARATION

When the decision to move forward with an undercover operation is made, careful plans must be prepared, drawing in the appropriate individuals. In this phase, an investigative team is formed, the investigation's objectives are decided, an investigative agency and operative are selected, and the remaining phases are planned. Planning is the key to an effective undercover investigation.

Investigative Objectives

Before it embarks on an undercover investigative project, the organization should select an investigative team. At a minimum, the team should include a corporate decision maker, a representative from human resources, a corporate security professional, and an attorney familiar with state and local employment law.

This team should meet to decide on the expected outcome or objective of the investigation. Should employee misconduct be uncovered, the outcome could include employee discipline, prosecution, and restitution. Before deciding on which course of action to pursue, however, the organization should review past practices, industry precedent, organizational policies, applicable labor contracts, and the criminal definition of the suspected activity. In addition, the effect on employee relations, public opinion, and the organization's culture and reputation must be considered along with the potential return on investment when no other alternatives are available. Sometimes competing, these considerations must be thoroughly analyzed and weighed before realistic objectives can be decided. For example the risk of embezzlement may be greater in an organization where the culture's predominant value is economic.

The objectives of the investigation will drive the type and structure of the pending investigation. Although an undercover investigation may be conducted for one purpose, information unrelated to that purpose or subject may be unearthed. Anticipating that unexpected information will surface and establishing a mechanism to deal with it is a necessary part of the planning phase.

Some situations might produce information useful to the employer but inappropriate for an investigation. Trying to determine the relative strength of a union organization campaign by identifying the workers sympathetic to the union would be a prime example and could be determined to be an unfair labor practice.

The objectives of an undercover investigation could include the following:

- To identify the true nature, scope, and perpetrators of a problem.

- To gather information so management can enforce its policies and take corrective action.

- To collect information in a way that is the least disruptive to the organization and its operations.

- To ensure the process provides the best return on investment.

These objectives are not only achievable but also the hallmark of any successful undercover investigation. They communicate that those who will conduct the investigation understand the organization's needs and know how to fulfill them.

Selecting an Agency

Once constituted, the investigative team should seek out a vendor that can provide the undercover investigator and conduct the investigation. Although law enforcement agencies can conduct workplace undercover investigations, most have neither the time nor the resources to devote to a proper investigation. As such, most employers turn to private agencies that specialize in undercover operations.

When pursuing the selection of an undercover agency, the client should:

- Request a copy of the agency's license and required permits. In several states, private investigators and their agencies must be licensed.

- Ask to see an agency's training curriculum and operative training files. The agency selected should conduct thorough preemployment screening and periodic drug testing after hire and should provide professional training to its investigators.

- Elicit answers to difficult questions regarding the agency's knowledge of and experience with investigations similar to the type under consideration.

- Ask for references and check them thoroughly. The best agencies are well known in the business community and are active in their trade associations.

- Find out about the firm's litigation and claims experience. All undercover investigators must be willing to testify and see their cases through to their fullest completion.

- Ask for sample reports and examine them closely.

- Require the agency under consideration to provide a Certificate of Insurance naming the organization as an additional insured. Also ensure the coverage is "occurrence" based (protection is provided regardless of when the claim is made), not "claims-made" (protection is provided only during the duration of the policy).

- Ask the agency to provide police references and cases when law enforcement assisted during past investigations. While employee prosecution is not always necessary, investigations involving illegal drugs cannot be done without the assistance of the police.

In addition, the client should be made aware of the length of time needed for the job, all associated costs, and the method of communication that will be used between the client and the investigator. The company should also ensure that its corporate attorney meets with the potential vendors. He or she will play a critical role and should be an active participant during the investigation.

Selecting and Placing an Investigator

Once an agency is selected, the next step is to choose the investigator. For the most part, today's professional corporate undercover investigators are well educated, properly trained, and highly motivated. Better agencies also routinely test their operatives for drugs. Because investigators may never know when they will be exposed to workplace drugs and substance abuse, they must randomly be screened to ensure their credibility and discourage carelessness. Short of a life threatening circumstance, the operative must never use or even sample illegal drugs. To do so threatens credibility and jeopardizes the entire investigation.

Undercover investigators come in all shapes, sizes, and colors. They also vary in experience and ability. The client should assist the agency in choosing an investigator that will blend into the target workforce. To ensure that the investigator fits in with the target audience, a number of personal factors should be considered, including sex, age, job experience, education, and ethnicity. In addition, the investigator should easily fit into the socioeconomic background and lifestyle of the workers he or she will be joining. For example, if the investigator must work with an unskilled labor force in a job typically filled by persons with less than a high school education, the operative's style or mannerisms should not imply that he or she either possesses a college education or spends more than the typical employee.

Professional operatives must also have strong communication skills. Not only must they make written reports detailing their daily activities, they must also be able to effectively communicate verbally with the agency's supervisor and occasionally with the employer or client.

The client should provide a position for the operative that will allow the investigator a great degree of interaction with a great number of employees. The position must allow the operative sufficient mobility to effectively network and obtain the desired information in the shortest amount of time. To achieve this goal, the operative must be placed in a position that allows him or her to encounter large numbers of employees and still perform the responsibilities of the cover position.

While undercover operatives can pose as an on-site contractor, they can also be very effective as an internal employee. In these circumstances, the undercover investigator should be treated just as any other employee and should not receive any preferential treatment or special considerations.

Proper placement of the operative is crucial to the investigation because the job selected must be one from which the mission's objectives can be achieved. As an illustration, if the client suspected that finished goods were being diverted at the shipping platform of a distribution center, the optimal job would give the investigator maximum opportunity to be on or near the dock. The most important activity for an undercover operative is learning the job and becoming familiar with surroundings.

Some of the best internal positions for the undercover operative are in the following departments:

- Material handling
- Shipping and receiving
- Mailroom
- Customer service
- Uniformed security

If the position requires specialized skills, the operative should already have the skills required for the job. If necessary, remedial training can be provided before the investigator reports for work. However, should this question arise, the client may find it more cost effective to simply select another investigator who already has the required skill level. If a vehicle must be used, the client should ensure that it cannot be traced to the investigator.

The investigator can be placed into a cover position in two ways. In the first, a cold hire, the investigator applies for a position and is processed just like any other applicant. This type of entry is preferred but is the least practical. In the second, a controlled hire, the employment process is manipulated covertly so that the operative is hired in the desired capacity and placed in the targeted location.

Before reporting for work, the operative should devise a plausible cover story, a fictitious reason or motive advanced to conceal the true one. The cover story should explain specifics of the investigator's identity and how he or she came to obtain the job. The level of detail can be superficial or quite involved, depending on the circumstances. Generally, the more intimate the investigator must be with members of the target group, the more in-depth the cover story should be.

While the details will need to be tailored to the specific situation, an operative's cover story should include the following points:

- A connection with the operative's actual past. In the best circumstances, the operative will have held a similar job before.

- A sound "back story" that includes personal details that are not true but which are known to the targeted employee. For example, the operative might claim that he or she attended a specific school, worked at a certain location, or lived in the same neighborhood as the target.

- Back-up for the actions contemplated by the investigative plan. For example, if the operative must ask the target to meet his or her "fence," then the operative must have such a connection. Or if the operative claims to own a custom sport utility vehicle, then he or she must drive such an automobile.

- Documents that support the cover story. The operative should be able to produce the normal documents needed by any employee in a similar situation. However, no documentation that indicates the investigator's actual identity should ever be carried while on an assignment.

2.6.2 PHASE TWO: INFORMATION GATHERING

Once the client, the investigative agency, and the operative have agreed to the specifics of the undercover assignment, the information-gathering phase can begin. This phase involves two types of assets: people, or those involved in the project management team; and processes, or how information will be communicated, reported, and preserved in case files.

The Project Management Team

The project management team oversees the actual investigative casework. It can be built from the investigative team, but should include five distinct but interrelated individuals who work closely together: the undercover investigator, the project manager, the client representative, a corporate attorney, and, if necessary, a representative of law enforcement. Each participant plays a distinctly different role but coordinates and communicates every effort with the other team members. This active participation and teamwork makes a successful investigation possible.

The undercover investigator can make or break the investigation. Through his or her ability to think, plan, and execute under often difficult and dangerous circumstances, the investigation moves forward. Once the investigation begins, the investigator will first engage in "relationship building." During this most important phase, the operative will learn the job, become familiar with the surroundings, and make acquaintances. The investigator should resist the temptation to press for information or appear too inquisitive. To do so will create suspicion and will hamper the ability to gather information later.

The project manager, usually someone from the investigative agency, should be responsible for the day-to-day administration of the case as well as the daily care and maintenance of the operative. The project manager should also maintain regular contact with the employer as well as the others involved in the project. The project manager must also ensure that the other team members are kept abreast of the operative's progress. In this respect, the project manager functions as the vehicle through which all case information flows and is disseminated.

To be effective, the project manager should be good a communicator, have exceptional writing skills, and a sound background in investigations and management. Prior law enforcement or military experience, though helpful, is not absolutely necessary. The best project managers have high ethical standards, understand the intricacies of civil and criminal law as it applies to the investigative process, and have terrific people skills.

The project manager must also have patience. For the operative, the cover position can be hard, dirty, and tiring. Cases that drag on for six months or more can be boring and sometimes frustrating. The operative needs to be closely monitored and coached so the case remains focused and moves forward with purpose. The project manager must supervise and motivate the operative and keep the assignment on track.

The client representative acts as the primary point of contact for the employer, and all information passing into and out of the organization should pass by this individual. In this way, confidentiality is protected, and the risk of accidental compromise is significantly reduced. The person selected for this position should be high enough on the organizational chart to have the authority to make policy decisions and spend the organization's money. The individual should also be of strong character and, of course, trustworthy.

Many investigative agencies and their clients never consider involving an attorney in an undercover investigation. This remarkable lapse in judgment is evidenced by the lawsuits these ill-fated endeavors precipitate. Security professionals who rely on their own knowledge and the legal counsel of an investigative agency to weave through the complexities of the typical workplace undercover assignment put their jobs and careers at risk. A major reason to involve legal counsel as part of the management team is to protect the investigator's work product from discovery.

The counsel selected must be an employment law specialist with experience in cases involving employment claims. He or she must also understand the intricacies of criminal prosecution and its affect on employer liability. The attorney selected can be most effective if he or she joins the team during the investigation's planning phase because the pre-litigation preparation needed in undercover cases is sophisticated and unique in the investigative community. Unlike litigation, the prosecution has the obligation to present all of the evidence that will be used by the prosecution, even if it is damaging to the prosecution. The failure to do so makes any other evidence inadmissible and effectively useless for the purpose of prosecution. Therefore, the attorney must be qualified to address employment, contract, and prosecutorial questions as they arise.

Law enforcement agencies play a critical role in most workplace undercover investigations. In cases involving illegal drugs, for example, no drug purchases should take place without the approval of the law enforcement agency with jurisdiction. In other types of cases, law enforcement may provide resources and in some instances actively participate in the supervision of the operative.

Communication

The project team, however constructed, cannot function without effective communications. Information can be collected and shared through written reports, electronic communications, or the telephone.

Written reports are the most fundamental form of communication used in undercover assignments. Even before the operative reports to the workplace, he or she can start generating reports. Although practices vary from agency to agency, most firms require their operatives to make daily reports as soon as possible after every shift. These reports, in their most basic form, detail the who, what, when, where, how, and why of the investigator's daily observations and experiences. Whatever the format selected, reports must be easy to read and accurately describe the observations and experiences of the operative. Generated by the operative at the end of the workday, the reports are then transmitted to the project manager for review and dissemination.

In writing a report, the investigator should assume that the reader knows absolutely nothing about the case other than what is provided. For example, descriptions such as using "short" to describe a person's height or "small amount" to quantify drug use forces the reader to guess what the writer is trying to say. Even "late day" and "early hour" are relative terms. The use of simple, direct language enhances the accuracy and clarity of the report.

A basic operative report, using a timeline or chronological format, is shown in *Appendix A.* The information contained in the report is organized so that the facts follow one another in a logical sequence, and the material related to a particular incident or event can be easily located and understood.

One of the most popular formats for investigative reports today, the structured narrative, is shown in *Appendix B.* This simple, yet sophisticated format still presents information in chronological order, but includes more detail. It is also noteworthy for its simplicity and readability as it is conversational in tone.

The narrative report is written in the third person, using descriptive text or "the operative," instead of in the first person using the pronoun "I." This technique is preferred for two reasons. The first is very practical: if the report is written in the first person, it technically cannot be edited by anyone other than its writer. For example, suppose an operative submitted a report to the project manager, which included the following sentence: "I observed Ben Richards leave his assigned machine." Before the project manager could prepare a report for a client presentation, the sentence would need to be edited into the third person: "The operative observed Ben Richards leave his assigned machine." In this case, the report would have to be re-authenticated by the operative before it could be passed on. This dilemma is easily overcome by simply generating all reports in the third person, a practice that eliminates massive rewrites and saves time and effort.

The second reason for preferring third person reports is more complicated. Suppose the results of the investigation were challenged, and the project manager who edited the operative's reports was deposed or otherwise called on to testify. While under oath, the project manager could be asked to identify the document's writer. He or she would have to admit that the operative's report was altered (edited). When asked to identify the alterations, the manager might be unable compare the edited version with the original and could easily miss something or make a mistake. The error could be exploited in an attempt to show that the report presented to the client (and ultimately used to make decisions) was possibly inaccurate since the project manager could not even recognize what he or she had altered.

If the operative's report had been created in the third person, however, the project manager could logically explain that the report he or she generated for the client was not a doctored version of someone else's work. Thus the manager could attest to the accuracy of the document and explain any differences from the operative's originals. The version presented would not look like an edited operative report pawned off as an original.

To see this important distinction, compare the operative reports in *Appendix A* and *Appendix B* with the resulting project manager's report in *Appendix C*. Clearly it would be difficult to get from *Appendix A* to the client report provided in *Appendix C* without using a great deal of literary license and red ink.

Also note that each entry in *Appendix B* is a stand-alone paragraph preceded by an alphanumeric code. These codes allow the project manager to later merge the operative's daily reports and then sort them by topic or date. Electronically, the project manager can quickly prepare a report for the investigative team in which the information is sorted chronologically as well as by subject. This "investigative summary," also written in the third person, is provided to the appropriate members of the investigative team in the place of daily reports. *Appendix C* is an example of a typical investigative summary.

The frequency of investigative summaries depends upon the needs and desire of the user. Typically, such summaries are prepared after the operative has completed a consecutive ten days of work. This timing allows the accumulation of enough information to allow for thoughtful analysis of events and provides the content with some continuity.

Information from the operative's daily report can meld seamlessly into the investigative summary report—such as paragraph A-13 of the daily report in *Appendix B* and the last paragraph of the summary report in *Appendix C*. Because the operative's report was written in the third person, it easily slides into the summary report. Reorganizing the information by topic makes the investigative summary more readable and much easier to use by the project team.

Another report that is typically produced during the investigation is called the "special report." These reports document a special event observed by the operative or something other than the normal happenings in the course of the investigation. Although there is no established format for these special reports, they should be easy to read and prepare. An example of such a report is shown in *Appendix D*. Notice that it was created easily from the investigative summary report (*Appendix C*). If the document could be used as criminal evidence, it should to be reviewed and signed by the operative before it is submitted to the client company.

Another way for the project management team to effectively disseminate information is through electronic communications, which has replaced many traditional methods of communication in today's digital age. For example, e-mail, the preferred method of communications for much of the business world, has overshadowed written mail and other physical means of moving information because it is fast, efficient, and inexpensive. An operative's reports uploaded to the investigative agency's network at the end of the work day can be downloaded, edited, and resent within minutes of receipt to a recipient at the client location. Using digital video, the sophisticated investigative agency can transmit scenes of a workplace drug transaction to virtually anyone with Internet access.

Telephone communications, whether conventional or wireless, are a necessary component of today's modern undercover investigations. In addition to providing a daily written report, the operative should talk to the project manager every day. Typically, however, he or she does not need to take or preserve notes on telephone conversations. As a function of normal operations, the project manager may choose to document telephone contacts to assure the client that communication with the operative occurred. Ultimately, though, the tangible, written reports will be used by the parties involved as a basis for action.

Case Files

At the completion of the investigation, all case file documents, including original notes, reports, and investigative summaries as well as any evidence should be retained. The person designated to maintain and archive the closed case file is called the "custodian of record."

The management and format of case files is largely a matter of preference by the project manager. However, the system chosen should be simple and neat. Because undercover investigations tend to generate a lot of paper, large three ring binders work well as document holders.

At a minimum the file should include sections for the following documents: operative daily reports, investigative summary reports, special reports, correspondence, and billing and expense information.

The case binder should be marked "confidential," and no reference to the operative or the investigation should be on the outside cover. Even a code name or case number on the outside of the file could arouse suspicion and invite someone with accidental access to peek inside.

Electronic folders and files should be downloaded and stored safely, preferably on recordable CDs or DVDs. Each disk can hold hundreds of megabytes of information, enough space to hold the case file of even the largest investigation. Digital images, spreadsheets, and databases can also be downloaded to disk and stored for safekeeping. Although duplicate information and files can be deleted to save space on servers, original documents and files should always be retained.

2.6.3 PHASE THREE: VERIFICATION AND ANALYSIS

Once the operative has been removed, the other members of the project management team take on the task of bringing the case to its conclusion by conducting employee interviews. Interviews are the most critical component of the entire undercover investigation. For those who use this powerful tool will attest, most of the information gleaned during the investigative process comes from their interviews. Information on how to conduct proper interviews can be found in the *Chapter 5. Interview and Interrogation*.

One distinction should be noted. In most general investigations, the interview process closes in on the perpetrators over time. However, interviews that follow an undercover investigation often begin with those most involved and work toward those less involved.

Following the interviews, the project management team should compile all of the information gleaned during the investigation and separate it by individual. Typically, information can come from three sources: information developed by the operative, details provided by the employee during a personal interview, or accounts provided by others during their interviews. The project management team can then prepare to guide company representatives through the information, examining the totality of information on each offender.

2.6.4 PHASE FOUR: DISCIPLINARY AND CORRECTIVE ACTION

Once the interview process is completed, the project management team turns the information over to the client's decision makers who then determine how discipline will be administered. In this instance, the security professional and the other members of the investigation's project management team are the information gatherers; others in the company make the disciplinary decisions. Once the discipline and corrective actions have been taken, all files, records, tapes, and evidence should be provided to the case file custodian of record for storage and safekeeping.

Following the disbursement of discipline, communication with the remaining workforce is recommended. Communications, whether written or spoken, should not be done until after all the disciplinary and corrective action has taken place. Any meetings should be direct and straightforward.

2.6.5 PHASE FIVE: PREVENTION AND EDUCATION

No discussion regarding employee misconduct is complete without mentioning prevention. Generally, workplace crime is a function of three fundamental elements:

- The quality of people the organization hires.
- The environment in which those people are placed.
- The quality of supervision managing that environment and those people.

Most offenders exposed during an undercover investigation had no business enjoying the jobs they had, and they should never have been hired. Stopping the problem at the door through effective preemployment screening only makes sense.

Many lessons can be learned from an undercover investigation. The results may reveal training failures and expose educational deficiencies. The project management team should make appropriate recommendations to corporate management, which can select the ones that will provide the highest return on investment.

Frequently, supervisors and managers are not equipped with the skills or tools necessary to prevent problems from recurring. In this instance, education and training is the answer. Training modules developed for this purpose might cover the following topics:

- Workplace substance abuse detection and prevention
- Loss prevention and asset protection
- Employee theft prevention
- Workplace violence prevention
- Basic supervision and people management.

2.7 **REMOVING AN OPERATIVE**

The amount of useful information gathered in every undercover investigation eventually reaches a point of diminishing return. Typically, the investigation has simply yielded enough information to allow the operative to be removed. The timing of the removal of the operative is one of the most frequently debated subjects among undercover supervisors. However, the answer is simple: the operative should be kept in as long as possible. However, if the undercover operator is to be removed, he/she should depart with a plausible explanation.

In cases where interviews follow the undercover effort, the operative should stay in place until named as a co-offender by enough interviewees so that he or she illogically should be interviewed also. The best time to remove the operative is once he or she has been named as an offender. To remove the operative sooner would only raise suspicions. If removed before the interviews begin, it will be clear to everyone that the person in question was an informant.

If the undercover investigator is not compromised or otherwise exposed when the case is concluded, he or she can continue to be very valuable if left in place. Following a highly visible workplace investigation, communications should be open with all levels of the organization. Once disciplinary or other corrective action is taken by an employer following a high-profile case, offenders who have not been caught can become complacent. Some will even brag of their cunning and ability to slip through management's grasp. These individuals then become easy targets for the undercover operative and further investigation.

2.8 TYPES OF UNDERCOVER INVESTIGATIONS

While undercover investigations can reveal a host of loss prevention issues, two types have become most common in recent years: drug investigations and theft investigations.

2.8.1 DRUG INVESTIGATIONS

Contrary to popular belief, drug investigations for the most part are relatively easy and are not always dangerous. Once an undercover investigator has successfully joined the workforce and is accepted by co-workers, his or her efforts can become more focused. Drawing on the contacts made during the initial relationship-building phase of the investigation, the operative can begin to actively identify the substance abusers. With guidance from the project manager and law enforcement agencies, the operative can systematically pursue information about each substance abuser as they are identified. The operative may eventually have the opportunity to buy drugs from those willing to sell them, thereby separating the users from the dealers. To prevent problems, guidelines should be established to direct the operative during this important stage of the investigation.

Guidelines for workplace drug purchases are not a matter of public policy or law. Rather, they are drawn up by the investigative team to give direction to the operative. The guidelines should address the following specifics:

- *Qualify the Dealer.* Entrapment is best defined as inducing a person to commit a crime. To overcome any potential allegation of entrapment (which is actually not a crime, but a criminal defense), the operative should qualify each person from whom he intends to purchase. Qualifying can be done through a simple report covering two points. First, the operative should establish that the behavior or activity in question was preexisting, or that the dealer had sold drugs previously. Second, the operative should establish why the dealer wants to sell to him or her. The perfect motive would be financial gain. By establishing a proper motive, dealers cannot claim that they were improperly induced into engaging in an activity that they knew was wrong. To avoid any allegation of entrapment, the operative should never invite another employee to commit criminal activity.

- *Coordinate with Law Enforcement.* All workplace drug buys should be done under the control and supervision of law enforcement. Although this step is not always possible, every attempt should be made to ensure that the appropriate law enforcement agencies are aware of and approve the drug purchase. This is especially true during a "buy-bust" at the conclusion of an undercover operation. Without this immunity, the operative and the investigative agency could be faced with criminal prosecution for the possession, transport, or purchase of a suspected controlled substance.

- *Buy Down not Up.* As a matter of practice, law enforcement agents typically buy increasingly larger quantities of drugs from the dealers they pursue. They purchase their way up the distribution chain hoping to eventually eliminate the supply at its source. However, in workplace drug investigations, the operative should purchase the smallest quantity the dealer is willing to sell. The employer must only demonstrate that the dealer committed a policy violation. The quantity sold is not an issue. Furthermore, by buying small quantities the operative can buy more often and from more individuals. Best or larger buys should be made near the conclusion of the undercover operation.

- *Make Purchases on Company Time.* Under most circumstances, an employer cannot control what an employee does away from work. The focus of the workplace investigation should be workplace issues and misconduct, not the enforcement of public law.

- *Avoid Actual Drug Use.* Short of a life-threatening situation, the operative should not use illegal drugs. To help preserve the operative's credibility in the eyes of the client, routine drug testing should be done. The results of periodic hair and urine testing can demonstrate that the investigator is not a substance abuser and has not used an illegal drug.

Drug purchases give credibility to an employer's claim of workplace substance abuse. However, the lack of an actual drug purchase is not fatal in a drug investigation. Many factors and situations may arise that force the investigator to forego an otherwise permissible buy. For example, a qualified dealer might insist that all drug purchases take place off company property at locations where he or she would be alone with the investigator. In other instances, the dealer might insist that the operative use the drug before he sells it. Regardless, the properly engineered investigation contemplates these situations during the planning phase and identifies solutions.

Experienced investigators (and arbitrators) know that drug purchases are not necessary to make good drug cases. Rather, good investigations make good drug cases. As a result, the investigation of potential drug use must include more than just an undercover operative. The investigative team can also draw on an assortment of investigative techniques. From chemical testing and ion scan technology to the use of trained narcotics dogs, the process of investigation should employ every information-gathering tool available.

If the investigation's objectives include prosecution, the team must be sure that it is necessary. Most importantly, the value of employee prosecution should be carefully calculated when determining the investigation's overall return on investment. Surprisingly, employee prosecution rarely provides any real return on the company's investment. Disciplinary action is a preferred recourse, since prosecution, from a business perspective, only further erodes the corporate bottom line and has been shown to have little deterrent value.

2.8.2 **THEFT INVESTIGATIONS**

Undercover investigations are often used to determine if theft is occurring at the workplace. Theft investigations mirror any other undercover investigation. However, special care should be taken during the planning phase.

Strategy and tactics play important roles in almost every successful theft investigation. The investigator must become visible and accessible to those who are stealing. Because the identity of the perpetrators may not be known at the beginning of the investigation, this part of the investigation can be particularly difficult, expensive, and time consuming.

As an alternative, operatives should try to attract the thieves to them. In one of the most basic tactics used to investigate employee theft, the operative appears to already be involved in some form of criminal activity. Employees who are involved in breaking the law in one way will often find it easy to join the operative in trying to break the law in other ways as well, a phenomenon known as cognitive consistency.

A well-known undercover axiom says that where one finds substance abuse one will also find theft. Therefore, the prudent undercover investigator looking to solve a theft problem should first look for a substance abuse problem. By seemingly being in the middle of the client's substance abuse problem, the operative can gain direct access to those involved in theft or diversion of company assets.

Another investigator, or third party, can pose as a shady associate of the operative with criminal connections. Without a great deal of lead time or preparation, this associate can be brought into and out of play. Without actually calling the associate a fence, a thief, or drug dealer, the operative carefully casts him or her as a highly trusted friend, relative, or gang member.

In theft investigations, it is perfectly acceptable for operatives to participate in a scheme to steal. But because their credibility is at stake, all of the theft activity should be done with an explicit purpose and be pre-approved by the project management team.

Everybody likes to get something for nothing, and criminals are no different. Offering small appliances, cigarettes, or common hand tools at ridiculously low prices is one such rouse to enhance the operative's criminal credibility by making coworkers think the products are stolen. Event tickets are another popular giveaway or item to sell.

One caution, however: Introducing weapons of any form into an investigation is unnecessarily dangerous and most likely unlawful. An investigator engaged in selling off-price merchandise might be asked to provide a handgun, for example. The investigator should not be allowed to do anything that will diminish his or her safety or that of the workplace or do anything else that is unlawful or otherwise inappropriate. A case can be worked in many ways without placing people at risk.

Buy-Busts and Sting Operations

The buy-bust is nothing more than arresting the perpetrator at the moment he or she is either buying or selling the property in question. Usually the other party to the transaction is a member of law enforcement or a designated agent. On some prearranged signal, the suspect is confronted and arrested on the spot. Arresting the offender at this stage of the investigation prevents the loss or destruction of valuable evidence and eliminates the need to chase down dangerous and possibly armed offenders later.

In theft cases, just as in most drug cases, this technique works best toward the end of the investigation. Because buy-busts usually culminate the investigation, the true identity of undercover operatives and law enforcement agents can, by design, be exposed during the bust, although this is not always the case nor it is always necessary.

Sting operations, on the other hand, are similar, but the term generally connotes a longer, more complicated investigative effort. Sting operations usually involve elaborate setups and buy-busts. They might include the actual setup and operation of a business as a front or place where stolen goods are sold or traded. Because of their complexity, good sting operations are usually expensive and time consuming.

Evidence Markers

Invisible evidence markers have been around for years. These interesting products allow the user to surreptitiously mark property so that if it is stolen and then recovered its rightful owner can be identified. Specific information on types of invisible markers can be found through an Internet search or in any law enforcement supply catalogue.

Corroborating Evidence

In most theft cases, corroborating evidence beyond that provided by the undercover investigator is often invaluable. The most common and most economical form of corroborating evidence is videotape. By carefully choreographing the action, the operative and the thief can be placed in perfect positions to be videotaped. In this way, the stolen property, the money, and entire transaction can be documented.

Multiple Buys

As in drug investigations, multiple buys from the thief makes a stronger case. As a matter of practice, the operative should always try to make more than one purchase from each player. Multiple purchases help eliminate the claim that the activity was spontaneous or an anomaly. Multiple purchases also help prove that the perpetrator is a true offender and not just someone who made a one-time mistake. Initially, the investigator should purchase a minimal amount.

Recoveries

Recoveries can be a big part of theft investigations. While determining who is stealing and what they are taking is most valuable, of equal value is why are they stealing and how the stolen property is being disposed. If other parties are receiving the property, civil recovery may be possible. Once these additional thieves are identified, the investigation can be engineered to allow recovery from them as well as the principle perpetrators. While typical recoveries include the property itself or consideration for the property, the costs of the investigation can be recovered as well. A settlement of this type significantly increases the return on investment of any investigation, not just undercover.

2.9 THE COST OF UNDERCOVER OPERATIONS

A successful undercover investigation requires money. The size, scope, and nature of the problem will determine the amount of money the employer must invest. Today, most experienced undercover investigation firms charge by the week (or some larger increment). The weekly rate is usually based on a forty-hour work week plus a minimum "cover pay," a wage paid to the undercover investigator. The weekly rate includes charges for both the investigator's time and that of his or her supervisor, as well as for report writing, transcription, postage, and communication with the employer's designated point of contact. This fee should cover everything except out-of-pocket expenses and the cost of other special investigations used to augment the undercover effort. When billed in this fashion, the investigator keeps the cover pay, and the agency pays the difference between it and the operative's normal salary.

Some less-experienced agencies charge by the hour and bill additional costs for report preparation, photocopies, and every telephone call, a practice that can cause the client to feel "nickeled and dimed to death." Clients tend to resent complicated invoices that suggest everything is passed on to them and every minute is billed. What's more, experienced clients know this billing scheme lays the foundation for hidden charges. Those who bill undercover by the hour will also bill for their investigators' report writing time, travel time, and overtime.

Some agencies claim to have several levels of skill or classifications for their undercover investigators. Another common manipulation of fees is charging a differential based on the investigator's experience. Some agencies go to great lengths to create the appearance of having huge flocks of investigators stratified by skill or experience. Should a potential undercover agency make such a claim, the client should ask to see written descriptions and qualifications for each level. The agency should then be able to tell how many investigators they currently have working undercover at each level. They should also be able to provide an investigator and a supervisor from each level for an interview.

The better agencies have no second- or tenth-tier employees. This system is just too complicated and expensive to maintain.

While overcharging can happen, undercharging is far more typical, a fact that is not a blessing for the potential employer. Undercharging or undercutting prices causes good but struggling agencies to cut corners and take unnecessary risks. It also unfairly erodes the profits of the healthy agencies. It diminishes every agency's ability to pay their investigators properly and provide them with proper benefits.

Businesses, even good businesses, do not continue to provide products and services if they cannot make a profit. Undercharging creates a market filled with inexperienced cutthroats that provide products and services of questionable quality. Unfortunately, the undercover business is no different.

2.10 THE FUTURE OF UNDERCOVER INVESTIGATIONS

In the future, the demands of an aging population and society's commitment to them will significantly alter the world's economy. Entrepreneurial businesses will seize the opportunity and fulfill these needs. And as is always the case, new industries spawn new problems and criminal opportunities.

One of the tools likely to be used to address these challenges will be undercover investigations. Already, the abuse and mistreatment of the elderly has made headlines. Unable to defend themselves and often unable to effectively report the abuse, the elderly are easy victims. Properly placed undercover investigators in these environments can help find a solution.

A similar opportunity is childcare. Again, the potential exposure to abuse and criminal conduct is not only enormous but horrific. Undercover investigators posing as staff, nurses, and doctors can infiltrate facilities and monitor the operation and its employees in a way no other form of investigation can. Not even covert cameras can learn what is said behind closed doors or what children are told to do or think. Properly managed undercover operatives can identify abuse and negligence.

A growing challenge is also evident in the healthcare industry. No longer can hospitals and healthcare institutions allow visitors and staff member to roam freely about the hospital or its campus. Baby thefts, equipment sabotage, and assault have heightened the concerns of every hospital administrator and security professional. Because of their open environment, hospitals are prime targets for thieves, vandals, and other forms of criminal activity. Unfortunately, more locks, cameras, or guards will not eliminate the problem. And although these tools play a critical role in keeping healthcare institutions safe, more will need to be done.

Undercover operatives effectively placed into the staff or posing as patients and visitors can easily serve as cost-effective tools to augment existing security architectures. Because of the high mobility most hospital employees and visitors enjoy, hospitals make perfect environments for effective and successful undercover investigations.

The technology companies of today will be tomorrow's has-beens if they cannot maintain their competitive edge. The very technological advances they have created will be used against them to steal their secrets, their ideas, and their people. Already, bolder enterprises are taking action. Discreetly, some of America's hi-tech powerhouses are using undercover operatives to monitor and protect their most important secrets. The effort is cost effective and terribly appropriate.

Governments can be a consumer of undercover services as well. A few possible applications include the investigation of discrimination complaints or the covert monitoring of food processing facilities and waste disposal sites. Entire corporate sectors could benefit from undercover operations, including the transportation industry and the food and drug industry. The interwoven chains of companies that comprise these industries and have high turnover among key financial positions leave them fraught with the potential for waste and fraud—the intentional deception perpetrated for the purpose of unlawfully taking another's property.

The future of undercover operations is bright as more organizations realize that this option may offer a solution where other security methods cannot. To stay competitive in today's global economy, companies cannot afford to absorb losses that can be discreetly discovered and corrected. Corporate awareness will turn into action, as it must.

APPENDIX A

CHRONOLOGICAL REPORT

THE XYZ INVESTIGATION COMPANY / DAILY REPORT

*** CONFIDENTIAL INFORMATION ***

AGENT: A1234B	ASSIGNMENT: 000-000-000
DAY: THURSDAY	DATE: 08/26/05

0600	I ARRIVED AT 000-000-000 AND CLOCKED IN.
0745	I TOOK BREAK AND OBSERVED BEN RICHARDS (EMPLOYEE, SUSPECT #1) AND MIKE MILLER (EMPLOYEE, SUSPECT #2) MEET IN A SUSPICIOUS MANNER.
1000	I WENT ON BREAK (UNSCHEDULED) AND TALKED ABOUT NOT BEING ABLE TO SLACK OFF AT WORK ANYMORE BECAUSE THE SUPERVISOR, CHRIS WATTS (EMPLOYEE, SUSPECT #3) HAD RETURNED FROM VACATION ON WEDNESDAY, 08/25/99. WATTS SAID FRIDAY WOULD BE A 12 HOUR SHIFT.
1200	I CLOCKED OUT AND DEPARTED FOR LUNCH WITH MIKE KILNER (EMPLOYEE).
1310	I LEFT MY WORK AREA TO TALK TO JOHN (LNU, JANITOR).
1315	I RETURNED TO MY WORK AREA. THIS WAS NOT A SCHEDULED BREAK TIME. NORMAL BREAK TIME IS 1345-1355 HRS.
1315	I PURCHASED MARIJUANA FROM RONNY SANDERS (EMPLOYEE, SUSPECT #7). SEE INCIDENT REPORT #7.
1450	I CLEANED UP MY WORK AREA.
1500	I CLOCKED OUT AND DEPARTED 000-000-000.
1530	I WENT J.J.'S BAR & GRILL AND DRANK BEER WITH SEVERAL EMPLOYEES.
1600	I DEPARTED J.J.'S.

END OF REPORT

APPENDIX B

NARRATIVE REPORT

Case Name:	Diamond-Back
Case Number:	000-000-000
Date:	Thursday, August 26, 2005
On Clock:	6:00 a.m.–3:00 p.m. (8.0)
Off Clock:	10:00 a.m.–11:00 a.m. (1.0)
Off Clock:	3:00 p.m.–4:00 p.m. (1.0)
Off Clock:	0.5 (report)
Expenses:	Social Activities $10.00 for beer, $1.00 tip

> For security purposes a code name is used in lieu of client's actual name

> For easy sorting, each entry is coded according to a checklist provided to the operative

OPERATIVE DAILY REPORT

A-13 Suspected Drug Activity.

On Thursday, August 26, 2005, at approximately 7:45 a.m., while in the production area, the operative observed **Ben Richards** (insert operator/temporary) leave his assigned machine accompanied with **Mike Miller** (production supervisor). **Richards** and **Miller** then entered the supplies closet and closed the door behind them. Both employees remained in the closet for approximately 3 minutes. **Richards** returned to his machine. **Miller** departed from the department. The operative intends to follow up and talk to **Richards** about this incident tomorrow.

E-23 Message from Management.

On Thursday, August 26, 2005, at approximately 10:00 a.m., while in the production area, **Chris Watts** (floor supervisor) informed the production department that Friday, August 27, 2005, was going to be a 12 hour mandatory shift due to excessive customer orders. Watts warned all the production employees not to be absent or tardy. Approximately 15 production employees complained about the overtime to **Watts**. **Watts** stated to everyone that it was normal to work long hours the first quarter of the year. The meeting ended and production resumed work.

B-2 False Time Records.

On Thursday, August 26, 2005, at approximately 1:10 p.m., while in the production area, **John** (last name unknown/Janitor/temporary) was observed clocking in three timecards. The operative asked **John,** to whom the timecards belonged. **John** explained they belonged to other janitors (names unknown) who were late. No further questions were asked due to **John's** behavior. **John** departed from the area and discontinued the conversation. **John** is described as a white male, approximately 22 years of age, 6'1", 200 pounds, brown short hair, brown eyes, and wore a blue janitorial jumpsuit uniform and white tennis shoes.

A-4 Marijuana Sale.

On Thursday, August 26, 2005, at approximately 1:15 p.m., while in the receiving department, **Ronny Sanders** (receiving clerk) handed what **Sanders** identified to be a 1/16 of an ounce of bud (marijuana) to **Mike Lance** (forklift operator) in exchange for $20.00 (two ten dollar bills). **Lance** placed the marijuana in his right side pants pocket. **Lance** thanked **Sanders** and exited the department through dock door 11. **Sanders** stated that **Lance** buys marijuana from him at least once a week at work. **Sanders** was paged over the intercom by **Tony Lucas** (receiving manager) to receive an order at dock door 14. **Sanders** responded to the page and discontinued the conversation. **Sanders** provided no further information concerning the marijuana transaction.

B-1 Absenteeism.

On Thursday, August 26, 2005, at approximately 2:10 p.m., while in the production area, **John** (last name unknown/Janitor/temporary) stated that he planned on calling in sick on Saturday (August 28, 2005). **John** further stated that he was going hunting for elk with several friends (non-employees/names unknown). **John** concluded the conversation by saying he often misses work. No further details were disclosed. **John** is described as a white male, approximately 22 years of age, 6'1", 200 pounds, brown short hair, brown eyes, and wore a blue janitorial jumpsuit uniform with white tennis shoes.

C-17 Sabotage.

On Thursday, August 26, 2005, at approximately 3:30 p.m., while at J. J.'s Bar & Grill (Cedar Springs, Colorado), **Kenny Sanchez** (truck driver) stated that he and two other driver's (names unknown) frequently puncture their work truck tires to avoid driving to certain delivery locations (locations unknown). **Sanchez** further stated that he has punctured the tires on his assigned truck on 3 occasions in a 12-month period. **Sanchez** changed the topic of conversation because **Randy Clark** (shipping lead) sat at the table with the operative and **Sanchez**. The conversation was changed to current affairs and sports. No further information was obtained.

Submitted by: A1234B ◄———— Because the report is submitted electronically and cannot be signed, this unique code authenticates it and the operative that submitted it.

End of Report

APPENDIX C

INVESTIGATIVE SUMMARY REPORT

The Very Big XYZ Company
Any Street
Any Town, USA 55555

Re: Diamond-Back
000-000-0000

INVESTIGATIVE SUMMARY REPORT

*** CONFIDENTIAL INFORMATION ***

The following Investigative Summary reflects the results of our investigative efforts at the Cedar Springs facility. The dates included are from Monday, August 16, 2005, through Friday, August 27, 2005. The operative developed information concerning the sale of cocaine and the talk of marijuana use/sales. Additionally, information was documented involving security/safety issues, employee misconduct, and employer/employee relations.

To date our efforts have yielded:

12 Cocaine purchases on company time and property

6 Cocaine purchases on company time off company property

7 Marijuana purchases on company time and property

Additionally, we have identified:

16 Employees using cocaine on company time and property

12 Employees using marijuana on company time and property

COCAINE SALE

On Tuesday, August 17, 2005, at approximately 11:35 a.m. while in the rail assembly area of the facility, **Ben Richards** (insert operator/temporary) motioned to the operative to step out the exit located behind the rail blaster. The operative walked out the exit at which time **Richards** reached into his left shirt pocket and pulled out a cigarette wrapper and dumped from it a large white rock wrapped in cellophane, and handed it to the operative. **Richards** explained that the operative could break off a piece, put it in a pipe and smoke it the way it is because it was so pure and better than the last "stuff" (cocaine), that he had sold the operative on Friday, August 13, 2005.

At approximately 11:40 a.m. the operative took possession of the cocaine **Ben Richards** (insert operator/temporary) had given him.

At approximately 11:45 a.m. the operative put the cocaine obtained from **Ben Richards** (insert operator/temporary) into an evidence bag that **Special Agent Kenny Berger** left with him, and then locked it in the evidence box in the trunk of his vehicle. The operative then proceeded to the First State bank to rendezvous with **Special Agent Berger**.

At approximately 12:00 p.m. the operative met **Special Agent Berger** and surrendered the locked evidence box. **Special Agent Berger** opened the box and removed the evidence bag. Upon satisfactory inspection of the bag and the evidence within it, **Special Agent Berger** provided the operative with a receipt (see Exhibit A) and returned the unlocked evidence box. **Special Agent Berger** allowed the operative to photograph the package after examining it himself (see Exhibit C). The operative placed the unlocked box in the trunk of his vehicle. **Special Agent Berger** retained the only key to the box. At approximately 12:10 p.m. the operative left the bank parking lot and returned to the facility.

At approximately 12:35 p.m. while in the rail assembly area of the facility, the operative gave **Ben Richards** (insert operator/temporary) $300.00 completing the cocaine transaction. The operative handed **Richards** three one hundred-dollar bills provided by the **Colorado State Police Narcotics Task Force**. The serial numbers of the bills are; AB67547008I, AL04508146D, and AJ35735194A (see Exhibit B).

SUSPECTED DRUG ACTIVITY

On Thursday, August 19, 2005 at approximately 11:00 a.m. while in the rail assembly area of the facility, the operative was engaged in conversation with **Ben Richards** (insert operator/temporary). **Richards** told the operative that **Chris Watts** (floor supervisor) likes to use crystal methamphetamine, because it leaves the body's system in two to three days. **Richards** further told the operative that when **Watts'** hand was cut open at work and he received stitches, he was not tested for drugs like other employees who are injured at work.

On Thursday, August 26, 2005, at approximately 7:45 a.m., while in the production area, the operative observed **Ben Richards** (insert operator/temporary) leave his assigned machine accompanied by **Mike Miller** (production supervisor). **Richards** and **Miller** then entered the supplies closet and closed the door behind them. Both employees remained in the closet for approximately 3 minutes. **Richards** returned to his machine. **Miller** departed from the department.

End of Report

Note that this paragraph came directly from the operative's daily report (Appendix B).

APPENDIX D

SPECIAL REPORT

The Very Big XYZ Company
Any Street
Any Town, USA 55555

Re: Diamond-Back
000-000-0000

SPECIAL REPORT # 16

Full physical description provided
to ensure positive identification

On Tuesday, August 17, 2005, at approximately 11:35 a.m. while in the rail assembly area of the facility, **Ben Richards** (insert operator/temporary, male Caucasian, 5' 11", 200 pounds, brown shoulder-length hair, blue eyes and large blue dragon tattoo on left forearm) motioned to **Confidential Informant #1** to step out the exit located behind the rail blaster. **Confidential Informant #1** walked out the exit at which time **Richards** reached into his left shirt pocket and pulled out a cigarette wrapper and dumped from it a large white rock wrapped in cellophane, and handed it to **Confidential Informant #1. Richards** explained that **Confidential Informant #1** could break off a piece, put it in a pipe and smoke it the way it is because it was so pure and better than the last "stuff" (cocaine), that he had sold **Confidential Informant #1** on Friday, August 13, 2005. At approximately 11:40 a.m. **Confidential Informant #1** took possession of the cocaine **Ben Richards** (insert operator/temporary) had given him.

At approximately 11:45 a.m. **Confidential Informant #1** put the cocaine obtained from **Ben Richards** (insert operator/temporary) into an evidence bag that **Special Agent Kenny Berger** left with him, and then locked it in the evidence box in the trunk of his vehicle. **Confidential Informant #1** then proceeded to the First State bank to rendezvous with **Special Agent Berger**.

At approximately 12:00 p.m. **Confidential Informant #1** met Special Agent Berger and surrendered the locked evidence box. Special Agent Berger opened the box and removed the evidence bag. Upon satisfactory inspection of the bag and the evidence within it, Special Agent Berger provided **Confidential Informant #1** with a receipt (see Exhibit A) and returned the unlocked evidence box. Berger allowed **Confidential Informant #1** to photograph the package after examining it himself (see Exhibit C). **Confidential Informant #1** placed the unlocked box in the trunk of his vehicle. Special Agent Berger retained the only key to the box. At approximately 12:10 p.m. **Confidential Informant #1** left the bank parking lot and returned to the facility.

Depending upon the needs of the prosecutor,
the operative's name may or may not be used.

At approximately 12:35 p.m. while in the rail assembly area of the facility, **Confidential Informant #1** gave **Ben Richards** (insert operator/temporary) $300.00 completing the cocaine transaction. **Confidential Informant #1** handed **Richards** three one hundred-dollar bills provided by the **Colorado State Police Narcotics Task Force**. The serial numbers of the bills are; AB67547008I, AL04508146D, and AJ35735194A (see Exhibit B).

End of Report

_____   _____

   Confidential Informant #1   Date

Because the document may be used as evidence, the operative may be required to sign it.

REFERENCES

Barefoot, J. Kirk (1995). *Undercover Investigation, 3ʳᵈ Edition*. Woburn, Massachusetts: Butterworth-Heinemann.

Columbia Encyclopedia, Sixth Edition [Online], (2004). *Molly Maguires*. Available: http://www.encyclopedia.com/html/M/MollyM1ag.asp [2004, October 1].

Ferraro, Eugene (2000). *Undercover Investigations in the Workplace*. Woburn, Massachusetts: Butterworth-Heinemann.

Pinkerton, Alan (1883). The Spy of the Rebellion. New York, New York: W. G. Dillingham.

Rosen, Mark B. (1992). "Going Undercover: An Inside or an Outside Job." *Security Management*, vol.36, no.6. Alexandria, Virginia: ASIS International.

Simmons, R. J. (1994). *Employer's Guide to Workplace Security and Violence Prevention*. Los Angeles, California: Castle Publications.

U.S. Department of Justice (1995). Crime Data Brief: Crime and Substance Abuse. Washington, DC: Government Printing Office.

U.S. Department of Justice (1993). *State Drug Resources: 1992 National Directory*. Washington, DC: Government Printing Office.

U.S. Department of Labor (1993). *Workplaces Without Drugs*. Washington, DC: Government Printing Office.

CHAPTER THREE

DUE DILIGENCE

3.1 **DEFINITIONS**

Due diligence is "a measure of prudence or activity that is to be expected from a reasonable and prudent person under the particular circumstances; not measured by an absolute standard, but dependent upon circumstances of a particular case" (ASIS International, 2007).

> *Black's Law Dictionary* (2004) defines it as follows:
>
> > The diligence reasonably expected from, and ordinarily exercised by, a person who seeks to satisfy a legal requirements or to discharge an obligation. –Also termed *reasonable diligence; common diligence.* Corporations & Securities. A prospective buyer's or broker's investigation and analysis of a target company, a piece of property, or a newly issued security. A failure to exercise due diligence may sometimes result in liability...

Common business usage defines due diligence as the investigative process for evaluating a target company or a company's assets for the purpose of acquisition by a potential buyer/acquirer.

The term *due diligence* loosely means doing one's homework on a particular subject. It takes place when an individual researches an issue, person, deal, or anything else, in an effort to determine whether it is legitimate—whether it "checks out." Merriam-Webster's Online Dictionary (2009) defines due diligence as follows:

> 1: the care that a reasonable person exercises under the circumstances to avoid harm to other persons or their property
>
> 2: research and analysis of a company or organization done in preparation for a business transaction (as a corporate merger or purchase of securities)

The term originated in the securities industry but has become a catchphrase for a methodology of risk management. The Securities Act of 1933 provided the first common use of the term *due diligence*. The act included a defense called "the Due Diligence Defense," which could be used by broker-dealers accused by investors of inadequate disclosure of material information. The Act absolved broker-dealers of responsibility for any information they failed to uncover about a company, as long as they conducted a due diligence investigation and disclosed their findings to potential investors. In other words, they were not held accountable for negative information they did not uncover. To protect themselves, broker-dealers adopted due diligence as a standard practice. Due diligence is now common vernacular for any investigations in almost any industry. Some types of due diligence investigations are financial, operational, covert, cultural, intellectual property, mergers and acquisitions, human resources, legal, information technology, and environmental.

Due diligence investigations are valuable in any situation where one or more parties are deciding future actions or non-actions based on existing conditions or on representations made by another party. In other words, anytime one party is trying to make a decision about whether to do something and depends on information from another person or conditions that need verification, due diligence is valuable.

As the ASIS definition notes, there is no absolute due diligence. Instead, the standard for a due diligence investigation depends on the type of investigation, the goals of the investigation, the individual conducting the research, and the available information. In fact, two investigators looking at the same problem may reach different conclusions based on their research and their analysis of the information they uncover. Although one can find some standard suggestions for ensuring due diligence (*Appendix A* provides a suggested due diligence checklist for a corporate acquisition), most cases are unique and should be approached from a distant perspective. If the matter under review results in litigation, one reviewer of the facts may find due diligence and another may not.

Whether due diligence was exercised is determined by looking backward. It can be difficult to ascertain whether a due diligence investigation was correctly conducted until after the deal is complete and observers review the investigation and compare it with the results. For example, if an investigation undertakes a due diligence investigation on a property, observers would argue the investigator conducted a thorough due diligence investigation. If, however, an investigator conducts a due diligence on a piece of property and finds no problems, but later the purchaser discovers the land cannot be developed because of zoning changes, observers will say the investigator failed to conduct a complete investigation. It is irrelevant whether the investigator had access to the information on zoning changes or intentions of the zoning board. The assumption is that the investigator should have uncovered the information that would have affected the purchaser's decision on whether to proceed with the deal.

Due diligence investigations may be required in any situation in which one or more parties expect to change position based on apparent conditions or on representations made by one or more other parties. For recurring situations, such as corporate mergers or the selection of a person to act in a fiduciary capacity, it is possible to develop models for ensuring due diligence. Although not all transactions can be reduced to a checklist, many can. Each case, however, is independent and must meet the "reasonably prudent person" rule.

The doctrine of due diligence can be compared to the doctrine of negligence. Diligence emphasizes the positive aspect of due care, while negligence describes the failure to exercise due care. Like negligent conduct, failure to exercise due diligence can result in legal damages if another party is harmed as a result. Lack of due diligence can also be costly to the person or entity that fails to exercise it, even if no damage occurs to others. Failure to exercise due diligence—due care in investigation—can result in enormous costs to all parties involved, including the loss of money, opportunities, and time.

3.2 RELEVANCE TO ASSETS PROTECTION

One of the most important reasons for conducting due diligence investigations is to protect assets. Without ensuring that a transaction or person is legitimate, a party gambles his or her assets.

Due diligence is a critical requirement for the protection of enterprise assets, particularly in transactions with outside parties. For example, if a manufacturer seeks a distributor for its products, it must vet potential vendors by ensuring candidates are competent to complete sales, have financial and logistical capabilities to maintain inventory, have a positive reputation so the manufacturer is not tainted by the association, and have a sure warehouse, among other matters. Without assurances about the distributor, the manufacturer risks losing product, time, and reputation, all of which have a cost to the manufacturer. In addition to direct loss, such as loss of product, the manufacture also can suffer cost in terms of lost opportunity, loss of market share, and negative reputation.

In this example, before contracting with the distributer, the manufacturer may want to know the following:

- *Business history of the potential distributor.* How long has it been in business? What is its level of success? What products does it currently distribute?

- *Distribution method.* How is product distributed? Does the distributor own trucks? How many?

- *Product tracking.* What system will the distributor use to track product and ensure safety from warehouse to distribution points? Are there methods of identifying the product to ensure its security throughout the distribution system? What are they?

- *Security and insurance.* How safe is the storage facility? The distribution network? What types of insurance does the distributor carry?

- *Relationships.* Is the distributor affiliated with other companies? Competitors? Does it have a history of positive business relationships or of problem relationships? Does it have the ability to partner with other companies who could assist in product distribution/sales/marketing?

- *Litigation.* Has the distributor been involved in previous litigation? With whom? Why? Do the suits reflect the general 'cost of doing business' or do they appear to reflect substantial problems with the distributor? Ws the distributor the plaintiff or defendant? Does it appear to break contracts? Does it regularly sue partners?

- **Reputation.** What is the reputation of the company? What is the reputation of the managers, officers, and other decision makers in the company? Will it hurt or help the manufacturer to be associated with the distributor?

- **Financial and credit issues.** What is the current financial and credit situations of the company? What is its credit and financial history? Does the distributor have enough resources to retain inventory? What are the source and extent of funds available to the company? How much debt does the company carry?

- **Sales and marketing.** Will the distributor assist with the sales and marketing of the product? What channels does it have in place? How large is its sales and marketing force? What media outlets does it use to advertise?

- **Officers and managers.** Who are the decision makers in the company? Do they have any "skeletons in the closet"? What is their business history? What is their reputation? What is their financial situation?

- **Total sales volume.** What is the sales volume currently booked by the distributor? How much capacity can it handle?

- **Facilities.** What facilities does the distributor currently own or lease? How large are they? What is the current state of the facilities? Where are they located?

- **Profitability.** What is the distributor's current and historic profitability (as a gauge of its operating efficiency)?

In finding reliable answers to these questions, the manufacturer exercises due diligence. These categories are not exhaustive, however, and the manufacturer could examine many other issues. Wider due diligence investigations may also examine a company's strategy, information technology, operations, human capital, and culture.

The difficulty of obtaining the information depends on the type of deal, and the type of information sought. Friendly deals may provide easy access to information, while hostile arrangements make it more difficult to obtain data from the target.

In a friendly acquisition or partnership, parties may readily exchange information to help facilitate the deal. However, one common error in due diligence investigations is relying on information from the target. While a target may attempt to provide accurate data, it is often skewed (sometimes inadvertently), or information may be omitted or ignored. If the target wants a deal to go through, it will attempt to provide the most favorable information possible. Verification of information from primary sources is critical to creating unbiased due diligence.

3.3 **EFFECTIVENESS OF DUE DILIGENCE INVESTIGATIONS**

Comprehensive, cohesive due diligence investigations are not only effective but also critical in weighing the pros and cons of mergers, hiring, alliances, acquisitions, investments, and other deals. Because there is no single "checklist" for due diligence, however, the results can vary widely. While a good due diligence investigation is the necessary cornerstone for making a decision, a poorly executed one can completely mislead parties.

True due diligence goes beyond verifying information provided by parties. It attempts to verify that information, but it goes beyond and uncovers new information, raises questions, and points to new areas for investigation. Failure to investigate fully can have disastrous consequences (for example, failing to uncover an internal investigation into the chief financial officer's fraudulent accounting activity could be a deal breaker). Parties involved in any transaction with other parties—even parties they believe they "know"—should undertake an unbiased, thorough due diligence investigation before proceeding.

In the United States, the USA Patriot Act of 2001 placed new responsibilities on financial institutions and multinational companies, which must make every effort to detect violations of the Foreign Corrupt Practices Act and Patriot Act. In a due diligence investigation after September 11, 2001, a company considering entering into a relationship with another company found that the second company's chief executive officer was affiliated with Osama bin Laden (Shaffer, 2004, p. 57).

Major business deals have failed because of inadequate due diligence investigations. In 1997, for example, Comp-U-Card (CUC) International merged with HFS, a travel services company. At the time of the merger, both companies were anxious to join, and neither side undertook serious a due diligence investigation. In 1998, after the merger, HFS accountants noticed irregularities in CUC's merger reserves. In April 1998, the company disclosed CUC's earnings problems, which caused Cendant's stock price to plummet—wiping out $14 billion in market capitalization in one day. In 2004, prosecutors put the two top officers of CUC on trial, charging they fabricated $252 million in non-existent earnings. HFS essentially lost everything because, in its enthusiasm to merge with CUC, it failed to conduct a comprehensive due diligence investigation.

A thorough due diligence provides information to assist in making a good decision, even if it does not include every piece of information. While a due diligence investigation does not guarantee the success of a venture, it provides valuable insight. Even incomplete or missing information can be useful. For example, if it is virtually impossible to obtain financials on a company, the company may have reasons to obfuscate financial information. Gaps in an individual's employment are technically a lack of information, but can speak volumes about an individual's history. Likewise, if a company has no reputation in its sector, no press coverage, and no recognition in trade journals, it may not have the track record it advertises. At a minimum, a strong due diligence investigation can raise issues for further research, verify or contradict given information, and point parties to new directions for information.

A due diligence investigation is not a guarantee of success, nor is it always possible to obtain all the information that would preclude making errors in judgment. However, if best practices are followed, the due diligence report serves as a foundation for further consultation and negotiation.

The Bernard Madoff scandal clearly shows the need for due diligence. In the case, Mr. Madoff lured investors to his hedge fund by promising and demonstrating returns higher than any other fund or securities investment. In late 2008, authorities discovered he was not actually making the investments he claimed. Instead, his fund was actually a $50 billion Ponzi scheme.

The strong reputation of the Madoff fund made potential investors giddy (and greedy) over the possible returns, so they ignored the usual due diligence process in exchange for fast action and entry into the fund. A proper investigation likely would have shown that it was virtually impossible for the fund to realize the level of gains Mr. Madoff represented. In fact, according to the *Wall Street Journal*, some of the analysts who performed due diligence investigation on Mr. Madoff were unable to replicate the fund's historic returns, conducting the same trades he reportedly made. They concluded it was doubtful Mr. Madoff made all or any of the required trades his strategy dictated. *Barron's* raised the possibility that his returns were most likely due to front running his firm's brokerage clients. Investors chose to ignore warnings and not to undertake additional due diligence because Mr. Madoff discouraged investigation and suggested that questioning him could limit individuals' ability to invest.

Details of several significant due diligence cases can be found at www.marketing-intelligence.co.uk/pubs/case-studies.htm and in *The Art of M&A: Due Diligence, Navigating Critical Steps and Uncovering Critical Data* (Lajoux, 2000).

3.4 **DUE DILIGENCE GUIDE**

As has been noted, there is no single, objective criterion for a due diligence investigation. The investigator must first look at the question at hand and determine what is important for the particular problem. Therefore, the first step in any due diligence investigation is to examine the issue at hand—the deal, the person, the investment, etc.—and understand what factors to focus on to answer the problem.

A due diligence strategy should include at least the following questions:

- What is the nature of the problem? What is at risk?

- What is the background of the situation? How well do the parties know each other?

- Who are the main players?

- What factors are important to the parties undertaking the deal?

- What potential problems would be most costly? What other minor problems could affect the issue?

- What type of transaction do the parties expect? What is the size of the transaction? How complex is it?

- What is the cost of the investigation in terms of time and money? How difficult will it be to obtain information?

- What are the risks for the players? What is the cost to the players if the transaction fails?

The key to a good due diligence investigation is to understand the needs of the client and the transaction at hand. If investigators lack an understanding of the object of the investigation, they almost certainly will fail in their due diligence because they will not ask the right questions.

3.5 **INFORMATION SOURCES**

Numerous investigative resources are available for conducting due diligence investigations. In general, resources can be broken down into primary and secondary research tools.

Primary sources include these:

- Interviews with individuals
- Direct observations of people, places, or events

Secondary sources include these:

- government-maintained public records
- commercial record sources
- annual reports and other company records
- news and other media sources

Many secondary resources are now available electronically, via the World Wide Web. Some are free, while others are available through pay sites. Some sites require users to have a valid private investigator license to access them, while others are available to the general public. Because access and available records change daily, investigators should regularly survey resources to ascertain the types and locations of available information. One advantage of government records is that they tend to be unbiased. The following are information sources that due diligence investigators may wish to consult:

- *Clerk records.* Each county clerk maintains records on liens, judgments, litigation, marriage, divorce, property ownership, mortgages, and other vital information. These records are important because they also show relationships, addresses, and patterns of behavior. They also often provide leads on other places to look for information.

- *Securities and Exchange Commission filings.* The United States Securities and Exchange Commission maintains records on public companies, providing valuable information concerning those companies. It also maintains records on licensed broker-dealers and investment funds. Public companies regulated by securities laws must file a variety of reports with the SEC. The annual report (10-K) and quarterly reports (10-Q) are extremely informative. The 10-K provides information on company organization, business activities, finances, legal activities, officers, and other issues related to the company. The quarterly reports update the annual reports, and contain any substantive changes since the annual report was filed. Private companies are not required to file reports with the SEC

  SEC reports are available online at www.sec.gov, or in person at SEC public reading rooms. Individuals wishing to access SEC filings can also request documents by mail. In Canada, each province has its own Securities Commission, which provides information to researchers online. *Appendix B* contains a list of security regulatory bodies in various other countries.

- *Secretary of State or Division of Corporations.* Each U.S. state has a Secretary of State or Division of Corporations that records and holds documents related to companies incorporated in that state. Depending on the state, these records may include annual reports and name change documents and may also provide information on mergers and acquisitions, date of incorporation, status, and names and addresses of officers. Many states provide access online, by phone or mail, or in person.

- *State regulatory agencies and licensing boards.* U.S. states have agencies that regulate individuals in various occupations, such as medical professionals, attorneys, therapists, private investigators, security guards, and persons who work in the gaming industry. These agencies or boards can provide information on individuals' licensing status, complaints, judgments, specialties, training, and other issues.

- *Uniform Commercial Code filings.* In the United States, sellers or creditors file Uniform Commercial Code (UCC) reports to record commercial debt. UCC filings note the type of transaction, the date of the transaction, the amount involved, the creditor and borrower (or seller and buyer), and the manner in which the debt is secured. UCC information is available on the Internet.

   In Canada, information similar to UCC filings can be obtained through provincial government agencies, such as those dealing with consumer and business relations.

- *Freedom of Information Act documents.* The Freedom of Information Act (FOIA) allows the public to request documents from government agencies that would not normally be considered public records. For example, the Federal Bureau of Investigation, local law enforcement, the Central Intelligence Agency, and the Department of State all have FOIA officers to provide access to previously classified documents. Some state and county offices also have FOIA access. While these documents can be valuable, often it takes a long time to obtain them. They also generally contain large blacked-out sections that are not releasable to the public.

- *Criminal records.* In the United States, the public can access criminal history records through the county clerk. There is no legal method for the public to search the entire country for criminal records.

   In Canada, the public can conduct a nationwide criminal check with a signed release, through the Canadian Police Information Computer.

   Several online sources offer international searches for over 200 countries. However, some of the information may be difficult to verify, and the process can be slow and expensive.

- *Property records.* Most U.S. counties have property appraisers' offices that offer information on property ownership, property value, sales information, deed transfers, and previous ownership. Google Earth, Yahoo Maps, and other free satellite services also offer overhead and street-level views of properties.

- *Patent records.* The United States Patent and Trademark Office offers free online access to patents. Other sites, such as Google Patents, also allow free patent searches.

- *Credit reports.* The major credit reporting companies—TransUnion, Equifax, and Experian—are valuable sources of financial, organizational, and personnel data on businesses and individuals. To obtain those documents, however, researchers must obtain signed releases and authorization from the target. Credit reports by themselves are not a good source of public information, and material from a commercial credit report should be confirmed through primary sources

- *Corporate reports.* Dun & Bradstreet provides corporate reports, primarily on publicly traded companies. Lexis-Nexis and Dialog are excellent sources for gathering news stories about public and private companies.

- *Watchdog data.* A number of watchdog organizations also provide information on companies. However, their information may skewed to reflect their particular point of view. One group, CorpWatch, provides links to other sites in a step-by-step guide to researching company background. Other groups include Corporate Watch (the UK version of CorpWatch), the Public Information Network, Public Citizen, Corporate Governance, CSRWire, and CSR Forum.

- *Interviews.* Interviews by professional investigators are valuable for a number of reasons. They provide information and background and direct the investigator to other sources of information. While the individual being interviewed likely presents information through his or her own filter, a skilled investigator can elicit important information.

- *Direct observations by investigators.* Professional investigators may need to visually inspect facilities, materials, or activities.

- *News media.* Print and televised media stories often are available online or on microfilm directly through the news service, through local libraries, or through services such as Dialog and Lexis-Nexis. These often contain valuable information on companies and individuals, as well as leads to other information sources.

- *General Internet searches.* The explosion of resources on the Internet has given investigators access to much corporate and personal information. General Web sties, blogs, and even social networking sites such as MySpace and Facebook provide large amounts of information. Investigators should independently verify all information from the Internet, however, as there is no guarantee that postings are accurate.

3.6 OUTSOURCING DUE DILIGENCE INVESTIGATIONS

Several types of companies advertise the ability to conduct due diligence investigations. These include private investigation firms, research firms, preemployment screening companies, law firms, and accounting firms. However, the firms have different views of "due diligence" and may not perform the same level of inspection. Clients should carefully interview such companies to understand their sources and methods before contracting with the company.

3.7 MANAGING DUE DILIGENCE INVESTIGATIONS

To receive the right type of service, the client of a due diligence company should provide detailed background information and work closely with the firm. Communication between the client and the investigating firm is critical for a successful investigation. The client and the investigator should discuss and specify the issues that are most important to the client.

Throughout the investigation, the client and the investigator should continue to communicate; the investigator reporting findings and the client assisting in deciding whether to pursue a lead or whether the information obtained is sufficient to answer the question.

The due diligence report should be coherent, easy to read, and comprehensive. The investigator must report findings in writing and should be prepared to defend the report if necessary.

Large, highly publicized fraud, such as the Madoff case, are making due diligence even more critical and more a standard part of any venture. The demand for international due diligence is heightened by the global economy and terrorism. For example, a company may want to know whether its potential joint venture partner participated in unsavory labor or environmental practices, or whether it was a target of animal rights extremists. Special international trade zones, too, raise the importance of—and demand for—international due diligence investigations.

APPENDIX A

DUE DILIGENCE CHECKLIST

Corporate Organization

- [ ] Articles of incorporation
- [ ] Bylaws
- [ ] Recent changes in corporate structure
- [ ] Shareholder list (showing outstanding shares and percent owned, as well as stock option or share appreciation rights plans)
- [ ] Parent, subsidiaries, and affiliates
- [ ] Shareholders' agreements
- [ ] Minutes of board of directors' meetings

Business Information

- [ ] Product offerings
- [ ] Depreciation method
- [ ] Patents
- [ ] Management information system

Business Plan

- [ ] Most recent five-year business plan
- [ ] Prior business plan

Capital Expenditures

- [ ] Last five years
- [ ] Five-year gross projection
- [ ] Detailed priority list with as much analysis as possible

Competition

- [ ] By product line (name, address and phone number, size of overall company, size of the business unit that is the competitor, market share, and competitive advantages and disadvantages)
- [ ] Trade publications (name, address, and phone numbers)

Contracts

- ☐ Major contracts listed by product lines (terms)

Debt and Leases

- ☐ Lender
- ☐ Terms
- ☐ Interest rate
- ☐ Payment schedule

Employee Relations

- ☐ Unions (name of union, name of local president, address and phone number, and copy of contract

Environmental Liabilities

- ☐ Description
- ☐ Environmental studies
- ☐ Five-year projected remediation cost
- ☐ Five-year projected compliance cost

Equipment

- ☐ List
- ☐ Age
- ☐ Appraisal (orderly liquidation value/replacement value)

Financial Statements

Five years of historical audited statements, including:

- ☐ Income statement
- ☐ Balance sheet
- ☐ Statement of cash flows
- ☐ Change in equity statement
- ☐ Year-to-date internally generated monthly statements
- ☐ Most recent five-year projections
- ☐ Monthly sales projections taking seasonality into account

Insurance

- ☐ Property
- ☐ Liability
- ☐ Workers' compensation
- ☐ Other

Last Corporate Transactions

- ☐ Description of each
- ☐ Purchase and sale agreement of each

Litigation

- ☐ Current (description, potential damages)
- ☐ Potential (description, potential damages)

Management

- ☐ Organizational chart
- ☐ Résumés
- ☐ Ownership interest
- ☐ Compensation and contracts
- ☐ Performance evaluation criteria
- ☐ Profit- or gain-sharing policies

Marketing

- ☐ Pricing strategy
- ☐ Patents
- ☐ Distribution channels
- ☐ Promotion tactics
- ☐ Customer base (top 10 customers by product line, showing volume)
- ☐ Market share by product line

Operating Data

- ☐ Accounts receivable (turnover or days, aging, control and credit policy, seasonality)
- ☐ Inventory (turnover or days, obsolescence policy, sources of supply, valuation method)
- ☐ Backlog (by product line, five-year history, current, seasonal issues)

Pension Plans

- ☐ Funding status
- ☐ Balance sheet treatment
- ☐ Ten-year projected cash expense

Property

- ☐ Description
- ☐ Recent acquisitions or spin-offs
- ☐ Expansion plans

Retiree Medical Benefits Liabilities

- ☐ Funding status
- ☐ Balance sheet treatment
- ☐ Ten-year projected cash expense

Tax Status

- ☐ Historical tax rate
- ☐ Net operating losses

APPENDIX B

SECURITIES REGULATORY BODIES

National Bodies

Australia	Australian Securities and Investments Commission	www.asic.gov.au/asic/asic.nsf
Brazil	Comissão de Valores Mobiliários	www.cvm.gov.br/ingl/indexing.asp
Canada	Canadian Security Administrators	www.csa-acvm.ca/home.html
France	Autorité des marchés financiers	www.amf-france.org
Germany	Bundesbank and German Financial Supervisory Authority	www.bafin.de/cgi-bin/bafin.pl
Greece	Hellenic Capital Market Commission	www.hcmc.gr
Hong Kong	Securities and Futures Commission	www.sfc.hk/sfc/html/EN/
Hungary	Hungarian Financial Supervisory Authority	www.pszaf.hu/english/start.html
India	Securities and Exchange Board of India	www.sebi.gov.in
Italy	Commissione Nazionale per le Società e la Borsa	www.consob.it
Japan	Financial Services Agency	www.fsa.go.jp/en/index.html
Jersey	Jersey Financial Services Commission	www.jerseyfsc.org
Lithuania	Securities Commission of the Republic of Lithuania	www.vpk.lt/en/index.php/
Malta	Malta Financial Services Authority	www.mfsa.com.mt/consumer
Mexico	Comisión Nacional Bancaria y de Valores	www.cnbv.gob.mx
Netherlands	Authority for the Financial Markets	www.autoriteitfinancielemarkten.com/english.htm
New Zealand	Securities Commission of New Zealand	www.seccom.govt.nz
Poland	Securities and Exchange Commission	www.kpwig.gov.pl
Portugal	Comissão do Mercado de Valores Mobiliários	www.cmvm.pt/en
South Africa	Financial Services Board	www.fsb.co.za
Spain	Comisión Nacional del Mercado de Valores	www.cnmv.es/index.htm
Switzerland	Swiss Financial Market Supervisory Authority	www.finma.ch/e/Pages/default.aspx
Turkey	Capital Markets Board of Turkey	www.cmb.gov.tr
United Kingdom	Financial Services Authority	www.fsa.gov.uk
United States	U.S. Commodity Futures Trading Commission	www.cftc.gov
United States	U.S. Securities and Exchange Commission	www.sec.gov

International Bodies

Bank for International Settlements	www.bis.org/index.htm
The Committee of European Securities Regulators	www.cesr-eu.org
Council of Securities Regulators of the Americas	www.cvm.gov.br/ingl/inter/cosra/inter.asp
Financial Stability Board	www.financialstabilityboard.org
International Accounting Standards Board	www.iasb.org/Home.htm
International Organization of Securities Commissions	www.iosco.org
International Federation of Accountants	www.ifac.org
International Finance Corporation	www.ifc.org
International Monetary Fund	www.imf.org
North American Securities Administrators Association	www.nasaa.org/home/index.cfm
Organisation for Economic Co-operation and Development	www.oecd.org/home
The World Bank	www.worldbank.org
World Federation of Exchanges	www.world-exchanges.org

APPENDIX C

SAMPLE DUE DILIGENCE REPORT

CONFIDENTIAL

December 7, 2005

Mrs. Mary Smith, Director
Anyville School District
Facilities Contracts Administration
555 Grand Avenue, 11th Floor
Anyville, CA 90000

Dear Mrs. Smith:

This is our due diligence report on the ABC Company. The review was initiated at your request. The report contains summary information regarding the company as it relates to financial issues and due diligence matters, including civil litigation, judgments, bankruptcies, and regulatory violations.

Please also note this report is marked "Confidential." Discussion and dissemination of this matter should be limited to only those District personnel having an official need-to-know.

If you have any questions, please contact me at (555) 555-6789.

Sincerely,

John Doe
Deputy Inspector General, Investigations

Work Performed

This report summarizes the results of online research conducted, pursuant to your request, regarding ABC Company and executives Joe Subject and Jane Subject. Regarding the entity, this phase of the investigation consisted of inquiries with available online public records in relevant jurisdictions, including litigation, bankruptcies, judgments, federal and state tax liens, UCCs, regulatory filings, professional licenses and business records, as well as a search of adverse media. Regarding the individuals, this phase of the investigation consisted of inquiries with available online public records in relevant jurisdictions, including identifier records, litigation, bankruptcies, judgments, federal and state tax liens, UCCs, regulatory filings, professional licenses and business affiliations, as well as a search of adverse media. Note that we focused primarily upon records positively identifiable with the individuals via known social security numbers, addresses, jurisdictions, dates of birth, or other identifiers.

Based upon residential and business addresses reported online for the subjects, our research focused upon online civil, criminal, and bankruptcy records related to the subjects at the following United States District and Bankruptcy Courts:

- Central District of California (for the individuals and entity)

Based upon these same addresses, we also conducted online searches for county-level criminal records, litigation, liens, judgments, and UCCs in the following counties:

- Los Angeles County, California (for the individuals and entity)
- Orange County, California (for the individuals)

We also conducted a nationwide search of relevant secretary of state records, limited partnership filings, fictitious business name ("dba") filings, and business reports to identify businesses with which the individuals currently are or formerly have been affiliated as an officer or director, as well as affiliates or subsidiaries of the business.

We reviewed available online files containing disciplinary actions and sanctions collected from various federal and state agencies such as the National Association of Securities Dealers, the Securities and Exchange Commission, HUD, stock exchanges, state mortgage and real estate regulators, the Department of Labor, and other federal and state agencies for any records naming the entity or executives.

We also searched the U.S. Department of the Treasury, Office of Foreign Assets Control, master list of Specially Designated Nationals and Blocked Persons/Entities, the U.S. Department of Commerce Bureau of Export Administration Denied Persons/Entities List, and other lists of U.S. and international securities risks for any records naming the entity or executives.

Note that online nationwide coverage of state/county-level criminal records is very limited in scope even where coverage is available. Unless otherwise indicated the jurisdictions in which the subjects are located are covered in the online searches to the extent that information is available online.

A worldwide review of online media from numerous English-language sources including newspapers, magazines, trade and industry journals, broadcast transcripts, and wire services was also conducted for any adverse references to the entity or executives. We constructed searches for adverse media using negative terms including, but not limited to: lawsuit, scandal, sexual, fraud, illegal, crime, incriminate, criminal, convicted, guilty, arrest, litigation, bankrupt, mafia, mob, indict, allegation, money laundering, racketeering, testify, corrupt, harassment, cooking the books, accused, smuggle, terrorism, DWI, driving while intoxicated, DUI, and driving under the influence.

Limitations to the Report

We assume no responsibility to update this report for events and circumstances occurring after the date of this report. Any written reports, schedules, other materials, or documents prepared or provided by us cannot be disclosed, published, or used in whole or in part without our prior written permission.

We use our professional judgment to identify the online sources to be searched, which is largely dependent upon the scope of the investigation, the location of the subjects, and budgetary considerations. While we have access to numerous potential data sources, we cannot possibly search all of them in the course of any one investigation. We caution that other professional services firms might reach different judgments about the databases to be searched or produce different findings.

In addition, since there may be additional information which has either not been reported or is not available through online sources, we cannot assume responsibility for the accuracy of the information obtained from these sources, nor can we guarantee that we will locate all relevant information that might exist regarding a certain subject.

Based on identifying information developed for the subjects, we focus our research in the jurisdictions specified in the report. However, the scope of available online public records varies in each jurisdiction searched. In most cases, the available records cover only the last five to ten years, but some jurisdictions are even more limited. Often, with regard to state/ county-level litigation, only business-related records are available online, not those relating to personal matters.

Note that SEC actions are not indexed until after the case is disposed. Therefore, it is possible that pending SEC actions against the subjects may exist, which cannot be identified at this time.

Regarding our searches for business affiliations of the subjects, note that although Secretary of State information can be searched by names of officers, in most states business entities are not required to provide these names when filing for incorporation or qualification. It is therefore possible that additional business affiliations exist that have not been identified through online inquiries. In addition, please note that fictitious business name ("dba") filings are generally not available online, and that manual searches in relevant counties are recommended to identify possible additional business names under which the subjects may be conducting business.

Executive Summary

No references to ABC Company, Inc., Joe Subject, or Jane Subject were found in the following searches:

- criminal filings
- federal litigation
- bankruptcy filings
- liens and judgments
- regulatory filings
- adverse media

Business Affiliations

Online business records provided general information regarding ABC Company, which is incorporated in the body of this report. ABC Company was found to be affiliated with an entity known as XYZ Company.

Joe and Jane were found to be affiliated only with ABC Company.

State Litigation

We located two records online naming ABC Company as a plaintiff and three records naming ABC as a defendant. Note that several of these cases also named one or both of the individual subjects of this report. Neither the nature nor the status of these disputes is reported online. Please see the body of this report for further details.

We located four records online which are a name match with Joe Subject. All of the cases were filed in Los Angeles County, California. Note that three of these cases also named ABC Company as a party. The status of these disputes is not reported online. Joe is named as a defendant in three of the four cases. Please see the body of this report for further details.

We located six records online involving Jane Subject. All of the cases were filed in Los Angeles County, California. Note that five of these cases also named ABC Company as a party. The status of these disputes is not reported online. Jane is named as a defendant in four of the six cases. Please see the body of this report for further details.

Uniform Commercial Codes

We located two records naming ABC Company. Both of the UCCs were filed in California; one of the two UCCs was reported as in force. Please see the body of this report for further details.

No UCC records were located naming Joe or Jane as a debtor or a secured party.

Detailed Findings

ABC COMPANY
234 MY STREET
TARZANA, CALIFORNIA 91356 (LOS ANGELES COUNTY)

Licensing

According to a nationwide review of professional license database resources, ABC Company is reported to maintain a professional license as follows:

- According to the State of California Department of Consumer Affairs, California Contractors State Licensing Board, ABC Company is licensed as a General Engineering Contractor, a General Building Contractor, and a Painting & Decorating licensee in the State of California. According to the online record, the entity's license (license number 123456789) is active. The license was issued on February 4, 1998, and expires on February 28, 2006. Note that Joe Subject is reportedly associated with the General Engineering Contractor class of this license and also held a Home Improvement Certification from March 6, 2000, until January 1, 2004. Jane Subject is reportedly responsible for the General Building Contractor and the Painting & Decorating classes of this license. A search of the State of California Department of Consumer Affairs, California Contractors State Licensing Board Web site confirmed this information.

Note that our investigation also disclosed a joint venture by ABC Company along with CBA Company, in which the two companies were licensed for General Building Contractor, Painting & Decorating, and Roofing under the name XYZ Company (license number 987654321). This joint venture license was issued on February 11, 1999, and expires February 28, 2007, but is not in good standing due to the lack of a contractor's bond, which was reportedly cancelled on February 9, 2004. CBA reportedly provided the Roofing portion of this joint venture's service offerings.

Business Affiliations

An online nationwide review of available Secretary of State records, limited partnership filings, fictitious business names filings, and business information reports was conducted for any entities related to ABC Company.

- **ABC Company.** According to the business information report provided by your office, this entity was started in 1993. Jane Subject is listed as president and founder. Joe Subject is listed as vice president. According to online California Secretary of State records, this entity was incorporated in California on October 1, 1997. John Doe is reportedly the registered agent. ABC was reportedly briefly suspended by the Secretary of State from November 9, 2004 until November 17, 2004. No additional information is provided online. According to information provided by your office, this entity was previously located at 123 City Street, Any Town, CA 999999.

The following additional entity was located:

- **XYZ Company.** This was reportedly a joint venture by ABC Company and CBA Company, in which the two companies provided general construction contracting, painting, decorating, and roofing services under the name XYZ Company. A license for this joint venture was reportedly issued on February 11, 1999, and expires February 28, 2007, but is not in good standing due to the lack of a contractor's bond, which was reportedly cancelled on February 9, 2004. Investigation regarding CBA was conducted under separate cover. Additional investigation regarding B&K Company will be conducted at your request.

Criminal Records

Based upon the addresses associated with ABC Company, online criminal records searches were conducted at the United States District Court for the Central District of California, as well as in relevant state/county-level courts in Los Angeles County, California, for any records naming the entity. In addition, we conducted an online nationwide search of available federal criminal filings for any matters naming the company.

No records were located online for ABC Company.

Lawsuits/Bankruptcies

Federal Litigation

Based upon the addresses associated with ABC Company, an online nationwide search of available federal civil filings was conducted at all United States District Courts, including the United States District Court for the Central District of California, for records naming the company.

No records were located online for ABC Company.

Bankruptcy Filings

An online nationwide search of available bankruptcy court filings was conducted for any matters naming ABC Company.

No bankruptcy records were identified online for ABC Company.

State Litigation

Based upon the addresses associated with ABC Company, online civil records searches were conducted in all available counties in the state of California, including Los Angeles County, for any matters naming ABC Company. An online nationwide search of available state-level lawsuit records was also conducted.

We located six records online naming ABC Company. Neither the nature nor the status of these disputes is reported online. Copies of relevant court documents will be retrieved at your request.

- *ABC Company v. Johnny Nobody*, case number BC 111111, was filed on February 21, 2003, in the Los Angeles County Superior Court in Los Angeles, California.

- *Jerry Somebody v. ABC Company*, case number BC 222222, was filed on April 10, 2001, in the Los Angeles County Superior Court in Los Angeles, California.

- *Marty Berry v. Joe Subject, Jane Subject, and ABC Company*, case number BC 333333, was filed on March 26, 2001, in the Los Angeles County Superior Court in Los Angeles, California.

- *Jane Subject v. Andy Wanabee*, case number BC 444444, was filed on March 13, 2001, in the Los Angeles County Superior Court in Los Angeles, California.

- *ABC Company v. Joe Subject*, case number BC 555555, was filed on January 23, 2001, in the Los Angeles County Superior Court in Los Angeles, California.

- *Jerry Somebody v. ABC Company*, case number BC 666666, was filed on October 19, 2000, in the Los Angeles County Superior Court in Los Angeles, California.

Liens and Judgments

An online nationwide search of state-level lien and judgment records was conducted in all counties whose records are available online, including Los Angeles County, California, for any records naming ABC Company. A nationwide search for any federal tax liens regarding the subject was also conducted.

No records involving ABC Company were located.

UCC Filings

An online nationwide search of Uniform Commercial Code (UCC) filings was conducted for any records naming ABC Company as a debtor or a secured party.

We located two records naming ABC Company.

- ABC Company is listed as a debtor in a UCC filed on August 8, 2001, number 112233445566, naming Citibank (West), FSB, Successor in interest by merger to California Federal Bank, and California Federal Bank as the secured parties. This UCC reportedly expires on August 8, 2006.

- ABC Company is listed as a debtor in a UCC filed on June 16, 2000, number 2233445566, naming Bank of America, NA, as the secured party. This UCC was reportedly terminated on July 3, 2001.

Regulatory Inquiries

We reviewed available online files containing disciplinary actions and sanctions collected from various federal and state agencies, such as the National Association of Securities Dealers, the Securities and Exchange Commission, HUD, stock exchanges, state mortgage and real estate regulators, the Department of Labor, and other federal and state agencies. These files generally date back to 1989, although coverage varies by agency. In addition, we reviewed online Securities and Exchange Commission administrative materials, including administrative decisions and administrative proceedings and rulings, dating back to 1933.

We also searched the U.S. Department of the Treasury, Office of Foreign Assets Control, master list of Specially Designated Nationals and Blocked Persons/Entities, the U.S. Department of Commerce Bureau of Export Administration Denied Persons/Entities List, and other lists of U.S. and international securities risks for any records naming the entity.

No records were located naming ABC Company.

Media and Trade Publications

A nationwide review of online media from numerous worldwide sources, including newspapers, magazines, trade and industry journals, broadcast transcripts, and wire services, was conducted for any adverse references to ABC Company.

No adverse articles were located for Joe Subject.

[Similar information regarding Jane Subject is omitted for brevity.]

REFERENCES

Arvedlund, Erin E. (2001, May 7). Don't ask, don't tell – Bernie Madoff is so secretive, he even asks his investors to keep mum. *Barron's*, [Online]. Available: http://www.sec.gov/news/studies/2009/oig-509/exhibit-0156.pdf. [2009, August 12].

ASIS International. (2007). International glossary of security terms. Available: www.asisonline.org/library/glossary/index.xml [2007, May 15].

Berenson, A., & Henriques, D. B. (2008, December 13). Look at Wall St. wizard finds magic had skeptics. *The New York Times*, [Online]. Available: http://www.nytimes.com/2008/12/13/ business/13fraud.html. [2008, December 15]

Cullinan, G., LeRoux, J-M, & Weddigen, R-M. (2004, April). The secrets of great due diligence. *Harvard Business Review.*

Garner, Bryan A., Editor. (2004). *Black's Law Dictionary, Eighth Edition.* St. Paul, MN: Thomson West.

Lajoux, A. R., & Elson, C. (2000*). The art of M&A: Due diligence, navigating critical steps and uncovering critical data.* New York, NY: McGraw-Hill.

Merriam-Webster. (2009). "Due diligence" entry, [Online]. Available: http://www.merriam-webster.com/dictionary/due diligence [2009, March 6].

Shaffer, S. (2004, November 1). Making the case for due diligence. *Franchising World.*

Thornton, C., & Ruskin, D. (2004). Due diligence: Learn from the past, but look toward the future. *Universal Advisor.* Publication of Plante & Moran (www.plantemoran.com).

CHAPTER FOUR

BACKGROUND
INVESTIGATIONS

PREEMPLOYMENT
SCREENING

A dishonest employee can wreak havoc with an enterprise. Just one bad hiring decision—one thief, drug abuser, or violent criminal—can significantly harm a company's productivity, earnings, reputation, and morale. A comprehensive, legally permissible, fairly executed background investigation and preemployment screening program is confirmatory and investigative in nature finds the most appropriate person of a particular job and can go a long way toward preventing losses and mitigating the damage caused by a bad hiring decision.

This chapter discusses the history of background investigations, benefits of preemployment screening, development of a policy and program, execution of the screening and investigation, and analysis and use of developed information.

4.1 HISTORY OF BACKGROUND INVESTIGATIONS

For centuries, obtaining background information on individuals was easy. People lived in smaller, less mobile communities and knew each other, at least by reputation. Today, society is much different. Companies are global, and job qualifications are more defined and specific. The preemployment screening industry is relatively new, only emerging in the United States in the 1980s (Rosen, 2005). Interest in preemployment screening has continued to rise as recent terrorist incidents around the world have spurred companies to review and enhance their screening policies.

At the same time that background investigations and preemployment screening become ever more important to businesses, institutions, and individuals, legislation in many countries is restricting preemployment evaluation and screening. The main concerns are privacy and data protection. Many countries provide exemptions when selecting applicants, for example, In the United States, Title VII of the Civil Rights Act of 1964 exempts defense contractors in the hiring of aliens. The types of information available and stipulations surrounding the use of personal information vary widely from place to place. Many countries are currently in the process of determining how to regulate and distribute information.

This chapter primarily uses U.S. and Canadian examples, but most of the information contained herein can be used to make sound hiring decisions around the world.

4.2 STUDIES AND RESEARCH ON BACKGROUND INVESTIGATIONS AND PREEMPLOYMENT SCREENING

Losses due to employee theft and fraud, workplace violence, and illegal drug and alcohol use are staggering. Applicant screening and employee socialization are primary loss prevention strategies. The best way to reduce internal theft and exposure to workplace violence is to hire employees with integrity. The grim fact is that crime does occur in the workplace and employees are often involved as perpetrators or victims.

4.2.1 RÉSUMÉ FRAUD

Hiring an honest, non-violent, drug-free employee is not easy. Honest and dishonest people look alike. As one security practitioner succinctly put it, "It would be nice if honest applicants wore blue suits and conmen wore plaid, but they don't" (D'Aaddario, 1990). Compounding the problem is that many résumés are misleading. A 2006 study by ADP Screening and Selection Services revealed a discrepancy between what the applicant provided regarding employment, education, or credential reference and what the source reported—in 49 percent of all background checks (ADP Screening and Selection Services, 2006).

Trends in résumé fraud have remained consistent over the past several years. With the recent focus on security, the number of companies performing preemployment screening is increasing. In fact, a survey by the Society for Human Resource Management (SHRM) showed that 96 percent of American companies conduct some kind of background or reference check on people applying for job openings. One in five companies surveyed by SHRM said they have added or updated screening services as a result of the 2001 terror attacks (Geller, 2005).

In the United States and other countries, preemployment screening and investigation can help minimize the risk of liability for improper hiring. It has been well established that an employer will be held responsible for the on-duty or job-related negligence of employees.

There is also significant legal precedent for holding an employer liable for the intentional misconduct of employees if it can be shown that the employer knew or should have known of any history that would suggest that they might engage in such misconduct. Thus, landlords have been held liable for hiring former convicts who attacked residents of the property, and employers have been held liable for hiring people with criminal histories who then injured fellow employees in a manner similar to their prior crimes.

4.2.2 **EMPLOYEE THEFT**

Employee theft is one of the major problems facing business today. In 2002, Ernst & Young conducted its 8th Global Fraud Survey (Ernst & Young, 2002), which included information provided by senior executives from major corporations in 43 countries. Here are some of the sobering findings:

- More than half of the organizations surveyed had been significantly victimized by fraud within the prior year.

- Fraud was not concentrated in any one geographic area, industry, or size of organization.

- Of the most costly frauds, 85 percent were committed by employees. Of those employees, 55 percent were in management.

- Most of the losses were relatively small, but 13 percent involved amounts over $1 million (U.S.).

4.2.3 **WORKPLACE VIOLENCE**

Workplace violence is a serious concern for security practitioners. In the United States, homicide, the most extreme form of workplace violence, is the fourth leading cause of fatal occupational injury. According to the Bureau of Labor Statistics Census of Fatal Occupational Injuries, in the year 2004, there were 551 homicides in the workplace out of a total of 5,703 fatal work injuries (Bureau of Labor Statistics, 2006).

4.2.4 **DRUG AND ALCOHOL USE AMONG WORKERS**

Everyone involved in a business—whether an owner or employee—is harmed by workplace alcohol and drug abuse. Some costly effects are obvious, such as absenteeism, accidents, and errors. Other effects, such as low morale and high illness rates, are less obvious but also costly and harmful.

In the United States, the vast majority of current illicit drug users are employed. Of the estimated 12.3 million current adult users of illicit drugs, 9.4 million (77 percent) work (Substance Abuse and Mental Health Services Administration, 2000).

4.3 BENEFITS OF PREEMPLOYMENT SCREENING

The primary purpose of a background investigation is to prevent losses and mitigate damages. From a legal perspective, preemployment investigations provide organizations mitigation from negligent hiring and discrimination. A bad hiring decision imposes many costs. For example, if a poorly chosen employee steals from the company, losses will include the value of the property or service stolen; the cost of the investigation; and the cost of recruiting, hiring, and training a replacement employee. (For information on calculating turnover cost, see *Appendix B*.) Once the costs are totaled, it becomes clear that an assets protection program needs to gather and analyze as much relevant information about employment candidates as is lawful. The policy should be cost-effective and conduct the most expensive components of the process last. Comprehensive preemployment screening programs arm managers with the critical information they need to make a successful hiring decision and should be conducted and evaluated prior to offering the potential employee a position.

A preemployment screening program benefits businesses in several ways:

- It discourages applicants with something to hide and encourages applicants to be honest during the interview process. Applicants know that the information they provide will be scrutinized.

- It demonstrates that a company has exercised due diligence, which may provide legal protection in a lawsuit and may also encourage good candidates to apply. One observer notes, "Job applicants have a desire to work with qualified and safe co-workers in a profitable environment" (Rosen, 2002).

- It ensures that a job candidate has the background, education, experience, and skills that he or she claims. Once that information is confirmed, hiring decisions can be based on facts, not instincts or promises.

4.4 DEVELOPING A SCREENING PROGRAM

Developing an effective background investigation and preemployment screening program requires the participation of many individuals and departments of the organization. This investigative function serves the best interest of the corporate organization by screening applicants in an effort to hire the best people. Upper management must first sanction and support the policy. Then, ideally, a team of security and human resources professionals should be tasked with developing and implementing the policy. Other functions of the organization, such as procurement or purchasing, may be instrumental in analyzing bid packages (if investigation is outsourced). Finally, because of the myriad judicial and compliance issues associated with collecting and using personal information, legal counsel must review and endorse the program.

Screening programs vary from organization to organization depending on the following factors:

- access to information
- nature of the position
- potential liability associated with incorrect performance of a job
- industry regulations

4.4.1 ACCESS TO INFORMATION

In today's global business environment, security practitioners face unique challenges in obtaining and verifying applicant information. International companies struggle to maintain consistency in hiring policies due to disparities in available information. Multinational candidates present unique complications.

Global customs and compliance issues vary tremendously, making screening even more complex. Throughout Latin America, for example, criminal history information is recorded under an individual's mother's maiden name. Australia considers education records off-limits to investigators, and Chinese law requires applications for criminal records to have the last name spelled in Chinese characters (Lashier, 2003).

In the United States, access to personal information such as credit, insurance and criminal history is governed by the Fair Credit Reporting Act (FCRA). Criminal history convictions are typically public information. Under the Freedom of Information Act "Public Interest Issues" records must be available for review. Credit History is not covered under this Act, and is not considered public information. Canada's information is protected by the Personal Information Protection and Electronic Documents Act (PIPEDA). The European Union protects privacy information according to a strict directive, and Japan recently enacted the Personal Information Protection Act.

Because of these differences, if an organization is outsourcing this service, it is generally best to use an investigative firm that is well versed in local criminal justice and privacy laws and is based in the country where the data resides.

4.4.2 NATURE OF THE POSITION

Not all positions in an organization require the same level of screening. Some employees are entrusted with highly sensitive information and large amounts of money or other financial instruments. Other employees are in close contact with the public or work in customers' homes or with children. Certain employees handle dangerous materials or are entrusted with protecting others. Such positions often merit an enhanced level of scrutiny. An organization must carefully review its position descriptions and select the appropriate level of screening.

4.4.3 LIABILITY ISSUES

Some positions allow little margin for error. Ship captains, pilots, doctors, child care workers, and many others are presumed to have the correct training, skills, and education. It is incumbent upon the employer to verify an applicant's background. Generally, the higher the level of responsibility is, the more involved the screening should be.

Consider the ramifications of incomplete or incompetent performance of particular jobs. What would happen if a pilot did not have the training or alcohol and drug history he or she reported? What if a child care worker had a violent criminal history? What if a company's chief financial officer had a history of embezzlement? Laws vary, but accidents and injuries that result from employee error or incompetence often become the employer's responsibility. Related lawsuits and settlements cost a substantial amount of money and may actually put a company out of business.

4.4.4 INDUSTRY REGULATIONS

In the Unites States, federal and state statutes set background screening requirements for many industries. These industries often require professional licensing; involve contact with vulnerable populations, such as children or the elderly; or in some other way present a high risk. Examples of regulated industries include banking, transportation, childcare, education, and security. A company must consider industry regulations when developing its screening program.

Despite the variation based on the preceding factors—access to information, nature of the position, liability, and industry regulations—preemployment screening programs have a common foundation:

- **data collection:** using a standardized, company-specific application and supplemental paperwork

- **background investigation and screening:** following standardized, written policies and processes

- **data analysis and hiring decisions**

4.4.5 SEVEN EASY STEPS TO A COMPREHENSIVE PREEMPLOYMENT SCREENING POLICY

The following steps can help in developing a legal, effective, and fair preemployment screening policy:

1. **Create clearly written, well-defined job descriptions for all positions.** The job description describes the duties to be performed in a position and the personal qualifications required for the successful completion of those duties. In compiling the job description, one must limit personal qualifications to those that are clearly required for the position. A prerequisite that cannot be shown as necessary for the successful completion of the prescribed duties can open the door to a complaint to a regulatory authority or even a civil action. In the United States, employers with at least 15 employees must comply with the provisions of the Americans with Disabilities Act in defining the necessary applicant qualifications.

   Because the requirements set out in the job description are the standards for preliminary screening of the applicant, an accurate, well-written job description is crucial to the success of the program.

2. **Assess the risk of each job classification in terms of reasonable (or foreseeable) potential for problems.** The following questions may aid in that assessment:

   — Will the employee have access to financial instruments or sensitive information?

   — Will the employee have regular or unsupervised contact with the public? (Examples of jobs with significant public contact include meter reader, appliance repair person, carpet installer, and many others.)

   — Will the employee be given keys, alarm codes, and after-hours access to buildings?

   — Does the position require the person to possess specific credentials, licenses, or professional standing?

   — Will the employee be required to handle a firearm?

   — Will the employee have access to dangerous materials, such as explosives or certain chemicals?

— Will the employee be required to drive a motor vehicle?

3. **Based on the preceding risk assessment, determine the scope of preemployment screening for each job classification**. This means establishing standardized and consistent screening measures for temporary, permanent, full-time, part-time, contract, and volunteer workers in various positions. The company screening policy must be administered scrupulously across the entire job classification to avoid charges of unfair or illegal hiring practices.

   Nevertheless, different levels of screening may be used for different positions as long as the level of screening is appropriate and is administered consistently and fairly. For example, a credit check may be warranted for an accountant but not a food service worker. If that is the policy, then all accountant applicants will be subjected to a credit check and all food service workers will not.

   The policy should also specify appropriate periods for each component of the program. For example, the policy might state that a seven-year felony check will be performed for all applicants in a particular job class. (In some cases, the standard may be mandated by law.)

4. **Work with human resources and legal personnel to develop an appropriate hiring packet.** This packet should include a thorough application and relevant authorization and release forms. Legal counsel can help ensure that the packet's contents comply with applicable laws. If, in the course of the preemployment background investigation, inconsistencies in the candidate's background are discovered, the human resource department should be advised that further investigation may be necessary.

5. **Establish criteria for evaluating information**. It is important to determine what will constitute disqualifying information and who will make the hiring determination. The criteria should specify, for example, what types of prior criminal behavior are significant enough to bar an applicant from employment for given positions. Many companies use a team of human resources, security, and legal personnel to review negative findings. The standard of proof necessary to refuse to hire the applicant is "good faith."

6. **Communicate the preemployment screening policy and its purpose to the workforce.** The policy and explanations can be posted on bulletin boards, on intranet sites, in the employee handbook, or in whatever place best fits the culture of the organization. The policy explanations should emphasize the benefits of increased safety and security, reduced turnover, and increased operational effectiveness.

7. **Periodically review policy compliance**. This step ensures that the policy is being followed consistently throughout the enterprise.

4.5 DATA COLLECTION: THE BASIC INFORMATION GATHERING TOOLS

A background investigation initially focuses on information provided by the applicant, which is typically found in the employment application, personal history questionnaire, résumé, and other biographical documents. Irrespective of whether the applicant offers a résumé, the employer should require the applicant to complete a standard application form, which should be designed by the company. No single screening tool should be used to asses an applicant. That approach helps the company obtain as much relevant and lawful information as possible about the applicant.

4.5.1 RÉSUMÉ

A résumé provides the first indication of whether an applicant is qualified for a position. As such, it is an important element in pre-screening applicants. If the résumé does not show the necessary experience or education, the applicant should be removed from the hiring pool. A résumé is a promotional device, and it is difficult to hold an applicant strictly accountable for the information it contains. Therefore, it is important for a company not to accept a résumé in lieu of an employment application or complete work history. A résumé can be an important source of additional information about an applicant and should always be reviewed as part of the preemployment screening process. However, the employer's own application form must be the main source for data gathering and should be reviewed prior to conducting the pre-hire investigation.

4.5.2 APPLICATION

Employment applications are the basic starting point for preemployment screening. The body of the job application consists of questions used to elicit information that will help the employer determine whether the applicant meets the minimum criteria for the position being filled. In drafting this section, the security manager can be instrumental in helping determine that the application contains sufficient information to chart an applicant's history and that only lawful questions are included. In the United States, applications are considered tests in the same sense as any other tool used to determine suitability. As a result, applications must be shown to have no adverse impact on applicants who are protected by federal employment discrimination laws. Legal counsel can help in making that determination.

Ideally, applications should address the following items:

- **Material omissions and misstatements.** An application should state that material (important or consequential) omissions and misstatements are grounds to terminate the hiring process whenever discovered.

- **Applicant's correct and full name.** The application should also request any other names by which the applicant was known at any place of education, residence, or employment.

- **Current and prior addresses.** It is necessary to know not only the applicant's current address (and permanent or legal address if different from the current one), but also all prior addresses at which the applicant resided during any period of employment or education or any other period for which activity is to be checked.

- **Education.** The following should be obtained for each level of education:

  — name and address of school

  — course or program pursued

  — dates of attendance

  — final status (e.g., graduated, degree awarded, withdrawn, etc.)

  — specific degree or certificate awarded, if any

  — average grades or standing

  — reason for withdrawal prior to completion, if applicable

  Many educational institutions are reluctant to disclose academic record information beyond the simple fact of attendance or graduation. Authorization from the applicant for the release of additional information is helpful in such cases.

- **Employment.** All employment history, including self-employment, should be required from the applicant for the period to be examined. If the organization will check the past five, seven, or ten years, the applicant should provide an orderly, chronological presentation of employment, self-employment, and unemployment during that period. Application forms that provide only two or three entry blanks in this section suggest that no more information is expected. Therefore, the application instructions must clearly state that a complete employment history is expected and that an extra sheet should be used if more space is necessary. There should be a place on the form for the applicant to indicate whether the current employer can be contacted as a reference.

  For each previous job, the following data are required:

  — name and address of employer

  — job title (initial and final)

  — period of employment

  — final compensation

  — reason for leaving

  — name and telephone number of the last immediate superior

- **References.** After several references have been interviewed, a trend should start to emerge in terms of the applicant's performance and work style. The application should request the names, business and residence addresses, and telephone numbers of at least three people who have known the applicant for one year or longer, who are not related to the applicant.

  A former employer who still knows the subject would provide an excellent source of reference. The applicant should also state the length of time known and the basis of the acquaintance (e.g., neighbor, friend, or coworker).

- **Military service.** The application should request the following information regarding U.S. military service. Outside the United States, one should first check with legal counsel.

  — period of service

  — branch of service

  — character of separation or discharge

  — rank or rating at time of discharge

  The Privacy Act and related regulations have imposed restrictions on what the military services may disclose about an applicant's unfavorable military service without a subpoena, but an applicant may voluntarily disclose such information. Therefore, an applicant should be asked to disclose an honorable or dishonorable discharge on the application form. The applicant can also be asked to produce the discharge document—Form DD 214—to confirm the character of separation.

- **Criminal history.** A criminal records check is the most common preemployment screening method. As this topic is probably the most variable, it makes sense to contact legal counsel before formulating the application's questions on criminal history. Ideally, criminal information should be requested in the broadest possible context such as requesting information on convictions, guilty pleas and nolo contendere. The application should also state that a criminal conviction is not automatic grounds for rejection.

- **Release.** The application form should indicate that the applicant consents to preemployment screening and that the release is valid for future screening for retention, promotion, or reassignment. Many information sources are either governed by statutes or have become cautious and reticent about disclosing data on former employees or students. In the United States, if an employer uses an outside screening service, the FCRA requires (1) a disclosure to the applicant that a consumer report maybe requested and (2) written authorization from the applicant. The disclosure and written authorization must be separate from the employment application.

4.6 EARLY APPLICATION REVIEW AND INITIAL INTERVIEW

The initial application review is an important tool in the preemployment screening process. Applicant falsifications generally fall into two categories:

- willful omissions of material facts

- misrepresentations of material facts

An applicant may attempt to omit information that could be a hindrance to employment. In fact, the applicant may have been falsifying the same information for years and become convinced that a prospective employer will not check it. All too often, the applicant is correct!

4.6.1 RED FLAGS IN EARLY APPLICATION REVIEW

Some of the most common misrepresentations or omissions found in employment applications are listed below:

- **Unsigned forms.**

- **Incomplete addresses or post office box numbers.** Some applicants list the names of schools but not the dates of attendance or the degrees conferred. A listed school with an unfamiliar name should always be verified.

- **Conflicting dates of employment, education, or military service.**

- **Gaps in employment.** All gaps in employment or life history—if more than one month— should be investigated.

- **Changes of occupation**. People tend to follow a general line of work for most of their lives, so any indication of an abnormal employment pattern should be closely examined.

- **Sketchy employment information or former employer out of business.**

- **Social security number variance (United States only).** The social security number may be at variance with the area of the country in which the applicant claims it was issued. By itself, this might not be a significant element of information, but it could serve as a valuable clue if the investigation must be expanded or the applicant questioned in further detail.

- **Omission of reasons for leaving**. Applicants may attempt to avoid giving their reasons for leaving, especially when they are unsure of the response a former employer might supply about their previous job performance. However, when asked directly, most applicants attempt to give an answer.

4.6.2 **INITIAL APPLICANT INTERVIEW**

Preferably, this step should be conducted in person and after the applicant provides the application paperwork. The initial interview provides a chance to clarify any omissions, such as missing signatures and dates, unanswered questions, or incomplete work histories. The interviewer should not ask negative questions or questions that prompt a source to render a judgment because it produces misleading answers. If the clarification process reveals that the applicant is clearly not qualified for the job, the company can tell the applicant immediately and spare him or her any false hope.

4.7 **FINAL SELECTION PHASE**

A cooperative effort within the organization will result in the optimum employee selection process. If the applicant makes it through the initial phases of the process, he or she will enter into the final selection phase, the point at which most in-depth screening occurs.

The terms background check, background investigation or screening, and pre-employment screening are often used interchangeably. In reality, they are related but distinct disciplines.

Generally, a background check is a confirmatory type of investigation. This would include verification of information provided by an applicant, such as education and job history.

Background investigation or screening actively searches for information, performing such tasks as developing references or searching criminal records. The goal is to uncover information that an applicant might try to hide, such as criminal activity or previous terminations. The ASIS Glossary defines background screening as an "inquiry into the history and behaviors of an individual under consideration for employment, credit, access to sensitive assets (such as national defense information), and other reasons." A background investigation or screening can vary widely, from merely checking prior employment experience and educational credentials to checking civil, criminal, and medical histories.

Preemployment screening is a process for determining whether a prospective employee is trustworthy or capable of performing the functions required for a particular job. It can include all of the above and may also include any of the following:

- drug or alcohol screening
- psychological testing (personality and integrity testing)
- general intelligence or aptitude testing
- medical screening and physical abilities tests
- polygraph tests

The legality of particular types of screening and the stages at which tests may be given are closely regulated in many places. It is best to consult legal counsel for specific requirements.

4.7.1 DRUG AND ALCOHOL SCREENING

Because illegal drug and alcohol use can be a serious problem for businesses, federal law in the United States requires mandatory testing for some positions. For any position where mandatory screening is not required, the risk assessment detailed earlier will help an organization determine appropriate screening levels. Any organization conducting drug testing of any kind should have a clear, written policy outlining when testing will be conducted, how it will be conducted, and what the ramifications of test results are. The policy must be communicated to all applicants and employees.

4.7.2 PSYCHOLOGICAL TESTING

The main goal of these pre-hire selection tools is to help an employer make informed hiring decisions.

Personality and Integrity Tests

Personality tests provide a psychological measure of an individual's basic characteristics, such as attitudes, emotional adjustment, motivations, interpersonal skills, and interests. This type of testing is particularly helpful in determining an applicant's compatibility with a position. For example, an individual who tests as shy or introverted would not necessarily be a good fit for a sales position. Integrity or honesty testing measures an applicant's propensity toward undesirable behaviors, such as lying, stealing, and drug or alcohol abuse. This type of testing is generally broken into two categories. Overt or direct testing asks explicit questions about an applicant's past dishonest acts or behaviors, while personality-oriented or indirect tests examine concepts such as dependability and respect for authority.

The tests are usually "paper and pencil" or conducted through specialized computer software. It is imperative that the test be administered, scored, and interpreted correctly. The results of psychological testing should be used as only one of the factors in making a hiring decision. As with other types of screening, improper use of these tests could have negative consequences for the organization. Before beginning a testing program, it is prudent to seek legal counsel. (The bibliography lists information sources that may help employers develop and administer preemployment testing programs.)

Intelligence and Aptitude Tests

Intelligence tests are sometimes part of preemployment assessments because intelligence is a good predictor of job performance. Intelligence tests could consist of logic problems, word problems, pattern identification, or other kinds of questions.

Aptitude tests measure cognitive ability in a particular area, such as memory recall, vocabulary, or numerical perception.

Intelligence and aptitude tests can be useful if administered and scored correctly, but they are not infallible and should be used as only one factor in making a hiring decision. The use of these tests should be discussed with legal counsel in advance.

Medical Screening and Physical Ability Tests

Medical screening is a sensitive area because of the personal nature of the tests and the legal risks they create. In general, medical screening may be performed if it specifically relates to a requirement of the job. If a medical exam discloses an illness or disability that is not directly related to the position for which the individual is applying, the organization may not refuse to employ that person. Physical ability tests measure specific characteristics, such as strength, endurance, or capacity for movement. Such tests tell an employer whether applicants would be able to perform the essential functions of a position without risking injury to themselves or others.

This type of testing and the program directing it must be reviewed and endorsed by legal counsel before implementation because of the potential for discrimination or disparate impact claims. Therefore, medical record information review is not found in a typical preemployment background investigation. Also, in the United States, this type of testing could be considered a medical exam and in some states can only be administered after an offer of employment is made.

Polygraph Tests

In the United States, before the passage of the Employee Polygraph Protection Act of 1988, which prohibits the use of a preemployment polygraph examination, the polygraph was considered the quickest and most effective method for verifying background information on applicants. Now it is used rarely.

4.8   INVESTIGATION PROCEDURES

Once the decision has been made to conduct preemployment screening and the policy is in place, one must determine how the screening will be accomplished. The three most common resources are these:

- security or assets protection department

- human resources department

- outside consumer reporting and investigative agency

These three resources are not mutually exclusive. Many organizations use different resources to conduct various segments of the investigation. The size and organizational structure of the enterprise are generally the principal factors in selecting the resources to be used. Staffing, expertise, efficiency, and cost-effectiveness should also be considered when deciding which services will be performed in-house and which services will be outsourced.

4.8.1 USING THE SECURITY OR ASSETS PROTECTION DEPARTMENT

If the security or assets protection department conduct investigations, it will need certain resources:

- experienced and well-trained investigative personnel

- sufficient reference materials

- adequate communications

Administrative support personnel can conduct some of the database searches and help to obtain and organize prior employment, education, and reference information. However, an experienced investigator must conduct the investigation and analyze the results of the search.

4.8.2 USING THE HUMAN RESOURCES DEPARTMENT

If it has enough staffing, the human resources department can play a significant role in the background screening process. Human resources professionals are versed in employment law and skilled in interviewing techniques. They are ideally suited for conducting preliminary screening, such as initial reference phone calls to determine whether an applicant has the appropriate skills and experience for a particular position. Often, as a result of this initial check, a determination is made as to whether the candidate will move forward in the process. If so, the remainder of the investigation must be conducted by an experienced investigator.

4.8.3 **USING A CONTRACT CONSUMER REPORTING AND INVESTIGATIVE AGENCY**

The number of firms offering preemployment screening services has grown phenomenally. If the organization is planning to outsource this function, careful consideration should be given to choosing a firm. The following questions can help in making the decision:

- Does the firm provide information to the client (the security manager's company) and the subjects in compliance with applicable laws (e.g., FCRA in the United States and PIPEDA in Canada)?
- Can the firm provide the client with regulatory guidance?
- Is the information supplied the most current and accurate available?
- Does the firm provide all the screening services needed by the client, or will the client need to use more than one vendor?
- Does the firm provide convenient methods of ordering?
- How long does it take to receive the information requested?
- What is the price for the services provided? How does the price compare to the price for similar services of competing firms?
- What steps does the firm take to establish an applicant's true identity?
- What quality control procedures does the firm follow to ensure accuracy?
- Does the firm have errors and omissions insurance or other applicable coverage?
- Does the firm have adequate procedures to ensure the security and confidentiality of the information?
- Has the firm provided similar services to organizations in the client's industry?
- Will the firm provide customer references that the client can contact?
- What client satisfaction guarantees does the firm provide?
- Does the firm provide its clients with resource materials or updates relating to legal and practical issues in preemployment screening?
- Will the firm provide a sample report?

4.8.4 **DATA ANALYSIS**

When all the screening results are returned, the process of analysis begins. In a best-case scenario, all of the applicant's information is verified and further screening shows no negative results. However, if negative results are found, the decision may become more complicated. The security manager should refer to the company's written policy on the types of prior criminal behavior that may disqualify an individual from employment. Privacy law may come into play in the company's particular location. In the United States, employers must disclose negative findings to an applicant and allow him or her to correct false or misapplied information.

Also, the employment application should state that material omissions and misstatements are grounds to terminate the employment process whenever discovered. Such a statement lays the foundation for terminating the process for dishonesty in supplying the information and not just for the negative information itself.

4.9 FUTURE OF BACKGROUND INVESTIGATIONS AND PREEMPLOYMENT SCREENING

Privacy legislation will significantly affect the future of background investigations and preemployment screening. Many countries are wrestling with the issues of data collection and storage and the secure transfer of information while balancing privacy and human rights. Around the world, recent changes have been toward restricting information.

On the whole, technology advances are streamlining the verification and investigation process and improving the economics of conducting research worldwide. Many databases can be accessed online, enabling almost instantaneous turnaround time. However, because these databases can have severe limitations and may contain unconfirmed information, the information they provide should be treated as supplemental. Technology is also improving how information is gathered and disseminated throughout the enterprise. These technological improvements can make a time-consuming and sometimes tedious process simpler and help ensure that employment information is collected, protected, and shared in an efficient and secure manner.

Preemployment screening is an essential component of any good security program. Security practitioners focus much attention on preventing employee theft, workplace violence, and other security incidents. Background checking and pre-employment screening can be instrumental in that effort.

APPENDIX A

SOCIAL SECURITY NUMBER TABLE—FIRST THREE DIGITS

Since 1973, social security numbers have been issued by the Social Security Administration's central office. The first three digits of a person's social security number are determined by the ZIP code of the mailing address shown on the application for a social security number. Before 1973, social security numbers were assigned by field offices. The number merely established that a person's card was issued by an officer in that state. The chart below shows the first three digits of the social security numbers assigned throughout the United States and its possessions.

001-003	New Hampshire	387-399	Wisconsin	525	New Mexico
004-007	Maine	400-407	Kentucky	585	
008-009	Vermont	408-415	Tennessee	645-649	
010-034	Massachusetts	756-763		526-527	Arizona
035-039	Rhode Island	416-424	Alabama	600-601	
040-049	Connecticut	425-428	Mississippi	764-765	
050-134	New York	587		528-529	Utah
135-158	New Jersey	588*		646-647	
159-211	Pennsylvania	752-755*		530	Nevada
212-220	Maryland	429-432	Arkansas	680	
221-222	Delaware	676-679		531-539	Washington
223-231	Virginia	433-439	Louisiana	540-544	Oregon
691-699		659-665		545-573	California
232-236	West Virginia	440-448	Oklahoma	602-626	
232	North Carolina	449-467	Texas	574	Alaska
237-246		627-645		575-576	Hawaii
681-690		468-477	Minnesota	750	
247-251	South Carolina	478-485	Iowa	751	
654-658		486-500	Missouri	577-579	District of Columbia
252-260	Georgia	501-502	North Dakota	580	Virgin Islands
667-675		503-504	South Dakota	580-584	Puerto Rico
261-267	Florida	505-508	Nebraska	596-599	
589-595		509-515	Kansas	586	Guam
766-772		516-517	Montana	586	American Samoa
268-302	Ohio	518-519	Idaho	586	Philippine Islands
303-317	Indiana	520	Wyoming	700-728	Railroad Board**
318-361	Illinois	521-524	Colorado	729-733	Enumeration at Entry
362-386	Michigan	650-653			

NOTE: When the same area is shown more than once, it means that certain numbers have been transferred from one state to another or that an area has been divided for use among certain geographic locations.

Any number beginning with 000 will NEVER be a valid SSN.

* New areas allocated but not yet issued.

** Issuance of these numbers to railroad employees was discontinued July 1, 1963.

APPENDIX B

TURNOVER CALCULATOR

Free Web-based turnover calculators can help determine the costs associated with replacing an employee. One example is found at http://www.uwex.edu/ces/cced/publicat/turn.html.

Replacing an employee due to poor selection and screening takes a high financial toll on an organization. By following the process below, one can calculate an estimation of the actual cost. The first step is to select a job that experiences high turnover due to poor selection or screening, and enter the average wage of that position on line 1. The next step is to multiply the average wage by 1.3 to include the cost of benefits. Multiplying the total wage by 25 percent produces the turnover cost per employee. That cost may then be multiplied by the number of former employees to calculate the total cost of turnover for the position.

Steps			*Example*	
1. Annual wage:	$		Assistant manager salary:	$48,400
Gross-up for benefits:		x 1.3	Gross-up for benefits:	x 1.3
2. Total wage:	$		Total wage:	$62,920
Turnover cost:		x 0.25	Turnover cost:	x 0.25
3. Cost per employee:	$		Cost per employee:	$15,730
4. Number of former employees:		x __	Number of former employees:	x 3
5. Total turnover cost:	$		Total turnover cost:	$47,190

CHAPTER FIVE

INTERVIEW & INTERROGATION

The purpose of an investigation is to determine the truth in a matter under question. The three tools that an investigator uses during an investigation are referred to as the three "I's": information, interrogation, and instrumentation. In this chapter we will concentrate on obtaining information through the principal tool of the interview/interrogation. The reason is that, in the majority of inquiries, the persons involved in the matter are the most available and valuable sources of information (Fay, 1993). Interviews of victims, witnesses, informants and confidential informants are considered the most critical aspect of an investigation as they are a primary source of information.

The value of each interview or interrogation is based on the investigator's knowledge, skills in eliciting information, and ability to evaluate the veracity of the information obtained. The most prize talent an investigator can have is the ability to obtain information from individuals through questioning. By questioning witnesses, subjects, and suspects, one can develop information that helps close an investigation successfully, cost-effectively, and on time. Throughout the process, it is vital to conduct interviews in accordance with statutes, regulations, and standards of fairness.

There are many types of interviews and interrogations, just as there are many types of investigations. For example, a private investigator may be involved primarily with domestic investigations, parental abductions, or traffic accidents. A corporation may employ private investigators to investigate corporate fraud or similar wrongdoing. The role of the corporate investigator is generally restricted to matters that may have an adverse effect on the personnel, financial stability, or reputation of the company. Information obtained from investigations can be used to improve loss prevention. Public sector investigators handle matters related to violations of the law.

An interview may be conducted in a private residence, on a street corner, or in a formal interview room. The purpose of the interview maybe to learn about an applicant's background, gain information on an individual who is indirectly involved in a matter under investigation, or obtain a written statement from a witness. When interviews are conducted in an accusatory or confrontational manner—for example, to obtain the confession of an employee who has defrauded the company of a large sum of money—they may be called interrogations. The quality of an interview or interrogation plays a crucial role in the successful completion of an investigation and in any ensuing litigation.

5.1 DEFINITIONS

Webster's New World Dictionary (Agnes, 2003) defines *interview* as "a meeting in which a person is asked about personal views." It defines *interrogate* as "to ask questions, especially formally." Many investigators refer to an interview as a process of gathering information and an interrogation as the questioning of an accused or suspect person.

Others have used a variety of definitions for the interview and the interrogation process. For example, *Interviewing Techniques* (Deming, 1997) uses the terms *informational interviews* and *confrontational interviews.* An informational interview is non-accusatory, while the confrontational interview can be accusatory and is generally highly structured. Deming's definitions are recommended for the corporate and private setting to further differentiate the investigative approach of the enterprise security professional from that of the law enforcement professional.

Undercover Investigations in the Workplace (Ferraro, 2000) uses the terms *administrative interview* and *investigatory interview* in describing the two functions. The administrative interview, which is simple and usually unstructured, is the process of interviewing witnesses, friends, supervisors, and anyone other than the subject or suspect in the investigation. The investigatory interview is a complex, structured process used when the subject is known to have committed the offense alone or with others and the investigator has reason to believe the subject committed the offense.

Criminal Interrogations and Confessions (Inbau, 2001), a leading text in the field, distinguishes between an interview and an interrogation as follows: an interview is a non-accusatory conversation in which both investigative and behavior-provoking questions are asked in order to develop investigative information; an interrogation is an accusatory process designed to persuade the subject to tell the truth about his or her involvement in, or guilty knowledge of, the issue under investigation. The interrogation is not a question-and-answer process but rather a monologue in which the investigator does the talking, offering the subject some type of psychological justification for the wrongful behavior.

In summary, a key difference between an interview and an interrogation is in the person being interviewed. The interview, informational interview, or administrative interview involves non-accusatory questioning of anyone with information that pertains to the matter under investigation. An interrogation, confrontational interview, or investigatory interview is a very direct and sometimes accusatory session with a person suspected of committing an offense.

This segment uses the terms general interview and confrontational interview, defining them as follows:

- **General interview:** non-accusatory questioning of a person to gather information that pertains to the matter under investigation. All persons in an investigation should be interviewed—victims, witness, and suspects.

- **Confrontational interview**: confrontational questioning of a person suspected of committing an offense or serious breach of corporate policy. Also known as an interrogation, this process should be reserved for individuals whose involvement in the issue under investigation is reasonably certain.

This discussion of interviews uses the following definitions of *suspect* and *witness*:

- **Suspect:** a person who is believed to have committed an offense based on accumulated evidence, proximity to the incident, motive, access to restricted areas, witness statements, etc.

- **Witness:** any person, other than a suspect, with information concerning an incident. The witness may not have directly observed the incident but may have facts that pertain to the matter under investigation or they may be a one-time informant who is eager to provide information based on moral grounds. Caution needs to be taken with anonymous informants, as they are the most likely to provide false or biased information. The safety and security of the informant is a priority.

In the most basic sense, the purpose of an interview is to aid an investigation into the truth. Questioning techniques should be objective, factual questions focused on obtaining evidence. However, the process has a variety of objectives, which are defined by the circumstances or the nature of the matter under investigation. John E. Reid and Associates, Inc., a firm that teaches interviewing and interrogation techniques, refers to at least four objectives in an interview (Fay, 1993, p. 422):

- to obtain valuable facts
- to eliminate the innocent
- to identify the guilty
- to obtain a confession

There are significant differences between the general interview and the confrontational interview (interrogation). The following list contrasts the two types of interviews (based on Fay, 1993, p. 423). The distinctions affect how the interviewer prepares for the session:

General Interview	*Confrontational Interview*
Non-accusatory	Accusatory
Dialogue	Monologue
Variable environment	Controlled environment
Private/semiprivate	Absolute privacy
Guilt unknown	Guilt indicated
No rights warning*	Rights warning*
Not lengthy	Lengthy
Cooperation	Hostility
Unstructured	Structured
Some planning	Extensive planning
Note taking acceptable	Note taking inhibits

*Varies by country.

5.2 **PSYCHOSOCIAL ASPECTS**

An interview is a process of human interaction between the interviewer and the interviewee. Each party brings emotions, experiences, and desires to the interview. To achieve the goal of the interview—truthful information—the interviewer must recognize the emotions and feelings of the interviewee. Moreover, the interviewer must be able to deal with those emotions and feelings with dignity and sensitivity. What follows is a look at the psychosocial needs, actions, and reactions of the interviewer and the interviewee.

5.2.1 **BEHAVIORAL SCIENCE**

The studies and theories of Abraham H. Maslow are instructive in this topic. Maslow names the following human needs (Maslow, 1987):

- physiological or survival needs, such as food, drink, and health
- safety or physical and emotional needs, such as clothing, shelter, and protection against attack
- affection needs, such as belonging to a family or other small group
- esteem needs, such as self-respect, accomplishment, and achievement recognized and appreciated by someone else
- self-fulfillment needs, that is, being able to use one's potential to the maximum in working with and for one's fellow beings

Maslow theorizes that once the primary needs are satisfied, they are no longer driving needs and are replaced by needs higher in the order. Thus, when primary needs are satisfied, higher-order needs are predominant.

These needs exist in every part of a person's life, including the interview. If the interviewer understands the needs of the interviewee and can relate to them, he or she can more effectively communicate with the interviewee. A successful interviewer fulfills as many of the interviewee's needs as possible.

5.2.2 **MOTIVATION**

All behavior is motivated by and directed to the attainment of some goal. The driving force is to satisfy a need. The direction of behavior is always toward a perceived reward or away from perceived punishment.

Explanations of why people steal have historically referred to the *theft triangle*, which consists of need or want (desire), rationalization (motive), and opportunity. The person must have a need or desire for the asset, be able to rationalize a basis for taking the asset, and have access to the asset (opportunity). For example, a bookkeeper who works excessive hours and seldom takes a vacation may be engaged in a dishonest activity and not want others to gain access to records.

Regarding the rationalization side of the triangle, need and want are not necessarily synonymous. A person might need additional life insurance but want a new, large-screen television. The person might rationalize that the pride that comes with owning the television exceeds the worry about dying. Another factor in the rationalization might be the perception of a low probability of theft detection or of minimal punishment when detected. A major factor in obtaining a confession is the interviewer's ability to help the offender form a socially acceptable rationalization for having committed the offense.

5.2.3 INTERVIEWER

The interviewer must appear professional, exude confidence, and interact well with others. The interviewer's demeanor sets the tone of the interview. A negative attitude quickly translates into negative results. By contrast, making positive comments on the investigation and the interview indicates professionalism and an expectation of a successful interview.

Interviewers must know their own skills and emotions and recognize the personal characteristics of the interviewee while eliciting information from that person. Interviewers must develop the skills to evaluate the truthfulness of the information furnished and simultaneously to formulate additional lines of questioning. By utilizing the floating point strategy of continuously re-evaluating a hypothesis as information is obtained, an investigator can adjust questions accordingly. Inexperienced investigators often neglect the skill of listening when interviewing suspects. Active listening includes attentiveness, concentration, acceptance, detachment, and patience. Interviewers must be able to assess facts previously established in the light of information provided by the interviewee.

Enlisting the cooperation of the interviewee is the key to a successful interview. The most important factor of a successful interview is the ability of the interviewer to establish a favorable rapport with the interviewee. The successful interviewer recognizes the personality characteristics of the interviewee that can be used to garner the required cooperation. The successful interviewer will make attempts to understand the interviewee's behavior and to satisfy the needs underlying the behavior.

The ability to persevere and listen attentively is critical. The interviewer must resist the temptation to mentally formulate the next logical question while the interviewee responds to the previous question. An inexperienced investigative interviewer is often impatient. Attentive or active listening is an acquired ability that takes patience and extensive practice. A good interviewer does not assume an adversarial role but should remain an objective and neutral fact finder.

Untruthful interviewees often experience a high degree of stress during interviews. They may exhibit their anxiety through a variety of verbal and nonverbal behaviors. Interviewers must be able to evaluate those behaviors to assess the truthfulness of subjects' responses.

5.3 **PREPARATION**

An investigator should take a number of actions in preparation for an interview. The most critical of these preliminary actions is to learn the case information thoroughly. The investigator normally has enough advance notice to take the appropriate steps. However, sometimes the need to investigate an incident immediately makes it impossible to complete all the steps.

5.3.1 **GATHERING INFORMATION**

The investigator should become familiar with all available historical information on the matter at hand before conducting an interview. Under ideal conditions, the investigator has time to research the matter in detail. Sometimes, however, it is only possible to take a few minutes to mentally review known facts. The investigator must use any available time to prepare for the interview.

Optimally, before the interview, the interviewer knows the following in detail:

- who will be interviewed
- what the interview is about
- the conditions under which the interview will be conducted

Matter Under Investigation

In the initial information phase of an investigation, the effort focuses on gathering all legally available basic information. Every investigation eventually develops a theory or theme that collates the disparate evidence and explains how the crime was committed. The interviewer should have a basic understanding of the case's current theory. All known facts on the matter under investigation should be reviewed. Particular attention should be paid to facts that have not been revealed to employees or the public. The interviewee who has knowledge of such facts is obviously a witness to or participant in the crime.

Background Information on the Interviewee

With knowledge of some personal characteristics of the interviewee, the interviewer can establish rapport more easily. A proper understanding of those characteristics aids in accurate evaluation of the interviewee's truthfulness. During a fraud investigation, for example, knowing the interviewee had motive, ability and opportunity to commit the crime are relevant facts. It is helpful to know the interviewee's age, residence, criminal history, work history, education, and hobbies. Criminal investigators go to great lengths to conduct a personality profile to identify an individual's mental, emotional and psychological characteristics. Ethnic influences on nonverbal responses are discussed later.

Records Review

Before conducting interviews, the interviewer should check the records of the organization and other entities for pertinent information. In a larger enterprise, investigative and personnel files are normally maintained in databases. If the matter under investigation is a shortage of product from a warehouse, the investigative records should be accessible by product name, product number, warehouse facility, and names of persons reportedly involved. Information from other investigations, open or closed, involving the product, facility, or personnel may suggest a course of investigation or method of interview.

Personnel files of individuals believed to be involved in the matter under investigation should receive high priority. Performance evaluations and reports of habitual tardiness, fights, or other unacceptable conduct are highly useful in assessing the individual.

Payroll files are helpful for evaluating the person's financial stability. Garnishment or attachment of wages and orders for support payments may indicate the need for additional funds.

Criminal justice files should be checked, to the extent possible, for adverse involvement with law enforcement. Access to criminal records must be sought in an ethical manner in accordance with statutes and policies.

Discussion with Legal Counsel

The policy of the investigating enterprise or that of the client frequently dictates which matters should be discussed with legal counsel. In many instances, the client is not aware of the nuances of legal counsel and will depend on the expertise of the investigator. Investigative action must be planned with the end in mind; possible civil or criminal actions should always be considered. For example, in the United States, investigations that include searches must comply with the Fourth Amendment to the Constitution. This includes locker searches where there is an expectation of privacy if the employees are allowed to use their own locks.

In some jurisdictions around the world, investigative reports, including statements taken in the course of interviews, are subject to discovery in civil or criminal proceedings. However, reports of investigative actions, including interviews that are taken on the advice of counsel may be protected from discovery as attorney work product. For example, In the United States any admission obtained by a private citizen who conducts an interrogation in violation of due process but otherwise follows constitutionally prescribed conduct may be admissible. An interviewer who is in doubt as to the proper course of action should consult with legal counsel.

5.3.2 **PLANNING THE INTERVIEW**

The nature of the situation may preclude detailed planning. However, if there is time, the interviewer should consider a number of key factors in planning the interview.

Location

An interview must be conducted in an environment that an objective outsider would consider fair. A judge, jury, or arbitrator may consider the circumstances of the interview in deciding a statement's admissibility or the outcome of a legal proceeding. Privacy for the interviewee is a major consideration. A quiet conversation in a secluded area at an incident scene might be acceptable. An intense conversation in a room where the interviewees faces a door that is open to a busy corridor during a shift change would be another matter. A competent, opposing counsel would quickly bring any apparently unfair condition to the attention of the judge, jury, or arbitrator.

The choice of interview site depends on the nature and phase of the investigation, the apparent involvement of the interviewee, the issue of interviewee confidentiality, and the desired level of formality. The experienced investigator evaluates all facets of the investigation to date when determining the optimum location for each interview.

A witness who has no other apparent involvement in the matter under investigation may be interviewed in the office or at home. In such settings, the witness may be less tense and feel more confident. However, normal household or office activity may disrupt the interview. In some circumstances, interviews should be conducted at or near the incident location.

For an interview with a subject who is expected to be uncooperative, a security office or interview room is the preferred location. Those locations provide a controlled environment with proper equipment and furnishings.

Flexibility and adaptability are required in the selection of interview locations. The need for interviewee confidentiality may dictate that the interview be conducted in a discreet location. Occasionally an interview is needed at a private residence, public restaurant, or other location not associated with the incident setting or security staff. Sometimes the age or infirmity of the interviewee requires an interview in a hospital or nursing home. The physical arrangements of the interview may thus be out of the interviewer's control. In every setting, privacy and confidentiality should be maintained.

The interview room should be free of unnecessary, distracting objects. Thus, the subject's office, which is likely to contain photos and mementos, is not an ideal interview location. If a room cannot be dedicated to interviews, a small conference room normally suffices. A straight chair with a padded seat and back, and without rollers, should be provided for the interviewee. Overstuffed and reclining chairs should be avoided, as they encourage slouching or leaning back. Such positions are psychologically undesirable, as a suspect who is too relaxed while being questioned may not give his or her full attention to the investigator.

The subject should face the interviewer, and any witness to the session should be seated to the side. The subject's forward view should not include distractions, such as a window. The interview should not be conducted across a desk or table, as such furniture inhibits rapport and precludes full observation of the subject's nonverbal responses. The particular investigation and interview techniques used by the interviewer will dictate the spacing of the chairs. Generally speaking, during the interview the distance between the subject and the investigator should be about five feet. The interviewer should avoid continuous eye contact as it may be perceived as an effort to dominate the interviewee.

The interview subject should always have a clear path to the room's exit. Otherwise, allegations of coercion or false imprisonment might be made and sustained.

To obtain accurate information, interviewers should interview only one interviewee at a time. Interviewing one person at a time and ensuring that the conversation cannot be overheard prevents one witness from influencing another.

The interviewee may use colloquial or street language in the course of the interview. Hence, it is advantageous for the interviewer to have a basic understanding of current jargon. However, the interviewer should not use expletives or street language himself or herself.

Time Factors

Several time issues must be considered in interviews:

- time since the incident
- time scheduled for interviews in other investigations
- availability of the interviewee
- availability of the interviewer
- anticipated length of the interview

In an incident investigation, the interviews should be conducted as soon as possible after the event to capture witnesses' recollections while they are fresh. Important details and nuances are quickly forgotten.

In a routine investigation, the considerate interviewer does not schedule an interview at an inconvenient time for the interviewee. In a business situation, the interview should be conducted during normal business hours when the interviewee is expected to be working. However, various circumstances may require different scheduling.

Generally, the length of time required for a general interview does not pose a problem. In interviewing a witness, the interviewer gathers the information and prepares a statement fairly quickly. Informational interviews of possible perpetrators, however, can take several hours. Nonetheless, these longer interviews must be completed in a reasonable length of time to preclude allegations of duress.

Questioning Order

Witnesses who should be questioned are, in descending priority, as follows:

- persons who are not likely to be readily available later, such as an employee scheduled to be transferred to a distant location
- persons believed to have the most pertinent information concerning the matter under investigation
- persons who are likely to be hostile witnesses

The offender or offending group is interviewed last. The theory of the case helps in identifying the person or persons. Information gathered from non-suspect persons may assist in confirming or refuting a suspect's guilt—before that suspect is questioned.

Questions to Ask

The salient points of the matter under investigation, along with the persons known or believed to be involved, should be firmly fixed in the mind of the interviewer. The interviewer should also be familiar with the elements of proof of the alleged offense. A general questioning format can be then be crafted, based on these two aspects of the investigation.

Whether to use prepared notes or commit questions to memory is a matter of interviewing technique. Prepared notes can indicate careful preparation for the interview. They can also be a disruptive factor if overused. Prepared notes are acceptable provided the interviewer does not refer to them regularly throughout the interview. The essential point is that the interviewer must prepare for the interview. In general, random questioning is not productive and indicates a lack of professionalism, which the interviewee can readily observe.

Persons Present

One or two interviewers and the interviewee are normally the only persons in the room. It is important not to fill the room with interviewers. However, the investigator may want to have a second person in the room who can insulate the interviewer from potential accusations by the interviewee and corroborate statements against interest, confessions, etc. If a witness to the interview is present (usually another investigator), he or she should sit to the side of both the interviewee and interviewer and at a reasonable distance from them. The seating arrangement should help keep the interviewee focused on the interviewer.

It is critical that the interviewee clearly understand all of the interview's proceedings. If the interviewee is not proficient in the language of the interviewer, a qualified interpreter must be brought in.

If the interviewer and interviewee are of different sexes, it may be wise to include in the interview a witness of the same sex as the interviewee. Otherwise, the door to the room should remain open. If interviewee confidentiality is a concern, the interviewee should sit facing away from the door.

5.4 DOCUMENTATION OF THE INTERVIEW

5.4.1 AUDIO AND VIDEO RECORDING

An audio or video recording of the interview is a valuable tool for confirming statements made by all persons present. It helps confirm the voluntary participation of the interviewee and preclude charges of coercion. With modern camera equipment, the recording process can be unobtrusive and is ideal for retaining information as recording is most reliable for verbatim documentation of evidence from an interview. The equipment should be tested before any interview. Because the recording may eventually reach a judicial proceeding, the audio must be reasonably free of scratching or hissing sounds generated by the equipment, and any video recordings must contain images that distinguish the interview participants. In both video and audio recordings, the participants' voices must be understandable. Interviewers should note that frequent use of the same tape will result in lower recording quality. The cost of new audio or video tape is negligible compared to the value of the information to be recorded.

Discretion and common sense must be exercised when determining whether the interview should be recorded electronically. To be useful in the case and to avoid damaging the case, the recording must be made in conformance with the law and under circumstances that a court would consider fair.

If the case requires audio recording, it is best if the interviewee consents and the recording is conducted openly. It may help to explain to the interviewee that the recording protects all participants.

When an interview needs to be recorded without the interviewee's knowledge, prior consultation with legal counsel is critical. It is poor practice to record the interview and assume that no one will know. If the interviewee does not consent and discreet recording is not feasible, the interviewer must take notes.

An interview recording should capture at least the following:

- consent of the interviewee at the beginning
- date, time, and place of the interview
- complete identification of the interviewee
- identification of all persons present
- statement of possible uses of the information furnished
- identification of persons leaving the room and time of exit
- identification of persons entering the room and time of entry
- start time, stop time, and purpose of any breaks
- reaffirmation of the interviewee's consent to the interview and recording

The book *Electronic Recording of Interrogations* (Buckley, 2005) describes the type of equipment that can be used; proper investigator conduct during recording; methods of testifying effectively about recorded interviews and interrogations; and the experiences and lessons learned from those who have performed recorded interviews for years. (For example, Minnesota and Alaska have long required that law enforcement electronically record interviews.)

5.4.2 NOTES

Note taking documents the subject's responses. To minimize distraction, the interviewer should briefly note all the subject's responses, using a form of shorthand. For example, it is critical to remain calm and document a response such as, "let's suppose I'm guilty." It is important that the interviewer watch the subject answer each question and then make a few brief notes about the response.

In the question-and-answer phase of the interview, the interviewer should note the interviewee's verbal and nonverbal responses (discussed later).

5.4.3 INTERVIEW LOG

A log of the interview should be made. It should include the same details required in an audio recording (listed previously).

5.5 **SUBJECT FACTORS**

Intoxication

Information obtained from a person under the influence of alcohol or another substance is unreliable to some degree. A statement taken from such a person may be invalidated in a judicial proceeding. The interviewee should be questioned as to alcoholic beverages consumed within the last 24 hours and as to any medication taken. The interviewer should note the quantity of alcohol and the name and dose of any medication.

Each situation must be considered on its own merits. It may be impossible to interview a homeless alcoholic in a state of sobriety; however, he or she may be the best available witness to an incident. Someone who is excessively active, has dilated pupils, hasn't eaten or slept in days may be under the influence of amphetamines and at best unreliable. The usefulness of the information gained must be weighed in light of the condition of the interviewee.

Physical and Psychological Condition

The physical and psychological condition of the interviewee can have a profound effect on the reliability and admissibility of the information obtained. For example, hostages may form an emotional bond with their captors (known as the Stockholm syndrome) that renders their interview suspect. Likewise an interviewer could have a Pygmalion effect on the interviewee influencing the behavior. A person who has been involved in a physically debilitating situation should be interviewed briefly on the event's crucial aspects before being allowed to rest. The psychological effects of an incident might not be readily apparent but are equally debilitating. Responses will be colored by the stress of the incident and may not be accurate. The psychological effects of a situation may persist, perhaps subliminally, for a long period. Questions concerning a long-past situation may trigger an unexpected emotional response.

A person who is physically debilitated or psychologically stressed should not be subjected to a lengthy interview. For example, a woman dependent upon economic assistance may remain in a physical abusive relationship and not be forthcoming. The length of the interview and the condition of the interviewee can be used at a later date by the person's counsel to invalidate any statement taken. The interviewee should be asked to verify that the interview would not be contraindicated by any physical or mental condition.

Prejudice

An interviewee's prejudice toward an individual or group can contaminate the interview process. The prejudiced person may answer questions in generalities that include the perceived traits of the individual or group. Responses may be swayed both positively and negatively. Such answers are useful in evaluating the interviewee but are rarely useful in gathering specific information concerning the case. The interviewer should ensure that the answers given apply to the matter under investigation and the specific people involved.

Prejudice on the part of the interviewer will harm the entire process. It may, in fact, render the interview nonproductive and have a negative effect on future interviews and the entire investigation. The interviewer must repress personal prejudice and remain neutral throughout the interview. It is tort of slander if an investigator deliberately and knowingly makes a false and damaging statement about the subject of an investigation. If the interviewer has a particular dislike for the individual or the group involved, it may be best for another investigator to conduct the interview.

Perception

The physical and mental perception of the interviewee should be established in the course of the interview. The interviewee's ability to have seen the events or documents pertinent to the investigation is critical in weighing his or her statements. Crucial factors include the interviewee's corrected visual acuity, available light, and distance to the event or document in question.

The mental perception of the interviewee is equally important. A member of the financial staff might immediately recognize a financial document but have difficulty with a detailed map of the facility. A maintenance worker might readily understand the facility map but not recognize the importance of a financial document.

Age

Age can have a serious effect on the interview process. In the corporate environment, interviews with children are rarely encountered. In some facets of the private investigation field, interviews with children are common. Interviews with elderly persons are necessary in all elements of investigative work.

It is not uncommon for children to be shy and distrustful of strangers. In fact, children are generally taught to be wary of strangers. If a young witness is interviewed, allowing the child to sit in the lap of a parent provides a physical sense of safety and facilitates cooperation.

The elderly frequently digress during interviews and may relish the interviewer's company. Moreover, an elderly person may pay extraordinary attention to the details of an incident. The investigator who spends a few extra minutes in friendly conversation maybe rewarded with unexpected cooperation and detailed information.

5.6 CONDUCTING THE INTERVIEW

5.6.1 OPENING PROCEDURES

The following are key steps to take at the beginning of an interview:

- **Identify the interviewee.** The person who is to be interviewed is identified by name, home address, date and place of birth, and, if applicable, job title, place of employment, and social security number or driver's license number.

- **Identify the interviewer.** The interviewee is told the interviewer's name, job title, and place of employment, as well as the name and function of others present.

- **Clarify the interview topic.** The topic of the interview must be made clear to the interviewee. This is best accomplished by asking for the interviewee's understanding of the reason for the interview. The interviewee's reply, using particular terms or nuances, may give insight into the matter under investigation. Any misconceptions on the part of the interviewee as to the purpose of the interview must be clarified. Details of the investigation are not necessary at this point. Further explanation can be given as the interview progresses.

- **Establish rapport.** The function of the interviewer is to elicit information from the interviewee. To this end, clear communication is essential, so a good rapport must exist between the interviewer and the interviewee. A haughty or superior approach by the interviewer will hamper this goal. Showing authority, standing over a sitting interviewee, or pointing an accusatory finger elicits a defensive response and precludes good rapport. If an interviewee verbally attacks an interviewer, the interviewer should remain controlled, understanding, and nonjudgmental.

- Experienced interviewers frequently finish introducing other persons present by inviting them to spend a few minutes with the interviewee. This technique, known as "yes conditioning," generally elicits an affirmative response and facilitates the cooperation of the interviewee. The interviewee should exhibit signs of congruence that signal a positive attitude.

Rapport can be accomplished by using hidden persuaders initiating a general discussion before direct questioning. The interview situation is usually fraught with tension for the interviewee, whose image of an interview was probably gained from television detective shows. Casual conversation about pets, gardening, sports, or similar topics puts the interviewee into an amenable state of mind. Insight as to the personality of the interviewee, gained in this casual conversation, can be highly useful later in the interview. The objective is to get to know the interviewee and to establish the interviewer as a helpful, understanding person. Maintaining eye contact with the interviewee promotes rapport.

5.6.2 INVESTIGATIVE QUESTIONS

An interview with a witness, record custodian, or other person who is not directly involved in the matter under investigation is normally an uncomplicated process. The interviewer and the interviewee are identified, the nature of the investigation is briefly explained, and the requisite information is gathered.

The interviewer should begin with broad, general questions and then ask more specific ones. Even if the theory of the case has been formulated and the interviewer has prepared a questioning format, the response to a broad question may suggest other questions to ask. The response to any question may lead to a correction in the case's theory or an adjustment to the questioning format.

The initial question in the interview is normally a request for the interviewee to relate the events in the matter under investigation. As much as possible, the interviewer should refrain from interrupting or guiding the interviewee at this stage. However, if the interviewee strays far from the matter under investigation, the interviewer must guide him or her back to the main topic.

While the interviewee relates the events, the interviewer makes mental notes of points to be further developed. When the recitation is completed, the interviewer asks questions about pertinent points, and the interview's focus shifts to more narrowly defined questions. In interviews, the two types of questions generally asked are open and closed. To put an interviewee at ease, the beginning of the interview should contain "Closed" questions, which are specific questions that offer a limited number of possible responses. In the primary phase of an interview, a narrative type of questioning should occur.

As the interview progresses, questions should be phrased to elicit a narrative answer, not a simple yes or no. The basic interrogatives (who, what, when, where, why, and how) are most useful in formulating open-ended questions. A request such as "Please tell me how that account is verified at the end of the business day" is most productive. Leading questions should be avoided.

Questions should be as simple as possible, given the nature of the matter under investigation and the interviewee's involvement in the matter. It is critical that the interviewee have a precise understanding of each question. If there is any doubt as to the interviewee's understanding, the question should be rephrased.

The response to each question should be complete before another question is asked. Multiple open questions can result in mixed, multiple responses that must then be clarified to avoid confusion.

5.7 **VERBAL AND NONVERBAL BEHAVIOR**

Throughout the interview process, the investigator should carefully observe the subject's verbal and nonverbal responses because the collection of information is based upon communication and observation, particularly as the subject answers questions about the details of the matter, any alibi, and the subject's relationship to the victim. In the primary phase this is particularly important. The interviewer must analyze and compare both the factual evidence or information and the behavior of the person who is the source of the information. Every investigator who questions a person about procedures followed, the sequence of events on a given day, or the reasons an action was executed in a particular manner evaluates the person's behavior and draws conclusions as to the person's truthfulness or deception.

5.7.1 **DIFFERENT TYPES OF RESPONSES**

Verbal responses include both spoken words and gestures that serve as word substitutes, such as nodding the head to indicate yes or a shaking the head to indicate no. Also within the category of verbal responses are such vocal characteristics as tone, speed, pitch, and clarity.

The careful listener considers not only the words themselves but also the interviewee's timing and emphasis. The normally socialized individual does not enjoy lying; deception leads to a conflict that results in anxiety and stress. A suspect who offers an evasive answer or an objection in response to a direct question does so because of an attempt to avoid the internal anxiety associated with outright denial.

Nonverbal responses include body movements and position changes, gestures, facial expressions, and eye contact. Nonverbal behavior is internally motivated to reduce anxiety. Whether through distraction (such as shifts in body posture, bringing a hand to the face, or crossing the arms) or displacement behavior (such as picking the lint off clothing, pacing, or repetitive fast movement), all nonverbal behavior that accompanies a deceptive response emanates from a guilty suspect's efforts to relieve anxiety.

5.7.2 **PRELIMINARY CAUTIONS**

The following cautions are in order:

- No single word or nonverbal behavior automatically means a person is lying or telling the truth. Each behavior characteristic displayed must be considered in the context of the environment and intensity of the setting and in comparison to the subject's normal behavior.

- The assessment of a subject's truthfulness should be based on the overall behavioral pattern displayed, not on any single observation.

- Behavioral indications should be evaluated on the basis of when they occur (timing) and how often they occur (consistency). To be reliable indicators of truth or deception, behavioral changes should occur immediately in response to a question or simultaneously with the subject's answer.

- Evaluation of behavior symptoms should consider the subject's intelligence, sense of social responsibility, and maturity. As a general rule, the more reliable behaviors are displayed by persons who are socially responsible—who have more at stake in the outcome of a case (such as their family, job, or reputation)—or are more mature. Caution must be used in evaluating the behavior of persons who are emotionally or psychologically unstable.

- Some behavioral characteristics that suggest deception may also be displayed by a truthful subject who feels fear, anxiety, anger, or mistrust.

5.7.3 VERBAL RESPONSES

Generally, a truthful person answers questions in a direct, straightforward, spontaneous, and sincere manner, particularly if the question is simple and unambiguous. Conversely, a deceptive person may delay response or repeat the question to gain time to contrive a false answer. For example, the subject may say, "Let me see now," trying to remember previous statements or camouflage reactions with pretended, serious thought. The truthful person does not have to ponder over an answer and an effective interviewer will use silence to enhance the interview. Truthful subjects have only one answer for any given question, and it will be substantially the same answer regardless of any repetition of the inquiry. In contrast, if a deceptive subject is asked whether he stole money from a safe, he may give an evasive answer, such as "I was home all day" or "I don't even know the combination." Some deceptive subjects may answer questions too quickly, even before the question is completed.

A lying subject will sometimes speak in an irrational manner or use fragmented or incomplete sentences, such as "It's important that…," "If you think…," or "I…I hope that you…" A deceiver may also develop a memory failure when confronted with a probing question and may respond with a half-lie, such as "I don't remember," "As far as I know," or "I don't recall." He or she may try to bolster an answer with such phrases as "To be perfectly honest with you…" or "To be quite frank…"More sophisticated liars usually plan ahead and give their answers a protective verbal coating, such as "At this point in time," "If I recall correctly," "It is my understanding," "If my memory serves me right," or "I may be mistaken, but…" By these tactics, deceptive subjects seek to establish an escape hatch rather than risk an outright lie. Some lying subjects may exhibit an unreasonably good or selective memory. The end result, however, will be so implausible as to reveal the attempted deception.

Deceptive subjects respond to questions with complicated, detailed explanations that include factual information and are overly broad for the question. Pathological liars are likely to invent stories when relating the actual facts would be simpler and more convenient.

Truthful subjects tend to use harsh, realistic words, such as *steal, rape, kill, rob,* or *stab,* while deceptive subjects usually avoid such language in order to assuage their guilty feeling. A person who uses an insincere facade of religion or oaths to support an answer is, in many instances, not telling the truth. Typical examples of expressions used by lying subjects who try to make their statements believable are "I swear to God, sir," or "I'll swear on a stack of Bibles," or "With God as my witness." Some may even state, "On my poor mother's grave, sir." A subject who uses religion as a defense—stating, for example, "I couldn't do something like that, sir. I am a [religious affiliation]"—is usually not telling the truth.

Truthful persons not only respond directly but also speak clearly, for example, "No, I didn't steal the money." Some liars mumble or talk so softly that they cannot be heard clearly, while others may speak rapidly or display erratic changes in the tone or pitch of their voice. Similarly, a verbal response coupled with nervous laughter or a wisecrack is a common attempt to camouflage deception.

Deceptive subjects are more likely to challenge minute details of factual information on a case, perhaps saying, "They said this thing happened at 1:30 and I didn't come back until 1:45." Deceptive subjects tend to offer excuses or justifications to support their claims of innocence and may give very specific denials: "I did not take that $12,437.18." The truthful subject will generally offer much more general denials: "I did not steal that $12,000 or whatever it is. I didn't steal a penny of it."

In summation, the verbal behavior of a person who is telling the truth differs from that of one who is withholding relevant information.

The truthful person:

- makes general, sweeping denials;
- offers unqualified, direct, and spontaneous answers;
- exhibits a reasonable memory; and
- responds to questions in a rational manner and a clear tone of voice.

The deceptive person:

- offers very specific denials;
- avoids realistic words;
- makes seemingly irrelevant comments;
- gives delayed, evasive, or vague answers;
- exhibits an unusually poor, selective, or remarkable memory;
- qualifies answers or uses religion or oaths to support statements; and. speaks in an irrational, fragmented, mumbled, or subdued manner.

5.7.4 **NONVERBAL RESPONSES**

Nonverbal behavior is responsible for more than half of the information and meaning of a message communicated in a conversation. While the verbal statements a person makes are usually carefully thought out and certainly under the person's conscious control, most people do not pay the same attention to their physical movements and gestures. As a result, the true meaning of a person's statement, in many cases, may be discerned only by considering the verbal content in conjunction with the nonverbal behavior that accompanies it.

For example, if the interviewer asks a person whether he or she was involved in a particular act (such as embezzlement), and the person responds in a firm voice, saying, "Absolutely not; I had nothing to do with that," while leaning forward in the chair, in an open posture and maintaining steady eye contact, the entire message conveyed is one of sincerity and directness. But if the interviewee responds in a variety of tension-relieving gestures, in a weak tone of voice, shifts positions in the chair, drops eye contact to the floor, crosses his or her arms and legs into a closed posture, and leans back in the chair while completing the answer, even if the same words are used, an entirely different message is conveyed—one of insincerity and lack of candor and maybe an indication of deception. Most people would recognize the difference even if they could not explain it.

Activities Suggesting Deception

A number of specific, observable nonverbal behaviors can be consciously evaluated for indications of deception. Physical activities of the deceptive person may be categorized into the following general types:

- Significant posture change. This includes quick and sudden movements of the upper and lower body or perhaps even leaving the room while being questioned.

- Grooming gestures and cosmetic adjustments. Such gestures include rubbing and wringing the hands; stroking the back of the head; touching the nose, earlobes, or lips; picking or chewing fingernails; shuffling, tapping, swinging, or arching the feet; rearranging clothing or jewelry; dusting, picking lint from, or pulling threads on clothing; adjusting or cleaning glasses; and straightening or stroking the hair.

- Supportive gestures. Among these are placing a hand over the mouth or eyes when speaking, crossing arms or legs, hiding the hands or feet, holding the forehead with a hand, or placing the hands under or between the legs.

- When a suspect repeatedly combines any of these nonverbal reactions with verbal responses, there is a strong indication the verbal responses may not be truthful.

Comparative Postures

Truthful people tend to exhibit a different posture than deceptive people do.

A truthful person:

- sits upright but not rigid;
- positions himself or herself in front of the questioner;
- leans toward the questioner when making a point; and
- appears relaxed and casual.

A deceptive person:

- slouches or leans back in the chair;
- sits unnaturally stiffly;
- sits off to the side, not directly in front of the questioner;
- pulls elbows close to the side, arms folded and locked in front, with legs crossed; and
- exhibits rapid and erratic posture changes.

Eye Contact

An important nonverbal sign is the suspect's degree of eye contact with the interviewer. Deceptive people generally do not look directly at the interviewer; they look down at the floor, over to the side, or up at the ceiling. Anxiety is relieved—and it is easier to lie—if their eyes are focused somewhere other than on the questioner. Consequently, deceivers either try to avoid eye contact with the interrogator by making compensatory movements or else overreact by staring in a challenging manner.

Truthful people, on the other hand, are not defensive in their looks or actions and can easily maintain eye contact with the questioner. Their speech is fluid and straight to the point; they do not move excessively during the questioning and refrain from fidgeting when responding. Truthful persons remain relaxed and display confidence even though apprehensive. They show no concern about the credibility of their answers. They are attentive, and their casual manner is natural.

Evidence is the cornerstone of any investigative decision. An investigator's ability to elicit full and complete information from others and to assess the truth of that information affects the direction of the investigation. An investigator with knowledge of these behavior symptoms and the ability to analyze them can be far more effective in distinguishing fact from fiction. The skill is a valuable tool for determining whether the truth was told.

Influence of Culture

In evaluating behavior displayed during the interview, the cultures of the interviewer and interviewee must be considered. Comments and actions that are normal and acceptable in some cultures are considered offensive in others. The interviewer who shows respect for the culture of the interviewee will establish rapport more easily. These cultural considerations, if well understood, can also be used to the interviewer's advantage during the interview.

In Western cultures, eye-to-eye contact indicates sincerity. In Asian cultures, however, eye contact with a person in a superior position is considered impolite. A person from an Asian culture might appear to be insincere in avoiding eye contact, but he or she may actually intend politeness.

In some cultures, the frequent use of hand gestures to emphasize verbal comments is common. A demonstrative person may use frequent hand gestures to emphasize verbal responses in the course of the interview. A less demonstrative person may avoid hand gestures, but that practice cannot be equated with truth or prevarication.

5.8 BEHAVIOR ANALYSIS INTERVIEW

The Behavior Analysis Interview (BAI) was first developed about 40 years ago by John E. Reid, founder of John E. Reid & Associates, Inc. A BAI is a systematic evaluation of a subject's verbal and nonverbal behavior during the course of a structured interview in which both investigative and behavior-provoking questions are asked. Investigative questions (about the who, what, when, where, why, and how of the incident) have already been discussed. What follows is a discussion of behavior-provoking questions.

Behavior-provoking questions in a BAI are designed to draw out specific verbal responses or behavior that can be studied to distinguish between a truthful person and a person who is lying. Theoretical models were developed and statistically tested and validated for the predicted differences in the type of responses given by truthful and deceptive subjects. More than 30 behavior-provoking questions have been developed and used during BAIs (Horvath, 1994). Five of these questions are presented here to illustrate some of the differences in message characteristics.

The following questions are asked in the context of an investigation into credit cards stolen from a mail room. Each question is followed by examples of response types normally offered by truthful and deceptive subjects.

- **Purpose question:** "What is your understanding of the purpose of this interview?" The truthful response provides an accurate description of events. The subject may use direct words, such as *steal*, and may mention numbers of cards stolen or victims' names, if known. The deceptive subject's response is a vague and nonspecific description of events. It may use non-descriptive language (an incident, something happened, etc.), or use qualifiers such as *apparently*, *evidently*, or *may have*. It does not mention any details about the number of stolen cards or the victim's names.

- **"You" question:** Often a novice investigator will not come right out and ask the suspect if he committed the offense, but often it is the shortest distance to identifying the offender. "Over the past several weeks we have had a number of credit cards disappear from the bank and specifically the mail room. If you had anything to do with stealing these missing credit cards, you should tell me now." A direct and unequivocal brief denial—for example, "No, I didn't steal any credit cards" characterizes the truthful response. It may use broad, all-encompassing language: "Absolutely not! I haven't stolen anything from here." The deceptive response is a longer and unemotional denial—for example, "I do not know anything about this" (an evasive response) or "I didn't even know credit cards were missing," or the objection, "Why would I risk my job by doing something like that?"

- **Knowledge question:** "Do you know for sure who did steal any of the missing credit cards?" Truthful subjects often volunteer suspicion: "Not for sure, but I have some ideas." They may express concern or anger: "I wish I did know, but I just don't have any idea." The deceptive subject gives a brief, unemotional denial: "No, I do not." The subject does not offer spontaneous thoughts or feelings.

- **Suspicion question:** "Who do you suspect may have stolen these missing credit cards?" The truthful subject gives the question careful thought and when offering a suspicion can substantiate its basis. A deceptive response would be, "I don't have any idea," without giving the question any careful thought. Deceivers may name improbable suspects, such as people without opportunity or access.

- **Vouch question:** "Is there anyone with whom you work who you feel is above suspicion and would not do anything like this?" This question is also known as a "Trust" question. The truthful subject will give the question thought and typically eliminate possible suspects. The deceptive one, however, will not vouch for others so as not to narrow the field of suspects. Doing so could increase the chance of exposure.

By incorporating these types of behavior-provoking questions into the interview process, in conjunction with the investigative questions, the investigator can develop a greater insight into a subject's probable truthfulness or deception. The investigator can more confidently eliminate people from suspicion and conduct a confrontational interview (interrogation) of the suspected guilty person.[1]

5.8.1 CONFRONTATIONAL INTERVIEW

When all the appropriate general interviews have been conducted and the accumulated evidence points to a specific person as the likely perpetrator, a confrontational interview or interrogation should be conducted.

The following is a description of what is generally considered the most effective process for persuading a deceptive suspect to tell the truth about the act under investigation: the Reid Nine Steps of Interrogation. The process should be conducted only when the investigator is reasonably certain about the suspect's involvement in the act.

Step One: Positive Confrontation

Most interrogators enter the room with a file summarizing the investigation results. After an exchange of greetings, the interrogator confronts the suspect with an accusation of guilt. This type of accusation is made only when the suspect's guilt seems very clear. Otherwise, the statement should be less direct. Following the confrontation, the interrogator pauses to evaluate the suspect's reaction to the statement, then repeats the initial statement of involvement. Then the interrogator sets the investigation file aside, sits down directly opposite the suspect, and makes a transition to a sympathetic and understanding manner.

---

[1] A complete list of BAI's behavior-provoking questions appears in *Criminal Interrogations and Confessions* (Inbau, 2001).

Step Two: Theme Development

The next step is to present moral justification for the suspect's criminal behavior. One way of doing so is to place moral blame for an illegal activity on another person or an outside set of circumstances. This effort appeals to a basic aspect of human nature—the tendency of a wrong doer to minimize responsibility for his or her actions by blaming someone or something else. In a credit card case, for example, the interrogator could suggest that the suspect was not paid enough by the employer or that someone left the card where it was an open temptation. Other moral justifications include unusual family expenses, desperate circumstances, the influence of a friend, retribution for an argument, or drug or alcohol dependence. By minimizing the situation, the investigator will make it easier for the subject to admit guilt.

The moral justification should be presented in a sympathetic and understanding way. An interest in working with the suspect to resolve the problem breaks the ice. The interrogator should voice the justification in a monologue, not giving the suspect an opportunity to speak until ready to admit guilt.

Step Three: Handling Denials

The more often the suspect denies guilt, the more difficult it becomes to admit guilt later. Therefore, the interrogator should interject a blocking statement whenever the suspect enters an "I didn't do it" plea. By sticking to theme development, the interrogator weakens the guilty suspect's denials. Many guilty people change from a defensive position to an offensive one, offering objections. The innocent suspect generally will not ask to make a statement but will, instead, without any display of etiquette, promptly and unequivocally maintain innocence. An innocent suspect never moves past this denial stage and remains steadfast in the assertion of innocence.

Step Four: Overcoming Objections

Most suspects' objection statements can be categorized in two general groups: trait objections (e.g., "I wasn't brought up that way" or "A person who would do something like that is really stupid") and factual objections (e.g., "I don't even have the safe combination," "I didn't even know him," or "I don't need the money"). Statements from either group are feeble explanations, even when they may be partly true. In any event, the interrogator should not argue about the statement or show surprise or irritation. A detached reaction discourages the suspect, who then perceives that the statement was wrong or at least ineffective. If the interrogator overcomes the objections, a suspect often withdraws into a shell and focuses on impending punishment.

Step Five: Keeping a Suspect's Attention

Following the objection stage, the guilty suspect often becomes pensive, apathetic and quiet. It is most important during this stage to ensure that the suspect listens attentively to the theme (psychological justification for the suspect's behavior) and does not concentrate on punishment (which would serve to reinforce a resolve to deny the crime). To keep the suspect's attention, the interrogator should draw nearer to him or her. This proximity often regains attention, and the suspect will watch and listen more intently. The interrogator begins to channel the theme down to the probable alternative components.

Step Six: Handling a Suspect's Passive Mood

At this stage, some suspects may cry, a reaction that often expresses remorse. Many other suspects do not cry but express their emotional state by assuming a defeatist posture—slumped head and shoulders, relaxed legs, and a vacant stare. To facilitate the impending inculpatory statement or admission of guilt, the interrogator should intensify the theme presentation and concentrate on the psychological justification for the unlawful act. Gestures of sympathy, such as a hand on the suspect's shoulder, also aid truth-telling.

Step Seven: Presenting an Alternative Question

The alternative question consists of two incriminating choices concerning aspects of the incident or crime. Elements of the alternative are developed as logical extensions of the theme. If the theme contrasts impulsive behavior with premeditated acts, the alternative question is, "Did you plan this thing or did it just happen on the spur of the moment?" Either choice is an admission of guilt. The alternative question should be based on an assumption of guilt. It should not ask, "Did you do this or didn't you?" A poorly phrased question invites denial. A suspect who accepts one alternative has made a first admission of guilt. The task, then, is to develop this admission into an acceptable confession.

Step Eight: Having the Suspect Relate Details

Once the alternative question has been answered, the interrogator responds with a statement of reinforcement. Essentially, this is a statement that acknowledges the suspect's admission of guilt. The objective is to obtain a brief oral review of the basic sequence of events while obtaining sufficient detail to corroborate the suspect's guilt. In seeking a confession, it is important to help the interviewee rationalize actions and avoid embarrassment. In attempting to obtain a confession, the investigator should not ask ambiguous questions.

Questions asked at this time should be brief and clear, calling for only limited verbal responses from the suspect. It is premature to say, "Well, just tell me everything that happened." Questions should be open-ended and free of emotionally charged words. Once the interrogator has obtained a brief statement about the crime sequence, he or she should ask detailed questions to obtain information that can be corroborated by subsequent investigation. After this full statement is complete, it may be necessary to return to the suspect's choice of alternatives, or to some other suspect statement, to establish the actual purpose and intent at the time of the crime.

Step Nine: Converting an Oral Confession

After advising the suspect, the interrogator leaves the room, ostensibly to check on something. He or she then returns with a witness, who may be introduced as someone who has been involved in the investigation. The interrogator repeat the essential details of the suspect's confession, and then the witness asks a few confirming questions. This is the time to convert an oral confession into a written one. One of four formats can be used:

- statement written by the suspect
- statement authored by the interrogator but read and signed by the suspect

- statement taken down by a secretary or stenographer and transcribed into a typed document for the suspect to read and sign

- recorded statement (audio or video) by the suspect

The statement of guilt must be legible and understandable by someone who is not familiar with what the suspect has done. Therefore, it must include a recitation of the facts or events. The statement should be made using the general vocabulary, grammatical irregularities, profanity, and idiomatic abnormalities that the person making the statement would use in everyday speech.

Any errors, changes, or crossed-out words should be initialed with an OK written in the margin by the suspect. The statement should reflect that the suspect was treated properly, that no threats or promises were made, and that the statement was freely given by the suspect. A suspect who has completed reading the written statement is instructed to "write your name here" while the interrogator points to the signature line. It is better to avoid asking the suspect to "sign here" because "sign" connotes too much legal significance. The suspect signs each page of the statement in front of the interrogator and the witness, and then both of them sign as well.

For a written statement or confession to be credible and admissible in U.S. court, it must be given voluntarily, be trustworthy, and include the following essential information:

- date, time, and place where the statement was prepared

- complete identification of the person making the statement: full name, date and place

- of birth, residence address, and social security number or driver's license number

- all pertinent points of the interview discussion, with particular emphasis on the elements of proof of the crime under investigation

- an affirmation that the statement is made freely after fair treatment in the course of the interview and without remuneration, threat, coercion, or promises

- sequential numbering of every page, with each page signed by the person making the statement

- initialing of any additions to, deletions from, or alterations of the statement by the person making the statement

- signature, on the last page of the statement, of the person making the statement, the interviewer, and a witness

Obtaining the written confession at the end of the interrogation is not the capstone. Every effort should be made to verify the statement and obtain the supporting evidence necessary for trial. Prior to going to trial, a formal deposition, given under oath, may be requested by either counsel to determine how the investigator conducted the investigation, what evidence was obtained, and what the witness(es) and suspect(s) said during the investigation.

5.9 CLOSING PROCEDURES

The close of the interview may not be the last time the interviewer and the interviewee meet. Developments in the case may require another interview, or the interviewee may be called as a witness in a legal proceeding.

The interviewer should display appreciation for the interviewee's cooperation. Even though the interviewee may have been uncooperative, the interviewer should avoid ending the interview on a hostile note. Cases have been resolved as the result of an individual contacting again the investigator with information that was not previously revealed. The best closing strategy besides general conversation would be asking the interviewee if there is anything he or she would like to add and, if necessary, may he or she be called on again.

5.10 GENERAL LEGAL ASPECTS

Interviewers should have a clear understanding of the legal requirements regarding interviews in the jurisdiction in which they work. Interviewers in the United States should particularly be informed about the requirements of the *Weingarten* decision (*NLRB v. Weingarten, Inc.*, 420 U.S. 251(1975)) regarding the right of the interviewee to have others present at an interview.

Statements and Confessions

A confession or sworn statement must be competent, material, relevant, and obtained voluntarily under legally acceptable circumstances so it will be admissible in any subsequent legal proceeding or hearing.

Promises and Guarantees

In the course of the interview, it may be necessary to make a promise to the interviewee. The interviewer must be certain that whatever is promised can be legally performed (Grau, 1981). The interviewer should avoid making any promise or guarantee, explicit or implied, that is illegal, that cannot be confirmed by the client or senior management, or that cannot be fulfilled.

An interviewee may ask for an opinion as to the outcome of the matter under investigation. The investigator usually cannot guarantee a specific outcome and, in fact, should not be in a position to do so. The function of the investigator is to gather the facts. A claim by the interviewer that cooperation on the part of the interviewee will lead to a more favorable outcome will, most probably, invalidate any confession obtained.

Threats, Intimidation, and Duress

Any coercion, duress, or psychological constraint placed on the interviewee is unacceptable and may make a confession inadmissible. Likewise, verbal abuse, threats, and intimidation are unprofessional, unethical, and unacceptable. Either type of abuse invalidates confessions or statements obtained and may call for civil or criminal action against the interviewer. Interviewees must understand that they are free to leave the interview location. An indication, expressed or implied, that the interviewee is not free to leave creates the conditions for allegations of false imprisonment.

Consent

The interviewee must consent to the interview and to making any statement. The consent must be fully voluntary and cannot be coerced in any manner. Otherwise, a confession or statement will be ruled inadmissible in subsequent legal proceedings.

The interviewee must be legally competent to give consent. For example, a minor cannot give consent, nor can a person under the influence of alcohol or other intoxicants.

The interviewee must also understand that consent, once given, may be withdrawn at anytime.

Access to Restrooms and Meals

The interviewee must have access to restroom facilities at reasonable intervals and especially on request. In a lengthy interview, time for meals should be scheduled at appropriate times. Coffee or other beverage breaks are useful when the interviewer wants to change the mood. If meals and breaks are taken in a public area, the environment is generally not conducive to a discussion of the interview topic. However, meals and breaks can enhance communication between the interviewer and interviewee. To preclude the possibility of interruption during the interview, the investigator should ask, "Are you in any way sick? Are you thirsty? Do you have to use the restroom?"

5.11 **CONCLUSION**

The key to the investigative process is the investigator's ability to interview suspects involved in the matter under investigation. While television shows perpetuate the idea that when investigators carefully examine a crime scene they usually find a clue that leads them to the offender, most cases are solved with information developed during interviews and the subsequent efforts to corroborate or disprove interview findings.

Skilled interviewers must be patient, persistent, and prepared. They must conduct every interview in a professional manner, always treating the subject with respect and carefully adhering to all legal requirements. In the future, it may become a requirement to electronically record all interviews and interrogations. Consequently, all interviews and interrogations should be conducted in such a manner that they can withstand the scrutiny of judicial review. The practices and techniques outlined in this discussion provide the foundation for effective and respectful techniques.

REFERENCES

Agnes, M. (2003). *Webster's new world dictionary*. New York, NY: Pocket Books.

Buckley, D., & Jayne, B. (2005). *Electronic recording of interrogations*. Chicago, IL: John E. Reid and Associates.

Deming, P. S. (1997). *Interviewing techniques*. King of Prussia, PA: Philip S. Deming and Associates.

Fay, J. J. (1993). *Encyclopedia of security management*. Woburn, MA: Butterworth-Heinemann.

Ferraro, E. F. (2000). *Undercover investigations in the workplace*. Woburn, MA: Butterworth-Heinemann.

Grau, J. J. (1981*). Criminal and civil investigation handbook*. New York, NY: McGraw-Hill.

Horvath, J., & Buckley, D. (2004, May). Differentiation of truthful and deceptive criminal suspects in behavior analysis interviews. *Journal of Forensic Sciences*.

Inbau, F. E., Reid, J. E., Buckley, J. P., & Jayne, B. (2001). *Criminal interrogation and confession* (4th ed.). New York, NY: Aspen Publishers.

Maslow, A. H. (1987). *Motivation and personality*. New York, NY: HarperCollins.

ADDITIONAL SOURCES

Association of Certified Fraud Examiners (Producer). (1994). *Beyond the numbers* [Motion picture].

Bilek, A. J., Klotter, J. C., & Federal, R. K. (1980). *Legal aspects of private security*. Dayton, OH: Anderson Publishing Company.

Buckley, D. M. (1993, April). Dealing with artful dodgers. *Security Management*.

Buckley, J. P. (1983, May). The nine steps of interrogation. *Security Management*.

Buckley, J. P. (1986, March–April). How do I know if they told me the truth? *Internal Audit Advisor*.

Buckley, J. P. (1991, first quarter). The behavioral profile of a liar. *NEWS* (International Association of Credit Card Investigators), Vol. 118.

Buckley, J. P., & Jayne, B. C. (1987, June). Read between the lines. *Security Management*.

Buckley, J. P., & Jayne, B. C. (1992, October). Criminal interrogation techniques on trial. *Security Management*.

Buckley, J. P., & Mullenix, P. A. (1985). The use of behavior symptoms in the search for the truth. *Prosecutor*, Vol. 19, No. 1.

Buckwalter, A. (1983). *Interviews and interrogations*. Stoneham, MA: Butterworth Publishing.

Fennelly, L. J. (1996). *Handbook of loss prevention and crime prevention*. Woburn, MA: Butterworth-Heinemann.

Fischer, R. J., & Gree, G. (1998). *Introduction to security* (6th ed.). Woburn, MA: Butterworth-Heinemann.

Fisher, R. P., & Geiselman, R. E. (1992). *Memory-enhancing techniques for investigative interviewing*. Springfield, IL: Charles C Thomas Publishers.

Force, H. R. (1972, September). Interrogations. *Security Management*.

French, S. R., & Van Houten, P. (1987). *Never say lie*. Boulder, CO: Paladin Press. Hinerman, J. W. Self-incriminatory statements. *Security Management*.

Inbau, F. E., Farber, B. J., & Arnold, D. W. (1996). *Protective security law*. Woburn, MA: Butterworth-Heinemann.

Jannsen, M. J. (1995, September). The case of the missing money. *Security Management*.

Jayne, B. C. (1994, February). Interviewing strategies that defeat deceit. *Security Management*.

Link, F. C., & Glenn, F. D. (1989). *The kinesic interview technique*. Riverdale, CA: Interrotec Associates.

MacHovec, F. J. (1989). *Interview and interrogation: A scientific approach*. Springfield, IL: Charles C Thomas Publishers.

Marshall, K. D. (1985, January). Unmasking the truth. *Security Management*.

Maxwell, D. A. (1993). *Private security law*. Woburn, MA: Butterworth-Heinemann.

McDonald, P. (1993). *Make 'em talk: principles of military interrogation*. Boulder, CO: Paladin Press.

Morgan, R. C. (1986). Interviewing *techniques in the detection of deception*. Idaho Assessment Center.

O'Hara, C. E., & O'Hara, G. L. (1994). *Fundamentals of criminal investigation*. Springfield, IL: Charles C Thomas Publishers.

Penley, W. J. (1979, November). Interviews Do Not Always Lead to the Truth. *Security Management*.

Pupura, P. P. (1998). *Security and loss prevention: An introduction* (3rd ed.). Woburn, MA: Butterworth-Heinemann.

Rabon, D. (1992). *Interviewing and interrogation*. Durham, NC: Carolina Academic Press.

Royal, R. E., & Schutt, S. R. (1976). *The gentle art of interviewing and interrogation*. Englewood, NJ: Prentice-Hall.

Royal, R. F., & Schutt, S. R. (1978). The art of interviewing and interrogating. *Security Management.*

Rudacille, W. C. (1994). *Identifying lies in disguise.* Dubuque, IA: Kendall/Hunt Publishing Company.

Scanning words for true confessions. (1992, August). *Security Management.*

Sennewald, C. A. (1981). The process of investigation: Concepts and strategies for the security professional. Woburn, MA: Butterworth-Heinemann.

Wygant, J. R. (1986, September). The language of truth. *Security Management.*

Yeschke, C. L. (1993). *Interviewing: A forensic guide to interrogation.* Springfield, IL: Charles C Thomas Publishers.

Yeschke, C. L. (1987). *Interviewing: An introduction to interrogation.* Springfield, IL: Charles C Thomas Publishers.

Zulawski, D. E., & Wicklander, D. E. (1993). *Practical aspects of interview and interrogation.* Boca Raton, FL: CRC Press.

E V I D E N C E

Evidence is that which provides proof or an indication of an assertion. New types of evidence continually appear and are accepted in court as medicine, technology, and diagnostic tools advance. Because of private security's broad concerns (criminal, civil, contract, and corporate), security personnel need advanced evidence-gathering skills.

This chapter describes the types of evidence and the means of collecting, protecting, examining, and transporting evidence according to the stringent standards required for criminal cases. Even if the evidence will not be used in a criminal case, handling it according to that standard preserves the option.

Evidence appears in oral, documentary, and physical forms, which are described in detail below. There are three classifications of evidence that the courts will consider, they are direct, circumstantial and real. Throughout history some have referred to evidence as inanimate (that which is less subject to human error) or animate (that which can be misleading), but for the purpose of this chapter we will be breaking it down two basic categories: direct (real, material) and indirect (circumstantial & hearsay). Direct evidence is first-hand knowledge. For example, if a witness sees a driver in an automobile pass through a red light and strike another automobile that had the right of way, that witness has direct evidence of the incident. Direct (real) evidence may also be the voucher the witness observed being forged by a bookkeeper). By contrast, indirect evidence is a highly informed inference. For example, perhaps a witness was around the corner, heard a screech of brakes and then the impact of two cars, ran to the scene, and then saw the light change from red to green. That witness can make an informed inference that the driver wrongfully passed through a red light. Indirect evidence is also known as circumstantial evidence where something is inferred to have happen because testimony given on a series of events leads one to believe that it did have happened. Hearsay evidence also falls into this category but with the exception of a dying declaration of an individual to a credible witness, hearsay evidence is normally not admissible in a trial. An exception to the hearsay rule is when a person making the statement about what another person said made statements against self-interest. The rule that applies most often in determining the importance of evidence and its ability to prove a point is called "Materiality". What are its quality, substance and connection to the incident or case?

Res gestae (a Latin phrase meaning "things done") is an exception to the rule against hearsay evidence. *Res gestae* is based on the belief that because certain statements are made naturally, spontaneously and without deliberation during the course of an event, they leave little room for misunderstanding/misinterpretation upon hearing it by someone else (i.e. by the witness who will later repeat the statement to the court) and thus the courts believe that such statements carry a high degree of credibility. Evidence which can be admitted into evidence as *Res gestae* fall into three headings:

1. Words or phrases which either form part of, or explain a physical act,

2. Exclamations which are so spontaneous as to belie concoction, and

3. Statements which are evidence as to someone's state of mind.

After an incident, security practitioners should gather evidence carefully, regardless of whether law enforcement will become involved. Such evidence can be used to establish a timeline, resolve the issue, analyze how the incident occurred, and if necessary modify security measures to prevent future incidents. If the case should go to trial the competency and materiality of the evidence will be determined by the judge, usually following case law. In non-criminal cases there may be more open interpretation and allowances made on the presentation of evidence. In both criminal and non-criminal cases the defense is entitled to the information during discovery. Investigators must be able to recognize when an incident scene staging has occurred to purposefully alter the scene to mislead the investigation.

When physical evidence is presented at a trial, a chain of custody, the uninterrupted control of evidence must be clearly shown, the evidence must be properly identified and it must be relevant to the case before the court. Evidence should be marked with the investigator's initials at the time it is gathered. Limiting the individuals who handle the evidence to the smallest number possible and properly documenting each transfer will maintain the chain of custody and assist the prosecution when introducing it at trial as the same evidence that was seized. For example, during the investigation of embezzlement, the documents that clearly indicates the fraudulent appropriation of property and criminal intent by the person to whom it has been entrusted is critical and should be controlled by the least number of people.

6.1 ORAL EVIDENCE

Oral evidence is a spoken statement regarding a person's knowledge, which may be direct or indirect and gained through any manner. The following discussion of oral evidence is adapted to a security audience from *Eyewitness Evidence: Trainer's Manual for Law Enforcement* (National Institute of Justice, 2003).

6.1.1 INITIAL REPORT AND FIRST RESPONSE

Answering the Call

Principle: The call taker should obtain, in a non-suggestive manner, complete and accurate information from the caller. This information may include the name or a description of the perpetrator. The call taker should also be alert for signs that may question the credibility of the complainant and the plausibility of the allegation.

Preliminary Scene Investigation

Principle: For a thorough preliminary investigation, it is necessary to preserve and document the scene, including information from witnesses and physical evidence. The methods used by the preliminary investigator have a direct impact on the amount and accuracy of information obtained throughout the investigation.

Policy: The preliminary investigator should obtain, preserve, and use the maximum amount of accurate information from the scene.

Procedure: After securing the scene, calm the victim and attend to any injured persons. The preliminary investigator should then do the following:

- Identify any perpetrators and detain them if still present at the scene.

- Determine what type of incident has occurred.

- Broadcast an updated description of the incident, perpetrators, and vehicles.

- Verify the identity of the witnesses. Witnesses will need to be contacted later.

- Separate witnesses, and instruct them to avoid discussing details of the incident with other witnesses. Witnesses should not hear others' accounts. It also may be helpful to ascertain whether witnesses have spoken with each other about the incident before being separated.

- Canvass the area for other witnesses. Witnesses may be reluctant to come forward or may have departed the scene before security personnel arrived. Also, other employees, contractors, guests, or invitees in the vicinity may have heard or seen something that could assist in the investigation.

Obtaining Information from Witnesses

Principle: The manner in which the preliminary investigating officer obtains information from a witness affects the amount and accuracy of that information.

Policy: The preliminary investigator should obtain, accurately document, and preserve information from witnesses.

Procedure: When interviewing a witness, the preliminary investigating officer should consider the following approach:

- **Establish rapport with the witness.** The witness will then be more comfortable during the interview and will likely provide more information. In the course of developing that rapport, the investigator can learn about the witness's communication style (e.g., how the witness describes everyday events compared with how the witness describes the incident).

- **Inquire about the witness's condition.** A simple question, such as "How are you doing?", contributes to rapport and may also alert the investigator to physical or mental conditions (e.g., intoxication, medication, shock) that could impair the witness's ability to recall or report information effectively.

- **Use open-ended questions** ("What can you tell me about the car?"), **augmented with closed-ended questions** ("What color was the car?"), **and avoid leading questions** ("Was the car red?"). An open-ended question allows for an unlimited response from the witness in his or her own words, thereby generating a greater amount of unsolicited information. Open-ended responses also tend to be more accurate and promote more effective listening on the part of the investigator. A closed-ended question, in contrast, limits the amount or scope of information that the witness can provide ("Did the perpetrator have a beard?" or "What color was the car?"). The investigator should follow with more directed questions if the witness is unresponsive to open-ended questions or provides imprecise responses. If, when answering an open-ended question, the witness states that the perpetrator was dressed in shabby clothing, the investigator should ask the witness to elaborate on the type of clothing ("What do you mean by shabby?"). For each new topic, the investigator should begin with open-ended questions and augment them with closed-ended questions if necessary. Leading questions suggest an answer and may distort the witness's perception or memory. The investigator needs to determine only what the witness knows, uninfluenced by what the investigator might expect or know from other sources.

- **Clarify the information with the witness.** This step helps ensures that the investigator has understood and accurately recorded the information.

- **Document information obtained from the witness, including the witness's identity.** This information will be necessary when the witness is contacted for a follow-up interview.

- **Encourage the witness to contact investigators with any further information.** Witnesses often remember additional, useful information after an interview. They should be reminded that any information, no matter how trivial it seems, may be important. For example, if the witness later remembers that the perpetrator drank from a soft drink can at the scene, there could be fingerprints or saliva on the can. Additionally, in such cases as sexual assault or arson, the witness may later recall or recognize a distinct smell that was on the perpetrator (such as cologne) or at the scene (such as gasoline).

- **Encourage the witness to avoid contact with the media or exposure to media accounts concerning the incident.** Media information may contaminate the witness's memory. Media requests for a story or offers of compensation may encourage a witness to fabricate information.

- **Instruct the witness to avoid discussing details of the incident with other potential witnesses.** Witnesses should not hear others' accounts because they may be influenced by that information. The independence of witnesses is important so that investigators can judge whether the information they have provided is consistent with other witnesses' statements and other evidence developed in the investigation.

Summary: Information obtained from the witness can corroborate other evidence in the investigation. Therefore, it is important that this information be accurately documented.

6.1.2 **INTERVIEWS BY THE FOLLOW-UP INVESTIGATOR**

Pre-Interview Preparations and Decisions

Principle: Preparing for an interview maximizes the effectiveness of witness participation and interviewer efficiency.

Policy: The investigator should review all available witness and case information and arrange an efficient and effective interview.

Procedure: Before conducting the interview, the investigator should do the following:

- **Review available information.** This information may include police reports and incident scene information. The interview can then be tailored to elicit the maximum amount of information from the witness.

- **Plan to conduct the interview as soon as the witness is physically and emotionally capable.**

- **Select an environment that minimizes distractions and is comfortable for the witness.**

- **Obtain key materials (e.g., notepad, tape recorder, camcorder) in advance so the interview will not be interrupted.**

- **Separate the witnesses. Independent** witness statements can be used for corroboration. Witnesses should not hear others' statements because they may be influenced by that information.

- **Determine the nature of the witness's prior law enforcement, security, or corporate contacts.** This information can help put any information obtained from the witness into context for the purpose of assessing witness credibility or reliability. It also can assist later in rapport development.

Conducting the Interview

Several principles underlie the interviewing of cooperative witnesses:

- social dynamics between the interviewer and witness

- facilitation of the witness's memory and thinking

- communication between the interviewer and witness

Social dynamics.
The interviewer should maintain or reestablish rapport with the witness and encourage the witness to actively and voluntarily report information, rather than passively respond to questions. A rapport is especially helpful when the investigator seeks personal or intimate information from a witness. The interviewer should show understanding and concern by asking about the witness's health, empathizing with the witness's situation, avoiding judgmental comments, and establishing common ground with the witness. The interviewer should also personalize the interview by treating the witness as an individual.

This can be accomplished by avoiding questions that sound programmed or artificial (e.g., "Is there anything you can tell me that would further assist this investigation?") and referring to the witness by name. The interviewer should also ask questions that follow up on the witness's previous responses, repeat the witness's concerns, lean forward, and make eye contact.

To encourage the witness to volunteer information without prompting, the interviewer should do the following:

- **State expectations.** The witness may not know what to expect or may have incorrect expectations of his or her role in the interview. The interviewer should state explicitly that the witness is expected to volunteer information.

- **Ask open-ended questions.** These questions allow the witness to do most of the talking.

- **Avoid interruptions.** Interruptions discourage the witness from playing an active role and disrupt his or her memory. The interviewer should make a note and follow up later with any questions that arise during a witness's narration.

- **Allow pauses.** Pauses after the witness stops speaking allow the witness to collect his or her thoughts and then continue providing information.

Facilitation of the witness' memory and thinking.

Much of the information about an incident is stored in the witness's mind. The interviewer can promote information retrieval in several ways:

- **Minimize distractions.** The interviewer should ensure that physical distractions, such as noise or the presence of other persons, are minimized. In addition, the interviewer can encourage the witness to block out distractions by closing his or her eyes and concentrating on the memory.

- **Encourage the witness to mentally recreate the incident.** The interviewer should instruct the witness to mentally recreate the circumstances surrounding the incident (e.g., by thinking about his or her thoughts or feelings at the time of the incident).

- **Tailor questions to the witness's narrative.** The interviewer's questions should be tailored to the witness's current thoughts and narrative. For example, if the witness is thinking or talking about the perpetrator's face, the questions should be about the face and not about other aspects of the incident, such as a license plate. The interviewer should try to understand what aspect of the incident the witness is thinking about. The interviewer should then ask an open-ended question about that topic and then follow up with non-leading, closed-ended questions related to the topic.

Communication between the interviewer and witness.

The interviewer is concerned with many issues, such as resolving an incident, enforcing corporate rules, and preparing for civil litigation. The witness knows details about the incident. For the most productive interview, both individuals should communicate their needs and information to each other.

Oral evidence is given great weight by jurors and judges alike. It is paramount for the security employee tasked with investigating an incident to possess the professional skills for obtaining oral evidence to be used in later proceedings. It is also important that the investigator make no promises or offers of a reward to encourage a witness to make a statement, this will not only void the statement if discovered, but may also lead to a charge of witness tampering against the investigator.

6.2 **DOCUMENTARY EVIDENCE**

Documentary evidence is information, usually in the form of letters, figures, or other marks, that is contained on or in such items as paper products, rubber stamps, plastic bags, typewriters, and seals. If particular documentary evidence will not be examined by law enforcement laboratories, security practitioners may need to reach out to private labs and experts. *Appendix A* lists crime lab organizations.

The following discussion of questioned document examination is adapted from the Federal Bureau of Investigation's *Handbook of Forensic Services* (2003).

6.2.1 HANDWRITING AND HAND PRINTING

Examination of handwriting characteristics can sometimes determine the origin or authenticity of questioned writing. However, the following factors can lead to inconclusive results:

- insufficient quantities of questioned or known writing
- lack of contemporaneous questioned and known samples
- distortion or disguise in the questioned or known writing
- insufficient identifying characteristics
- submission of photocopied evidence instead of original evidence

Traits such as age, sex, personality, and intent cannot be determined.

Obtaining Known Writing Exemplars

The text, size of paper, space available for writing, writing instrument, and writing style (handwriting or hand printing) must be as close to the original conditions as possible. In obtaining a known sample, the investigator should do the following:

- **Give instructions (oral or written) only concerning the text to be written.** The investigator should not give instructions on spelling, punctuation, or arrangement of writing.

- **Ensure that all exemplars are on separate pieces of paper.**

- **Ensure that the writer and a witness initial and date each page of writing.**

- **Do not allow the writer to see the previous exemplars or the questioned writing**. The investigator should remove exemplars from the writer's sight as soon as they are completed.

- **Obtain exemplars from dictation until normal writing has been produced.** Normal handwriting is assessed by determining whether the writing is too quickly or slowly executed and whether the handwriting is consistent.

- **Obtain exemplars from the right and left hands.**

- Obtain hand printing exemplars in both uppercase and lowercase letters.

- Obtain exemplars written rapidly, slowly, and at varied slants.

- Obtain a sufficient quantity of exemplars to account for natural variation in the writing.

- Obtain undictated writing, such as business records, personal correspondence, and canceled checks.

Altered or Obliterated Writing

Altered or obliterated writing can sometimes be detected and deciphered.

Nongenuine Signatures

False signatures may be of several types:

- **Traced signatures** are prepared by using a genuine signature as a template or pattern.

- **Simulated signatures** are prepared by copying or drawing a genuine signature.

- **Freehand signatures** are written in the forger's normal handwriting with no attempt to copy another person's writing style.

6.2.2 TYPEWRITING

Questioned typewriting can occasionally be matched to the typewriter that produced it. This is most common when the typewriter is a typebar machine. The identification may be based on characteristics that develop during manufacturing and through use and abuse of the typewriter. Other kinds of typewriters (e.g., ball, printwheel, or thimble) are less likely to be successfully connected with questioned typewriting. Comparison of questioned typewriting with reference standards can sometimes determine a make and model of the typewriter or typewriter elements. Carbon film typewriter ribbons can sometimes be read for content or specific wording of questioned material. Carbon film ribbons can sometimes be identified with questioned typewritten impressions. Fabric ribbons cannot be read.

Obtaining Known Typewriting Exemplars

The following are steps that an investigator should take to obtain known exemplars of typewriting:

- **If the typewriter has a carbon film ribbon, remove it from the typewriter and submit it to the laboratory.** The investigator should also submit the correction tape and then insert a new ribbon in the typewriter before obtaining exemplars.

- **If the typewriter has a fabric ribbon, remove it from the typewriter and put the typewriter in the stencil position.** The investigator should then place a sheet of carbon paper over a sheet of blank paper, insert both into the typewriter, allow the typeface to strike the carbon paper, and then submit the fabric ribbon strike and the carbon paper strike exemplars to the laboratory.

- **Obtain two full word-for-word texts of the questioned text and type the entire keyboard (all symbols, numbers, and uppercase and lowercase letters) two times.**

- **Record the make, model, and serial number of the typewriter on the exemplars.** The investigator should also record the date the exemplars were obtained and the name of the person who directed the exemplars.

- **Obtain the typewriter's service and repair history.**

- If the laboratory examiner requests the typewriter, it must be packed securely to prevent damage during shipment. Typewriter elements (e.g., ball, printwheel, or thimble) must also be submitted.

6.2.3 PHOTOCOPIES

Photocopies can sometimes be matched to the machine producing them if the exemplars and questioned copies are relatively contemporaneous.

Obtaining Known Photocopy Exemplars

Investigators should take the following steps in obtaining known photocopy exemplars:

- Obtain at least 10 exemplars with no document on the glass plate, with the cover down.

- Obtain at least 10 exemplars with no document on the glass plate, with the cover up.

- Obtain at least 10 exemplars with a document on the glass plate, with the cover down.

- Record on each exemplar the date the exemplars were obtained, the name of the person who directed the exemplars, and the conditions under which the exemplars were made.

- Record the make, model, and serial number of the photocopy machine, information about the toner supplies and components, whether the paper supply is sheet- or roll-fed, and options such as color, reduction, enlargement, zoom, mask, and trim.

- Do not store or ship photocopies in plastic envelopes.

6.2.4 **OTHER MATERIALS AND IMAGES**

Graphic Arts (Printing)

Printed documents can sometimes be associated with a common source or identified with known printing paraphernalia, such as artwork, negatives, or plates.

Paper

Torn edges can sometimes be positively matched. The manufacturer can sometimes be determined if a watermark is present. Paper can be examined for indentations caused by writing. The investigator should not rub the indentations with a pencil or add indentations by writing on top of the evidence.

Burned or Charred Paper

Information on burned or charred documents can sometimes be deciphered. The document must be minimally handled. The document must be shipped in the container in which it was burned, in polyester film encapsulation, or between layers of cotton in a rigid container.

Age of a Document

The earliest date a document could have been prepared can sometimes be determined by examining watermarks, indented writing, printing, or typewriting.

Carbon Paper or Carbon Film Ribbon

Examination of used carbon paper or carbon film ribbon can sometimes disclose the content of the text.

Checkwriter Impressions

A checkwriter impression can sometimes be associated with the checkwriter that produced it.

Embossings and Seals

An embossed or seal impression can sometimes be identified with the instrument that produced it.

Rubber Stamps

A rubber stamp impression can sometimes be identified with the rubber stamp that produced it. The investigator should submit the rubber stamp to the laboratory uncleaned.

Plastic Bags

Plastic bags (such as sandwich or garbage bags) can sometimes be identified with the roll or a box from which they originated.

Anonymous Letter File

Security organizations should collect images of anonymous letters that were cause for concern. Investigators can then search the collection to associate a letter from one case with letters from others.

6.2.5 SHIPPING DOCUMENTARY EVIDENCE

Documentary evidence must be preserved in the condition in which it was found. It must not be folded, torn, marked, soiled, stamped, written on, or handled unnecessarily. In addition, investigators should do the following:

- Protect the evidence from inadvertent indented writing.

- Mark documents unobtrusively by writing the collector's initials, date, and other information in pencil.

- Whenever possible, submit the original evidence to the laboratory. The lack of detail in photocopies makes examinations difficult. Copies are sufficient for reference file searches.

- Refrain from storing or shipping photocopies in plastic envelopes.

If evidence needs to be shipped to a laboratory or other testing facility, properly packaged evidence must be sent via registered mail or a registered carrier (FedEx, DHL, etc.) to preserve the chain of custody.

6.3 **PHYSICAL EVIDENCE**

Physical evidence is tangible. It may consist of air particulates, a puddle of liquid, dirt or dust, clothing, tools, electronic devices, weapons, vehicles, bodily fluids, or anything else that can be touched or sensed physically or technologically. Physical evidence can be divided into five categories: *corpus delicti*, associative, identifying, tracing and trace. *Corpus delicti* relates to the evidence that proves a crime has been committed, such as the body at a homicide scene. Associative evidence (also known as circumstantial evidence) links a suspect with the scene of a crime, such as fingerprints, or DNA. Identifying evidence is the associative evidence that establishes the identity of a suspect such as a fingerprint, bite impressions, or blood found at the scene. Tracing evidence (not to be confused with "trace evidence") are those article that assist in the possible identification and location of a suspect, such as a credit card receipt or a laundry mark or tag on a piece of clothing. Trace evidence that will undergo examination in the criminalistics section of a crime lab includes fibers, paints, dyes, glass, and similar elements. Impression evidence includes firearms, tool marks, bite impressions, and footprints.

6.3.1 **EVIDENCE SEARCHES**

Success in the use of physical evidence increases when an incident scene search is planned, coordinated, and executed by knowledgeable security employees, who must keep in mind the following:

- The best search options are usually the most difficult and time-consuming.
- Physical evidence cannot be over documented.
- A search may be either a cautious search of visible areas (avoiding evidence loss or contamination) or a vigorous search of concealed areas.
- Searches must be timely so that they are conducted while the evidence may still be available. For example, a six year old bank forgery case may not yield any physical evidence of a false production or document alteration because the regulations require the bank to maintain records for only 5 years.

The security professional in charge should take these steps first:

- Discuss the search with involved personnel before arriving at the scene, if possible.
- Ensure that personnel are aware of the types of evidence usually encountered and the proper handling of the evidence.
- Make preliminary personnel assignments before arriving at the scene, if possible. Personnel may be assigned two or more responsibilities.

The following are the responsibilities associated with various roles at the scene of the search:

Person in charge:
- Ensure scene security.
- Prepare administrative log.
- Conduct preliminary survey (initial walkthrough).
- Prepare narrative description.
- Resolve problems.
- Make final decisions.

Photographer:
- Photograph and log evidence and scene.

Sketch preparer:
- Sketch and log scene.

Evidence recorder:
- Serve as evidence custodian and log evidence.

Scene supervisor:
- Establish communication with the appropriate corporate executives, including legal counsel if necessary, so issues arising from incident scene searches can be resolved. Coordinate agreements with all departments in multi-departmental incident scene searches.
- Obtain evidence collection and packaging materials and equipment.
- Prepare the paperwork to document the search.
- Provide appropriate protective clothing, communication, lighting, shelter, transportation, equipment, food, water, medical assistance, and security for search personnel.
- In prolonged searches, use shifts of two or more teams. Transfer paperwork and responsibility in a preplanned manner from one team to the next.
- Be alert for evidence.
- Take extensive notes.
- Consider the safety of all personnel.

The sections below describe the main tasks that the on-site team should perform.

Secure and Protect the Scene

- Take control of the scene immediately.

- Determine the extent to which the scene has been protected. Obtain information from personnel who have knowledge of its original condition.

- Designate one person to be in charge of final decision making and problem resolution.

- Take extensive notes.

- Keep out unauthorized personnel.

- Record who enters and leaves.

Conduct Preliminary Survey

The preliminary survey is a tool for planning a search.

- Cautiously walk through the scene.

- Maintain administrative and emotional control.

- Select a narrative technique (written, audio, or video).

- Take preliminary photographs.

- Delineate the extent of the search area. Usually expand the initial perimeter.

- Organize methods and procedures.

- Recognize special problem areas.

- Identify and protect transient physical evidence.

- Determine personnel and equipment needs. Make specific assignments.

- Develop a general theory of the incident.

- Take extensive notes to document the scene, physical and environmental conditions, and personnel movements.

Evaluate Evidence Possibilities

- Ensure that the collection and packaging materials and equipment are sufficient.

- Focus first on evidence that could be lost. Leave the least transient evidence for last.

- Ensure that all personnel consider the many varieties of possible evidence, not only evidence within their specialties.

- Search the easily accessible areas and progress to out-of-view locations. Look for hidden items. For example, in the case of a homicide, look for postmortem lividity which denotes the blood flow to the lowest point of gravity in a corpse.

- Evaluate whether evidence appears to have been moved inadvertently.

- Evaluate whether the scene appears contrived.

Produce Narrative

The narrative is a running description of the incident scene.

- Use a systematic approach in the narrative.

- Consider everything that catches one's attention to be worth recording.

- Generally, do not collect evidence during the narrative.

- Use photographs and sketches to supplement, not substitute for, the narrative.

- Include the following key points in the narrative:

    — case identifier
    — date, time, and location
    — weather and lighting conditions
    — identity and assignments of personnel
    — condition and position of evidence

Photography

- Photograph the incident scene as soon as possible.

- With the use of digital cameras take a few test shots to make there is no distortion of the crime scene in the photos. Distortion can be caused by an incorrect point of view, improper perspective and deceptive tones, such as shadows.

- Prepare a photographic log that records all photographs and a description and location of evidence.

- Establish a progression of overall, medium, and close-up views of the incident scene.

- Photograph from eye level to represent the normal view.

- Photograph the most fragile areas of the incident scene first.

- Photograph all stages of the incident scene investigation, including discoveries.

- Photograph the condition of evidence before recovery.

- Photograph the evidence in detail and include a scale, the photographer's name, and the date.

- Take all photographs intended for examination purposes with a scale. When a scale is used, first take a photograph without the scale.

- Photograph the interior incident scene in an overlapping series using a normal lens, if possible. Overall photographs may be taken using a wide-angle lens.

- Photograph the exterior incident scene, establishing the location of the scene by a series of overall photographs including a landmark. Photographs should have 360 degrees of coverage. Consider aerial photography.

- Photograph entrances and exits from the inside and the outside.

- Photograph important evidence twice—first, taking a medium-distance view that shows the evidence and its position to other evidence, and second, taking a close view that includes a scale and fills the frame.

- Before entering the scene, acquire, if possible, prior photographs, blueprints, or maps of the scene.

Sketches

- Use sketches to record location of items, conditions, and distance and size relationships.

- Number sketches in a way that coordinates with evidence log numbers.

- Include the following with each sketch:
  - case identifier
  - date, time, and location
  - weather and lighting conditions
  - identity and assignments of personnel
  - dimensions of rooms, furniture, doors, and windows
  - distances between objects, persons, bodies, entrances, and exits
  - measurements showing the location of evidence (in reference to two unmovable items, such as doors or walls)
  - key, legend, compass orientation, scale, scale disclaimer, or combination thereof

Physical Evidence Collection

The actual collection of evidence is most critical and the time when most errors occur, so special care is needed during the search, photographing, recovery, marking, identifying and packaging of the evidence by in evidence technician or investigator. It is also imperative that the crime scene be isolated and protected for the preservation of evidence. That is why it is important to teach the proper process of securing a crime scene in any basic law enforcement or security officer training course.

- The most common type of physical evidence is fingerprints, so care should be taken to collect and preserve them first.

- Use a search pattern (grid, strip or lane, spiral).

- Search from the general to the specific.

- Be alert for all evidence.

- Search entrances and exits.

- Photograph all items before collection and notate the photographic log.

- Mark evidence locations on the sketch.

- Complete the evidence log with notations for each item of evidence. If possible, have one person serve as evidence custodian.

- Arrange for two persons to observe evidence in place, during recovery, and being marked for identification. Mark directly on the evidence when necessary, but first attempt to place identifying marks on evidence containers. As a minimum, the best way to certify a piece of evidence is with the investigator's initials.

- The proper marking of evidence at the time of seizure and transfer establishes the actual chain of custody.

- Wear latex or cotton gloves to avoid leaving fingerprints.

- Do not excessively handle the evidence after recovery.

- Seal all evidence packages at the incident scene.

- Time and temperature have an effect on organic materials, so measures need be taken to prevent deterioration.

- Obtain known standards (e.g., fiber samples from a known carpet).

- Make a complete evaluation of the incident scene.

- Constantly check paperwork, packaging, and other information for errors.

- Accounting for control and secure handling of all evidence is paramount to maintaining the chain of custody.

- For evidence to be admissible, it must be proven that the evidence was not tampered with, thus the chain of custody must be maintained and documented throughout the process to identify all the individuals whom came in contact with the evidence.

Final Survey
The final survey is a review of all aspects of the search.

- Discuss the search with all personnel.

- Ensure that all documentation is correct and complete.

- Photograph the scene, showing its final condition.

- Ensure that all evidence is secured.

- Ensure that all equipment is retrieved.

- Ensure that hiding places or difficult access areas have not been overlooked.

Release

- Release the incident scene after the final survey.

- Note in release documentation the time and date of release, to whom the scene was released, and by whom it was released.

- Ensure that the evidence is (1) collected according to legal requirements, (2) documented, and (3) marked for identification.

- Consider the need for specialists (e.g., human resources, labor relations, safety) to observe the scene before it is released.

- Release the scene only when all personnel are satisfied that the scene was searched correctly and completely.

- Allow only the person in charge to release the scene.

6.3.2 REQUESTING EVIDENCE EXAMINATIONS

All requests for evidence examinations should be in writing, on organizational letterhead, and addressed to the appropriate laboratory. Submission requirements vary by laboratory but typically include the following:

- submitting person's name, organization, address, and telephone number

- any previous case identification numbers, evidence submissions, and communications relating to the case

- description of the nature and basic facts of the case as they pertain to evidence examinations

- names and descriptions of individuals involved (such as the subject, person of interest, or victim)

- submitting organization's case number

- list of evidence enclosed or sent under separate cover (along with means of shipping)

- types of examinations requested

- address to which the evidence should be returned

- address to which the laboratory report should be sent

- statement regarding whether the evidence was examined by another expert, there is local controversy, or other organizations have an interest in the case

- reasons for an expeditious examination if needed

- separate communications for separate cases

6.3.3 **SHIPPING EVIDENCE**

Several steps are important in transporting evidence to laboratories:

- Before packaging and shipping evidence, call the laboratory for specific instructions.

- Take precautions to preserve the evidence.

- Wrap and seal each item of evidence separately to avoid contamination.

- Place the evidence in a clean, dry, previously unused inner container.

- Seal the inner container with tamper-evident or filament tape.

- Affix "EVIDENCE" and "BIOHAZARD" labels, if appropriate, on the inner container. If any of the evidence needs to be examined for latent prints, affix a "LATENT" label on the inner container.

- Affix the evidence examination request and all case information between the inner and outer containers.

- Place the sealed inner container in a clean, dry, previously unused outer container with clean packing materials. Do not use loose foam materials.

- Completely seal the outer container so that tampering with the container would be evident.

- In the United States, all shipments of hazardous materials must comply with U.S. Department of Transportation regulations. 49 CFR 172.101 identifies items considered hazardous for the purpose of transportation. It also addresses special provisions for certain materials, hazardous materials communications, emergency response information, and training requirements for shippers. A trained and qualified evidence technician must assist with the typing, labeling, packaging, and shipping of all hazardous materials.

The following guidelines must be followed when shipping live ammunition:

- Package and ship ammunition separately from firearms.

- Label the outside of the container "ORM-D, Cartridges, Small Arms."

- Note on the Declaration of Dangerous Goods the number of packages and the gross weight of the completed packages in grams.

In addition, evidence shipments must comply with the International Air Transport Association's *Dangerous Goods Regulations* detailing how to prepare and package shipments for air transportation.

It is advisable to use shipping services that track shipments carefully. Security staff should record the method of shipment and the tracking numbers on the chain of custody form.

A related concern is disposal of hazardous materials. The U.S. Environmental Protection Agency's Resource Conservation and Recovery Act (RCRA), commonly referred to as the "cradle-to-grave" regulation, was established to track chemicals from "cradle" or generation to "grave" or disposal. This system imposes requirements on both generators and transporters, as well as on transport, storage, and disposal facilities. RCRA specifies that once a material is determined to be hazardous, it is the generator's complete responsibility.

The process for determining whether a material is a hazardous waste should be done by qualified personnel. Even new material in its original container may be waste if there is no use for it. Hazardous waste contractors and transporters can be used to help remove materials from scenes. Hazardous materials that are removed from incident scenes are considered evidence and would not fall under RCRA waste provisions. However, when a case has been adjudicated or the material for other reasons is not needed, the immediate assistance of a qualified contractor knowledgeable about local regulations must be sought. Clandestine drug laboratories and environmental incidents are examples of scenes that may require the removal of waste.

6.3.4 **HANDLING PHYSICAL EVIDENCE**

The following are recommendations that investigators should follow in handling various types of physical evidence:

Abrasives

- Employ personnel familiar with engine and machinery operations and mechanics to recover abrasives.

- Submit the oil and fuel from the engine sump and filters, as abrasives settle in oil and fuel.

- Submit bearings and other parts in which abrasives become embedded.

- Submit abrasives in heat-sealed or resealable plastic bags or paint cans. Do not use paper or glass containers.

Adhesives

If possible, submit the item to which the adhesive, caulk, or sealant is adhered. If not, remove a sample of the material with a clean, sharp instrument and transfer it to a resealable plastic bag or leakproof container, such as a film canister or plastic pill bottle.

Ammunition and Related Materials

Bullets
Fired bullets can be examined to determine the general rifling characteristics such as caliber and physical features of the rifling impressions and the manufacturer of the bullets. The microscopic characteristics on evidence bullets can be compared to test-fired bullets from a given firearm to determine whether the evidence bullet was fired from that firearm.

Bullet Jacket Alloys
Ammunition components, such as bullets, cartridge cases, and shotshell casings, should be packaged separately with the date, time, location, collector's name, case number, and evidence number written on the container.

Cartridge Cases or Shotshell Casings
Examination of cartridge cases or shotshell casings can determine the caliber or gauge, the manufacturer, and whether there are marks of value for comparison. The images of questioned cartridge cases and shotshell casings can be scanned into the National Integrated Ballistics Information Network to compare with evidence from other shooting incidents. The microscopic characteristics of evidence cartridge cases and shotshell casings can be examined to determine whether they were fired from a specific firearm.

Gunshot Residue on Clothing
The deposition of gunshot residue on evidence such as clothing varies with the distance from the muzzle of the firearm to the target. Patterns of gunshot residue can be duplicated

using a questioned firearm and ammunition combination fired into test materials at known distances. These patterns serve as a basis for estimating muzzle-to-garment distances. Clothing submitted for gunshot residue examination must be carefully handled, air-dried, and wrapped separately in paper. Clothing with blood must be air-dried and labeled "BIOHAZARD" on the inner and outer containers. The date, time, location, collector's name, case number, and evidence number must be on the container.

Shot Pellets, Buckshot, or Slugs
Examinations of shot pellets, buckshot, or slugs can determine the size of the shot, the gauge of the slug, and the manufacturer.

Unfired Cartridges or Shotshells
Examinations of unfired cartridges or shotshells can determine the caliber or gauge and whether there are marks of value for comparison. Examinations can also determine whether the ammunition was loaded in and extracted from a specific firearm. Unfired and fired cartridges or shotshells can be associated through manufacturing marks.

Wadding
Examinations of wadding components can determine the gauge and the manufacturer.

Anthropology

- Clean and air-dry bones, if possible. Pack in paper bags and wrap in protective material, such as bubble wrap or paper. If tissue is present on the skeletal material, refrigerate until mailing, and then ship in a foam cooler.

- Collect insect samples found on the remains in leak proof containers such as film canisters or plastic pill bottles. Call the laboratory for additional instructions or contact an entomologist.

Arson

Contact the local fire or police department or the federal Bureau of Alcohol, Tobacco, Firearms, and Explosives.

Audio

- Write-protect the original recording.

- Submit original audio recording.

- Identify known and questioned voice samples.

- Label the outer container "FRAGILE, SENSITIVE ELECTRONIC EQUIPMENT" or "FRAGILE, SENSITIVE AUDIO/VIDEO MEDIA" and "KEEP AWAY FROM MAGNETS OR MAGNETIC FIELDS."

Building Materials

- When building materials are penetrated or damaged, debris can adhere to people, clothing, tools, bags, and loot and can transfer to vehicles. If possible, submit the evidence in such a way that lab examiners can remove the debris themselves. Package each item of evidence in a separate paper bag. Do not process tools for latent prints.

- Collect known samples from the penetrated or damaged areas.

- Ship known and questioned debris separately to avoid contamination. Submit known and questioned debris in leakproof containers, such as film canisters or plastic pill bottles. Do not use paper or glass containers. Pack to keep lumps intact.

Chemicals (General Unknowns)

General unknowns include powders, liquids, and stains that are of indeterminate origin or cannot be readily classified. Full identification of an unknown may not be possible, but general classification of a substance usually is. When comparison samples are available, it may be possible to comment on the consistency of the unknown substance with a known comparison sample.

- Submit powder and liquid samples in leakproof containers.

- Do not submit large stained evidence. When possible, cut a small sample of the stained area and submit it in a heat-sealed or resealable plastic bag. Collect an unstained control sample, package separately, and submit it with the stained evidence. When cutting is not possible, transfer questioned stains by rubbing with a clean cotton swab (dry or alcohol-dipped). Air-dry the swab and pack in a heat-sealed or resealable plastic bag. Submit an unstained swab as a control.

Computers

Examinations can determine what type of data files are in a computer, compare data files to known documents and data files, determine when and in what order files were created, recover deleted files via a bit stream backup, convert files into different formats, search files for word or phrases, recover passwords, decrypt encoded files, and analyze source code. The FBI's Computer Analysis Response Team uses both investigations and laboratory support to conduct computer forensic examinations as in the case of malicious programs known as viruses or a trojan horse wherein it appears to do something desirable but actually does something unexpected. Investigators will seize printouts and other data copies, mark and control them so that the forensic team can conduct a sterile examination to maintain the integrity of the original media. It is critical to:

- Determine the type of computers and operating systems.

- If applicable, determine the type of network software, the location of the network servers, and the number of computers on the network.

- Determine whether encryption or password protection is used.

- Decide whether to seize computers and media or conduct an on-site examination.

- Generally, submit only the central processing units and the internal and external storage media.

- Use a sturdy cardboard container when shipping computer components. If possible, use the original packing case with the fitted padding. Use large, plastic bubble wrap or foam rubber pads as packing. Do not use loose foam pieces because they lodge inside computers and components and create static charges that can cause data loss or damage to circuit boards. Seal the container with strong packing tape.

- Pack and ship central processing units in the upright position. Label the outside container "THIS END UP."

- Pack disks, cartridges, tapes, and hard drives to avoid movement during shipping.

- Label the outer container "FRAGILE, SENSITIVE ELECTRONIC EQUIPMENT" and "KEEP AWAY FROM MAGNETS OR MAGNETIC FIELDS."

Appendix B contains a sample policy on seizing computer equipment.

Controlled Substances

Controlled substance examinations can establish trace-drug presence, identity, and quantity.

- Submit evidence in separate heat-sealed or resealable plastic bags.

- Fold clothing to preserve trace evidence.

- Do not submit used drug field test kits with evidence.

DNA

Deoxyribonucleic acid (DNA) is analyzed in body fluids, stains, and other biological specimens recovered from evidence. The results of DNA analysis of questioned biological samples are compared with the results of DNA analysis of known samples. The analysis can associate victims or persons of interest with each other or with an incident scene.

Two sources of DNA are used in forensic analysis. Nuclear DNA (nDNA) is typically analyzed in evidence containing blood, semen, saliva, body tissue, and hairs that have tissue at their root ends. Mitochondrial DNA (mtDNA) is typically analyzed in evidence containing naturally shed hairs, hair fragments, bones, and teeth.

If DNA evidence is not properly documented, collected, packaged, and preserved, it will not meet the legal and scientific requirements for admissibility in a court of law. In particular:

- If DNA evidence is not properly documented, its origin can be questioned.

- If it is not properly collected, biological activity can be lost.

- If it is not properly packaged, contamination can occur.

- If it is not properly preserved, decomposition and deterioration can occur.

When DNA evidence is transferred by either direct or indirect means, it remains on surfaces by absorption or adherence. In general, liquid biological evidence is absorbed into surfaces, and solid biological evidence adheres to surfaces. The appropriate methods for collecting, packaging, and preserving DNA evidence depend on the liquid or solid state and the condition of the evidence. The more the evidence retains its original integrity until it reaches the laboratory, the greater the possibility of conducting useful examinations.

<u>Blood</u>
- Ensure that only qualified medical personnel collect blood samples from a person.

- Have medical personnel collect at least two 5 milliliter tubes of blood in purple-top tubes with EDTA as an anticoagulant for DNA analysis. Have them collect samples for drug-or alcohol-testing in gray-top tubes with sodium fluoride.

- Identify each tube with the date, time, subject's name, location, collector's name, case number, and evidence number.

- Refrigerate (do not freeze) blood samples. Use cold packs, not dry ice, during shipping.

- Pack liquid blood tubes individually in foam or cylindrical tubes with absorbent material surrounding the tubes.

- Label the outer container "KEEP IN A COOL DRY PLACE," "REFRIGERATE ON ARRIVAL," and "BIOHAZARD."

- Submit sample to the laboratory as soon as possible.

For blood on a person, the investigator should do the following:

- Absorb liquid blood onto a clean cotton cloth or swab. Leave a portion of the cloth or swab unstained as a control. Air-dry the cloth or swab and pack in clean paper or an envelope with sealed corners. Do not use plastic containers.

- Absorb dried blood onto a clean cotton cloth or swab moistened with distilled water. Leave a portion of the cloth or swab unstained as a control. Air-dry the cloth or swab and pack in clean paper or an envelope with sealed corners. Do not use plastic containers.

For blood on surfaces or in snow or water, these steps apply:

- Absorb liquid blood or blood clots onto a clean cotton cloth or swab. Leave a portion of the cloth or swab unstained as a control. Air-dry the cloth or swab and pack in clean paper or an envelope with sealed corners. Do not use plastic containers.

- Collect blood that is in snow or water immediately to avoid further dilution. Eliminate as much snow as possible. Place in a clean, airtight container. Freeze the evidence.

The following steps should be followed for bloodstains:

- Air-dry wet bloodstained garments. Wrap dried garments in clean paper. Do not place wet or dried garments in plastic or airtight containers. Place all debris or residue from the garments in clean paper or an envelope with sealed corners.

- Air-dry small, wet bloodstained objects. Preserve bloodstain patterns. Avoid creating additional stain patterns during drying and packaging. Pack to prevent stain removal by abrasive action during shipping. Pack in clean paper. Do not use plastic containers.

- When possible, cut a large sample of bloodstains from immovable objects with a clean, sharp instrument. Collect an unstained control sample. Pack to prevent stain removal by abrasive action during shipping. Pack in clean paper. Do not use plastic containers.

- Absorb dried bloodstains on immovable objects onto a clean cotton cloth or swab moistened with distilled water. Leave a portion of the cloth or swab unstained as a control. Air-dry the cloth or swab and pack in clean paper or an envelope with sealed corners. Do not use plastic containers.

A blood examination request letter should contain the following information:

- brief statement of facts relating to the case
- claims made regarding the source of the blood
- whether animal blood is present
- whether the stains were laundered or diluted with other body fluids
- information on the victim's medical condition or that of any persons of interest, such as AIDS, hepatitis, or tuberculosis

Buccal (Oral) Swabs

- Use clean cotton swabs to collect buccal (oral) samples. Rub the inside surfaces of the cheeks thoroughly.

- Air-dry the swabs and place in clean paper or an envelope with sealed corners. Do not use plastic containers.

- Identify each sample with the date, time, subject's name, location, collector's name, case number, and evidence number.

- Buccal samples do not need to be refrigerated.

Hair

- Pick up hair carefully with clean forceps to prevent damaging the root tissue.
- Air-dry hair mixed with body fluids.
- Package each group of hair separately in clean paper or an envelope with sealed corners. Do not use plastic containers.
- Refrigerate and submit as soon as possible to the selected laboratory.

Saliva and Urine
- Absorb liquid saliva or urine onto a clean cotton cloth or swab. Leave a portion of the cloth unstained as a control. Air-dry the cloth or swab and pack in clean paper or an envelope with sealed corners.

- Submit small, dry saliva- or urine-stained objects to the laboratory. Pack to prevent stain removal by abrasive action during shipping. Pack in clean paper or an envelope with sealed corners.

- When possible, cut a large sample of saliva or urine stains from immovable objects with a clean, sharp instrument. Collect an unstained control sample. Pack to prevent stain removal by abrasive action during shipping. Pack in clean paper.

- Pick up cigarette butts with gloved hands or clean forceps. Do not submit ashes. Air-dry and place the cigarette butts from the same location (e.g., ashtray) in clean paper or an envelope with sealed corners. Do not submit the ashtray unless a latent print examination is requested. Package the ashtray separately.

- Pick up chewing gum with gloved hands or clean forceps. Air-dry and place in clean paper or an envelope with sealed corners.

- Pick up envelopes and stamps with gloved hands or clean forceps and place in a clean envelope.

- These samples should not be packed in plastic containers.

Semen and Semen Stains
- Absorb liquid semen onto a clean cotton cloth or swab. Leave a portion of the cloth or swab unstained as a control. Air-dry the cloth or swab and pack in clean paper or an envelope with sealed corners.

- Submit small, dry semen-stained objects to the selected laboratory. Pack to prevent stain removal by abrasive action during shipping. Pack in clean paper.

- When possible, cut a large sample of semen stains from immovable objects with a clean, sharp instrument. Collect an unstained control sample. Pack to prevent stain removal by abrasive action during shipping. Pack in clean paper.

- Absorb dried semen stains on immovable objects onto a clean cotton cloth or swab moistened with distilled water. Leave a portion of the cloth or swab unstained as a control. Air-dry the swab or cloth and place in clean paper or an envelope with sealed corners.

- These samples should not be packed in plastic containers.

Tissues, Bones, and Teeth
- Pick up tissues, bones, and teeth with gloved hands or clean forceps.

- Place tissue samples in a clean, airtight plastic container without formalin or formaldehyde. Place teeth and bone samples in clean paper or an envelope with sealed corners.

- Freeze the evidence, place in foam containers, and ship overnight on dry ice.

Dyes

- Do not submit large stained evidence (e.g., car seats). When possible, cut a small sample of the stained area and submit in a heat-sealed or resealable plastic bag.

- Collect an unstained control sample, package it separately, and submit it with the dye-stained evidence.

- When cutting is not possible, transfer questioned stains by rubbing with a clean cotton swab (dry or alcohol-dipped). Air-dry the swab and pack it in a heat-sealed or resealable plastic bag. Submit an unstained swab as a control.

Electronic Devices

It is possible to extract data from such devices as mobile telephones, personal digital assistants (PDAs), pagers, global positioning system (GPS) devices, and facsimile machines. It is also possible to examine "interception of communication" devices, which consist of transmitters and receivers for eavesdropping. It is also possible to identify devices' operating characteristics and modifications. In some cases, it is necessary to disassemble devices during examination.

- Label the outer container "FRAGILE, SENSITIVE ELECTRONIC EQUIPMENT" and "KEEP AWAY FROM MAGNETS OR MAGNETIC FIELDS."

Feathers

Feather examinations can determine bird species and can compare feathers found on clothing, vehicles, and other objects with feathers from the incident scene.

- Submit feathers in heat-sealed or resealable plastic bags or paper bags.

Fractures

Fracture examinations can be used to determine whether evidence was joined together and subsequently broken apart.

Guns and Gun Parts

Gun parts examinations can determine the caliber and model of gun from which the parts originated. Before examination, it is important to ensure that all firearms are unloaded.

Firearms must be minimally handled to avoid loss or destruction of evidence. Objects must not be allowed to enter or contact the firearm's barrel, chamber, or other operating surfaces.

- Use figures to pick up a handgun by its knurl grips, never stick anything down the barrel of the weapon.

- When handing a recovered spent projectile/bullet, all care must be taken to protect the rifling marks.

- When handling a spent cartridge it is recommend that it is picked up by the open end using tweezers or some other tool so as not to destroy any partial figureprint or other evidence that may be on the outside of the cartridge.

- Do not mark the item. Firearm pieces must be identified with a tag containing the caliber, make, model, and serial number. The date, time, owners' names, location, collector's name, case number, and evidence number must be on the container.

Glass

Glass comparison examinations can determine whether particles of glass originated from a broken source of glass. Glass fracture examinations can determine the direction and type of the breaking force and the sequencing of shots.

Comparison
- Submit samples of glass from each broken window or source in leakproof containers such as film canisters or plastic pill bottles. Do not use paper or glass containers.

- Submit samples of laminated glass (e.g., windshield) from each side of the glass. Label the samples "INSIDE" and "OUTSIDE" and package separately in leakproof containers such as film canisters or plastic pill bottles. Do not use paper or glass containers.

- Submit relevant air-dried clothing. Each item must be packaged separately in a paper bag.

- Search for particles in hair, skin, and wounds. Submit particles in leakproof containers such as film canisters or plastic pill bottles. Do not use paper or glass containers.

- Search for particles in vehicles by vacuuming each section of the vehicle separately. Do not use tape for recovering glass particles. Submit vacuum sweepings in leakproof containers. Do not use paper or glass containers.

- Ship known and questioned debris separately to avoid contamination.

- Do not process evidence for latent prints.

Fracture
- Label the sides of the glass in the frame ("INSIDE" and "OUTSIDE"). Label the glass where it was removed in the frame ("TOP," "BOTTOM," "LEFT," and "RIGHT").

- Submit all glass pieces so that the pieces can be fitted together to identify the radial cracks near and at points of impact and to increase the probability of matching edges. Pack all glass separately and securely to avoid shifting and breaking during shipping.

- Submit the entire piece of laminated glass, if possible. Secure the glass between plywood or sturdy cardboard. Do not place any objects into the impact area.

- Do not process evidence for latent prints.

Hairs and Fibers

Hairs

Hair examinations can determine whether hairs are animal (including which species) or human. Race, body area, method of removal, damage, and alteration (e.g., bleaching or dyeing) can be determined from human hair analysis. Examinations can associate a hair to a person on the basis of microscopic characteristics in the hair but cannot provide absolute personal identification. Hairs can be submitted for mitochondrial DNA analysis.

- Collect at least 25 known hairs from different parts of the head or pubic region. Comb and pull out the hairs. Submit hairs in clean paper or an envelope with sealed corners.

Fibers

Fiber examinations can identify the type of fiber, such as animal (wool), vegetable (cotton), mineral (glass), and synthetic (manufactured). Questioned fibers can be compared to fibers from clothing, carpeting, and other textiles associated with victims or persons of interest. A questioned piece of fabric can be physically matched to known fabric. Fabric composition, construction, and color can be compared, and impressions on fabric and from fabric can be examined. Clothing manufacturers' information can be determined by label searches.

- When possible, submit the entire garment or textile. Submit fibers in clean paper or an envelope with sealed corners.

Images

Photographic Comparisons

Examinations of film, negatives, digital images, photographic prints, and video recordings can compare persons in the questioned images with persons in known images (e.g., photographs, videos). Comparisons can also be made with firearms, vehicles, clothing, and other objects depicted in images.

Photogrammetry

Dimensions can be derived from photographic images through the use of mathematical formulas or on-site comparison. Examples of photogrammetry include determining people's height and the length of weapons or tools depicted in images.

Location, Time, and Date

Examinations of photographic evidence may be able to determine the location, time, and date that an image was taken.

Authenticity and Image Manipulation Detection

Examinations can determine whether an image is a composite, alteration, or copy.

Cameras
Examinations can determine whether a specific camera (film, digital, still, or video) created a specific image.

Videos
Still images can be produced from video images for enlargement and use in courtroom presentations.

Automobile Make and Model
Vehicles depicted in surveillance images can be compared with images in vehicle image repositories, such the National Automotive Image File in the United States, to determine make and model.

General Advice

- Write-protect original recordings. Never use the pause operation when viewing original video recordings.

- Submit original evidence (e.g., film or videotape) whenever possible because it contains the greatest level of detail. If the originals are unavailable, submit first-generation photographic prints or videotapes.

- Process all film, including bank surveillance film, prior to submitting.

- When requesting forensic examinations based on video images, cue the original videotape to the approximate time of the pertinent area. State in a communication the date and time of the pertinent area and use the date-time stamp on the images or the counter indicator (set from the beginning of the tape at 000). If prints from the relevant frames are available, submit them for reference.

- If a facial comparison is requested, ensure that the face or head fills more than half the frame. If questioned images show tattoos or marks, include photographs of the same areas on the known persons of interest. Whenever possible, images of persons should show several angles.

- Do not mark or cut items submitted for comparison (e.g., clothing or firearms) where they are visible in the questioned images.

- Submit items such as clothing and firearms for other examinations before submitting them for image comparison.

- If photogrammetry is requested, include the dimensions of the scene to the nearest 1/8 inch and include a diagram or print from the surveillance film indicating the location of the measurements. Include one diagram or print for every angle used in the scene. Do not touch or move surveillance cameras except to remove the film.

Ink

Examining inked writing in conjunction with other techniques (e.g., handwriting analysis, watermark identification) can provide details regarding document preparation. The composition of writing inks varies with the type of writing instrument (e.g., ballpoint pen, fountain pen, porous-tip pen) and the date of the ink manufacture. In general, inks are composed of dyes in solvents and other materials that impart selected characteristics. Ink analysis is usually limited to comparisons of the organic dye components. When ink formulations are the same, it is not possible to determine whether the ink originated from the same source to the exclusion of others. Examinations cannot determine how long ink has been on a document.

- Pack ink evidence separately from any document or surface with ink marks.

Latent Fingerprints

The laboratory is the best place to develop latent prints; however, it is sometimes necessary to develop latent prints at incident scenes. Caution should be taken to avoid destroying latent prints. The following are measures to ensure that incident scene latent prints are protected:

- Photograph latent prints prior to any processing. (See below.)

- Examine all evidence visually and with a laser or alternate light source before using any other latent print development process.

- When using latent print development processes, refer to the manufacturer's instructions and any safety guidance. Use personal protective equipment (e.g., safety glasses, masks, gloves, smocks).

- Consult the FBI's Processing Guide for Developing Latent Prints (2001), a comprehensive list of latent print processes and protocols. Following this guide will maximize the potential to develop latent prints and preserve evidence if other forensic examinations are required.

Photographing Latent Prints

- Use a tripod and cable release when photographing latent prints.

- Use a 35mm or medium-format camera with a macro lens capable of half-size to full-size reproduction.

- Photograph latent prints at each step in the processing sequence before moving to the next process.

- Photograph latent prints developed with fingerprint powders before lifting them.

- Use T-Max 400 film. Set the aperture to f/11 and use the metering system to select a suitable shutter speed.

- Take three exposures of each latent print by bracketing—that is, taking pictures one stop below the recommended exposure, at the recommended exposure, and above the recommended exposure.

- Photograph latent prints individually. This ensures that the target latent print is in focus.

- Fill the frame completely.

- Photograph latent prints with an identification label that includes a scale, reference number, date, collector's initials, and location of the latent prints. The identification label should be placed on the same plane as the latent prints.

- Maintain a log that records each shot, reference number, date, collector's initials, location of prints, and other pertinent information.

Lifting Latent Prints

- After photographing the prints, apply black, gray, or white powder to the surface with a long-hair brush. The color of the powder should contrast with the color of the surface (e.g., black for light surfaces or gray or white for dark surfaces).

- Use a short-hair brush to remove excess powder. Use caution when powdering. Avoid overbrushing a latent print and losing clarity.

- Use transparent tape or black-and-white rubber lifts to lift latent prints.

- When using transparent tape, ensure that the color of the backing card contrasts with the color of the powders (e.g., white backing card for black powder).

- Stabilize the evidence to avoid movement or friction during shipping.

- Place nonporous evidence (e.g., nonabsorbent, hard surfaces) in separate protective coverings such as thick transparent envelopes or suspend in a container so that there is minimal surface contact. Friction will destroy latent prints on this type of surface.

- Place porous evidence (e.g., paper, cardboard) in separate protective coverings. Friction will not generally destroy latent prints on this type of surface.

- Submit known fingerprints and palm prints of everyone who may have handled the evidence, including persons of interest, victims, those who had legitimate access, and investigative personnel. All fingerprint cards must include pertinent biographical or demographic information.

- Take palm prints on only one side of a separate card, not on the reverse side of a fingerprint card or on the reverse side of a card that has a recorded impression on the other side.

- On fingerprint cards, include, at a minimum, the name of the person printed, the name of the person recording the prints, date, incident identification number, and a brief statement of facts relating to the case.

- Include the notation "elimination prints" if the person printed is not a person of interest.

- When known prints are submitted separately from evidence, refer to previous communications, case identification numbers, and other pertinent information.

Lubricants

Lubricants include a range of substances, including petroleum products, natural fatty ester oils, and polyalkylene glycol oils. Automotive fluids (e.g., engine oil, brake fluid), certain cosmetics (e.g., bath oils, lotions), and some polishes contain lubricants. Lubricant examinations may be conducted in sexual assault, vehicular homicide, or heavy equipment sabotage cases.

- Submit entire items (e.g., clothing) when possible. Air-dry the evidence and package separately in paper bags.

- Absorb lubricants onto a clean cotton cloth or swab. Leave a portion of the cloth or swab unstained as a control. Air-dry the swab and pack in a heat-sealed or resealable plastic bag.

- Package lubricants separately in leakproof containers.

Metals

Comparison
Comparative examinations can determine whether two metals or metallic objects came from the same source or from each other. Metal comparisons can identify various surface and microstructural characteristics, including fractured areas, accidental damage, and fabrication marks to determine whether the objects share a common origin. Moreover, the manufacturing methods used to produce an object can be determined. Examinations can also determine mechanical properties, such as the response of a metal to an applied force or load. In addition, examinations can also determine chemical composition, including alloying and trace elements.

Broken or Mechanically Damaged Metal
The causes of failure or damage can be determined. The magnitude of the force or load that caused the failure, how the force or load was transmitted to the metal, and the direction it was transmitted can also be determined.

Specification Frauds and Noncompliant Materials
Metallurgical testing of materials can determine whether inferior components were substituted in contracting frauds. The composition and mechanical properties of materials can be examined to determine if the components meet contractual obligations or appropriate regulatory codes. In some cases, the country of origin can be determined. Precious metal contents can also be determined.

Burned, Heated, or Melted Metal
Examinations can determine the approximate temperature to which a metal was exposed, the nature of the heat source, and whether a metal was in an electrical short-circuit.

Cut or Severed Metal
Examinations can determine the method by which a metal was severed, such as sawing,

shearing, milling, turning, or thermal cutting. The nature of the thermal source (e.g., burner bar, electric-arc welder) can sometimes be determined.

Metal Fragments

Examinations can determine how metal fragments were formed. If fragments were formed by impulsive (short duration, high-strain rate) loading, it can be determined whether an explosive was detonated and what the magnitude of the detonation velocity was. The nature of the object that was the source of the fragments can also often be determined.

Watches, Clocks, and Timers

The conditions causing a watch, clock, timer, or other mechanism to stop or malfunction can be determined, as can the on/off condition of appliance timers damaged by a fire or explosion.

Lamp Bulbs

Examinations can determine whether a lamp bulb was glowing when its glass envelope was broken or when it was subjected to an impact force, such as a vehicular collision.

Internal Components

X-ray radiography can nondestructively reveal the interior construction and the presence or absence of defects, cavities, or foreign materials. The positions of on/off switches and other mechanical components can also be determined.

Paint

The layer structure of a questioned paint sample can be compared with known sources. The sequence, relative thickness, color, texture, number, and chemical composition of each of the layers can be compared. The color, manufacturer, model, and model year of an automobile can be determined from a paint chip (for factory-applied, original automotive paint). Paint on safes, vaults, window sills, and door frames can be transferred to and from tools. A comparison can be made between the paint from an object and the paint on a tool.

- Search the accident or incident scene to locate paint fragments. Note that paints can be transferred from one car to another, from car to object, or from object to car during an accident or incident.

- Collect control paint chips. Controls must be taken from an area close to, but not in, any damaged area. If no damage is obvious, controls should be taken from several areas of the substrate. Each layer can be a point of comparison. Controls must have all of the layers of paint to the substrate. This can be accomplished by cutting a paint sample from the surface with a clean, sharp instrument; lifting or prying any loosely attached chips; or dislodging the paint by gently hitting the opposite side of the painted surface.

- Package paint specimens in leakproof containers, such as vials or pillboxes. Do not stick paint particles on adhesive tape. Do not use plastic bags, cotton, or envelopes to package paint specimens.

Pepper Spray or Foam

Oleoresin capsicum, a resin in various peppers, may be used in self-defense sprays or foams. Ultraviolet dye or tear gas may be also be in the sprays or foams. Items can be analyzed for the presence of oleoresin capsicum, dye, or tear gas.

- Submit entire items (e.g., clothing) when possible. Air-dry the evidence and package separately in paper bags.

- Moisten a clean cotton cloth or swab with isopropanol (rubbing alcohol) and wipe over the sprays or foams. Prepare a second, moistened cloth or swab as a control. Air-dry the cloths or swabs and pack separately in heat-sealed or resealable plastic bags.

- Submit spray canisters when possible.

Pharmaceuticals

Pharmaceutical examinations can identify constituents, active ingredients, quantity, and weight.

- List the names of the pharmaceuticals and information on use.

- If possible, submit pharmaceuticals in original containers.

Polymers

Polymer evidence typically consists of pieces of plastic or other manmade materials. The source, use, or manufacturer of polymer evidence usually cannot be identified by composition analysis.

Motor vehicle trim can be compared with plastic remaining on property struck in hit-and-run cases. The manufacturer, make, model, and model year of a vehicle can be determined if a manufacturer's part number is on the trim.

Plastics in wire insulation and miscellaneous plastics such as buttons can be compared with known sources.

When a motor vehicle has been in an accident, fragments (e.g., of plastic lens covers) may be left at the scene. These pieces can be physically reconstructed with the remnants of the fixture left on the car if edges are intact.

- Search the incident scene and parties' personal effects to locate plastic fragments. Submit fragments in leakproof containers, such as film canisters or plastic pill bottles. Do not use cotton or paper containers.

- Remove damaged motor-vehicle parts and package separately in resealable plastic bags or boxes.

- If possible, submit entire items (e.g., clothing) with potential or smeared polymeric transfers. Package separately in paper bags. Pack to prevent stain removal by abrasive action during shipping. Pack in clean paper. Do not use plastic containers.

Product Tampering

Product tampering occurs when a commercial product is intentionally distorted to harm someone or for extortion purposes. Examples include drug tampering in medical environments and food adulteration in supermarkets.

- Submit control samples of the unadulterated product.

- Package and ship samples separately to avoid contamination. Submit samples in leakproof containers, such as film canisters or plastic pill bottles. Do not use paper or glass containers.

- Caution should be taken to avoid destroying latent prints.

Ropes and Cords

A piece of rope or cord can be compared with a questioned rope or cord. The composition, construction, color, and diameter can be determined. If a tracer is present, the manufacturer can be determined.

- Submit the entire rope or cord. If the rope or cord must be cut, specify which end was cut during evidence collection.

- Label the known and questioned samples.

- Handle the sections of rope or cord carefully to prevent contamination or the loss of trace material.

- Submit in heat-sealed or resealable plastic or paper bags.

Safe Insulation

Safe insulation can be compared to a known source. Examinations of safe insulation can sometimes determine the manufacturer.

- Collect safe insulation samples from damaged areas.

- Safe insulation can adhere to people, clothing, tools, bags, and loot and can transfer to vehicles. If possible, submit the evidence to the selected laboratory for examiners to remove the debris. Package each item of evidence in separate paper bags. Do not process tools for latent prints.

Serial Number

Obliterated serial or identification numbers on metal, wood, plastic, and fiberglass are often restorable.

- If possible, remove the material containing the serial number and note where it came from.

- Otherwise, make a cast to submit to the laboratory:

  — Call the laboratory regarding the appropriate cast kit.

  — Different formulas are used in different temperatures. If possible, move the evidence to a warm area.

  — Clean the serial number area, as casts duplicate foreign material in the stamped characters. Remove paint and dirt with a solvent, such as acetone, gasoline, or paint remover. Use naval jelly to remove rust. Use a soft brush, not a wire brush.

  — Build a dam around the stamped characters to retain the cast material while it hardens. The dam material must be soft and pliable (like modeling clay) to avoid having gaps in the dam.

  — Remove the cast when it is hard. If paint and rust are on the cast, make additional casts and submit the cleanest one to the laboratory.

  — Pack the cast to prevent breakage.

Shoeprints and Tire Treads

Shoeprint or tire tread impressions are routinely left at incident scenes. These impressions are retained on surfaces in two- and three-dimensional forms. Almost all impressions, including partial impressions, have value for forensic comparisons.

<u>Photographing Shoeprint and Tire Tread Impressions</u>
General incident scene photographs must be taken to relate the impressions to the incident scene. These photographs must include close-range and long-range photographs using 400 ISO color film.

Examination-quality photographs must then be taken to obtain maximum detail for forensic examination. They must be taken directly over the impressions using a tripod and lighting. A scale must be in every photograph. The purpose of these photographs is to produce a detailed negative that can be enlarged to natural size. Examination-quality photographs must be taken as follows:

- Place a linear scale such as a ruler next to and on the same plane as the impression. Place a label in the picture to correlate the impression with incident scene notes and general photographs.

- Images should be taken using a 35mm or medium-format film camera. Low-cost digital cameras do not provide sufficient image detail for examination-quality photographs. Use a manual focus camera. If the shoeprint is made from a colored substance (e.g., blood), color film maybe preferable to black-and-white. In most ambient light situations, use 100 ISO film. Use 200 or 400 ISO film if necessary.

- Place the camera on a tripod and position it directly over the impression. Adjust the height of the camera and if possible use a normal lens (50mm for a 35mm camera). Fill the frame with the impression and scale. Position the camera so the film plane is parallel to the impression.

- Set the aperture to f/16 or f/22 for a greater depth of field.

- Attach an electronic flash with a long extension cord to the camera.

- Block out bright ambient light with a sunscreen to maximize the light from the flash.

- Focus on the bottom of the impression, not on the scale.

- Position the flash at a very low angle (10-15 degrees) to the impression. This will enhance the detail of the impression. For consistent exposure, hold the flash at least five to seven feet from the impression. Shoot several exposures, bracketing toward overexposure to obtain maximum image detail.

- Take the exposures, move the light to another position, adjust the sunscreen, and take more photographs.

- In the case of wet footprints it is best to use oblique lighting.

Impressions in snow are difficult to photograph because of lack of contrast. It is best to attempt to photograph the impressions as if in soil. To increase the contrast, snow impressions can be lightly sprayed with snow print wax, a material used for casting snow impressions, or with colored spray paint. The spray can must be held at least two to three feet from the impression so the force of the aerosol does not damage the impression. A light application of spray must be directed at an angle of about 30 to 45 degrees so the paint only strikes the high points of the impression. Highlighted impressions will absorb heat from the sun and must be shielded until photographed and cast to prevent melting.

Casting Shoeprint and Tire Tread Impressions
If the evidence itself cannot be submitted to the laboratory, it can be cast with dental stone and the cast submitted to a laboratory. Dental stone is available through local dental supply houses. Colored dental stone is preferred.

- Store premeasured dental stone in resealable plastic bags.

- Add the appropriate amount of water to the bag and close the top. Mix the casting material by vigorously massaging it for three to five minutes through the bag. Ensure that the material in the corners of the bag is also mixed. After mixing, the material should have the consistency of pancake batter or heavy cream.

- If the impressions are numerous or large, it may be necessary to mix larger quantities of dental stone in a bucket or bowl. The dental stone should be slowly added to the water and continuously stirred for three to five minutes.

- Casting material has sufficient weight and volume to erode and destroy detail if it is poured directly on top of the impression. The casting material should be poured on the ground next to the impression, allowing it to flow into the impression. The impression should be filled with casting material until it has overflowed.

- If the mixture is too viscous to flow into the impression, vibrate a finger or a small stick on the surface to cause the dental stone to flow into the impression. Do not put the stick or finger more than 1/4 inch below the surface of the casting material because it can damage the impression.

- Before the cast completely hardens, write the date, collector's initials, and other identifying information on it. The cast should be left undisturbed for at least 20 to 30 minutes in warm weather (longer in cold weather). Casts have been destroyed or damaged when lifted too soon. If the cast is in sand or loose soil, it should lift easily. Casts in mud or clay may require careful treatment and excavation when being removed.

- Allow the cast to air-dry for at least 48 hours. Package the cast in paper, not plastic. A laboratory examiner must clean the cast.

<u>Lifting Two-Dimensional Impressions</u>
Lifting an impression allows for the transfer of a two-dimensional residue or dust impression to a lifting film. It also allows the impression to be shipped to the laboratory for photography and examination.

Electrostatic lifts. An electrostatic lifting device lifts footwear impressions from porous and nonporous surfaces without damaging the impressions. This device works on dry dust or residue impressions on clean surfaces but will not work if the impressions were wet or become wet. Electrostatic lifting devices have instructions regarding use.

Lifted impressions are easily damaged if the film is not properly stored. The film has a residual charge that attracts dust and debris and causes the film to cling to another surface. To preserve and store the lifting film containing an impression, tape one edge of the film securely in a clean, smooth paper file folder or tape the edges securely in a shallow photographic paper box. Low-grade cardboard boxes such as pizza boxes must not be used because the residual charge on the film will pull dust from the boxes and contaminate the impression.

Items that contain a dry residue footwear impression must not be wrapped or stored in plastic because a partial transfer of the impression to the plastic will occur.

Gelatin and adhesive lifts. Gelatin lifters can be used to lift impressions from porous and nonporous surfaces. Black gelatin lifters work well for lifting light-colored dry or wet impressions. White gelatin lifters can be used to lift impressions developed with fingerprint powders or impressions dark enough to contrast with a white background.

Adhesive lifters can only be used to lift impressions from smooth, nonporous surfaces. White adhesive lifters can be used to lift impressions developed with fingerprint powders. Transparent adhesive lifters can be used to lift impressions developed with black or fluorescent powders. Transparent tapes such as two-inch fingerprint lifting tape can also be used to lift powdered impressions if they are transferred to a white card.

<u>Shoeprint and tire tread files.</u>
A file of shoe manufacturers' designs and a file of tire treads and other reference material can be searched to determine brand names and manufacturers.

- For shoeprint and tire tread comparisons, submit original evidence whenever possible (shoes, tires, photographic negatives, casts, lifts).

- For shoeprint and tire tread file searches, submit quality photographs of the impressions. If photographs are not available, submit casts, lifts, or the original evidence. Detailed sketches or photocopies are acceptable. Images of impression evidence maybe submitted electronically.

- Unobtrusively write the collector's initials, dates, and other relevant information on the evidence.

- Air-dry and package evidence separately in bubble wrap; clean, smooth paper or laminated folders; or paper bags.

Soil

Soil examinations can determine whether soils share a common origin by comparing color, texture, and composition.

- Collect soil samples as soon as possible. Soil at the incident scene can change dramatically.

- Collect soil samples from the immediate incident scene area and from the logical access or escape routes.

- Collect soil samples where there are noticeable changes in color, texture, and composition.

- Collect soil samples at a depth that is consistent with the depth from which the questioned soil may have originated.

- If possible, collect soil samples from alibi locations such as a yard or work area.

- Submit a map identifying soil sample locations.

- Do not remove soil adhering to shoes, clothing, and tools. Do not process tools for latent prints. Air-dry the soil and the clothing and package separately in paper bags.

- Carefully remove soil adhering to vehicles. Air-dry the soil and package separately in paper bags.

- Ship known and questioned debris separately to avoid contamination. Submit known and questioned soil in leakproof containers such as film canisters or plastic pill bottles. Do not use paper envelopes or glass containers. Pack to keep lumps intact.

Tape

Tape composition, construction, and color can be compared with known sources. Comparisons can be made between a torn piece of tape and a roll of tape.

Laboratories examine duct, vinyl electrical, and packaging tapes but may not examine cellulose acetate tape (e.g., Scotch tape).

- Whenever possible, submit tape still adhered to the substrate. This minimizes the loss of trace evidence, latent fingerprints, or contact impressions. If it is not possible to submit the substrate, the tape may be manually removed and placed adhesive side down on a clean, colorless piece of plastic sheeting (e.g., transparency film or tubular rollstock), not on cardboard, paper, or vinyl document protectors. Do not distort or tear the tape during removal.

- If the tape is cut during removal, document and initial each cut. Use a method that produces a unique cutting pattern (e.g., pinking shears).

Toolmarks

Tools can bear unique microscopic characteristics due to manufacturing processes and use. These characteristics can be transferred to surfaces that the tools contact. Evidence toolmarks can be compared to recovered tools. In the absence of a questioned tool, toolmark examinations can determine the type of tool that produced the toolmark and whether the toolmark is of value for comparison. Toolmark examinations also include lock and key examinations.

- If possible, submit the toolmarked evidence.
- If not, make a cast to submit to the selected laboratory.
  - Call the laboratory regarding the appropriate cast kit.
  - Different formulas are used in different temperatures. If possible, move the evidence to a warm area.
  - Casts duplicate foreign material in the evidence. Clean the area before proceeding. Remove paint and dirt with a solvent such as acetone, gasoline, or paint remover. Use naval jelly to remove rust. Use a soft brush. Do not use a wire brush.
  - Build a dam around the evidence to retain the liquid while it hardens. The dam material must be soft and pliable (like modeling clay). Ensure there are no gaps in the dam.
  - Following the instructions in the kit, mix the liquid and powder for one minute and pour into the dam.
  - Remove the cast when it is hard. If paint and rust are on the cast, make additional casts and submit the cleanest cast to the selected laboratory.
  - Pack the cast to prevent breakage.
- Obtain samples of any material deposited on the tools. Submit samples in leakproof containers, such as film canisters or plastic pill bottles.

- To avoid contamination, do not place the tool against the toolmarked evidence.

- Submit the tool rather than making test cuts or impressions.

- Mark the ends of the evidence and specify which end was cut during evidence collection.

Photographs are useful for locating toolmarks but are of no value for identification purposes.

Toxicology

Toxicology examinations can disclose the presence of drugs and poisons in biological specimens and food products. The examinations can determine the circumstances surrounding drug- or poison-related incidents and accidents.

Because of the large number of potentially toxic substances, it may be necessary to screen for classes of poisons, such as volatile compounds (ethanol, methanol, isopropanol), heavy metals (arsenic), nonvolatile organic compounds (drugs of abuse, pharmaceuticals), and miscellaneous substances (strychnine, cyanide).

Biological evidence in drug-facilitated assaults must include a urine sample. The urine must be collected as soon as possible after the assault and not more than 96 hours after the alleged drugging.

The quantity of biological specimens submitted depends on whether the identity of a toxic substance is known, the route of administration, the time after exposure that biological specimens are collected, and whether the persons involved are living or dead. Call the laboratory before submitting the specimens to ensure that the correct quantity is submitted.

- Place each biological specimen in a separate, labeled, sealed glass tube, plastic cup, or heat-sealed or resealable plastic bag. Affix "BIOHAZARD" labels to the inside and outside containers. To avoid deterioration, biological specimens must be refrigerated or frozen during storage and shipping. Pack so that no breakage, leakage, or contamination occurs.

- Submit a copy of the incident report.

- Describe the symptoms of the person involved at the time of the incident

- List any known or questioned drugs consumed by or prescribed for the person.

- Describe any known or questioned environmental exposure to toxic substances by the person.

Video

The following are key points regarding video evidence:

- Authenticity examinations are conducted to determine whether video recordings are original, continuous, unaltered, and consistent with the recording device used to make the recording.

- Enhancement examinations are conducted to maximize the clarity of the video signal through video processors and time-base correctors.

- Enhanced prints can be produced from images depicted on videotapes.

- Videotapes can be converted from one standard to another (e.g., PAL to NTSC or SECAM) and from one format to another (e.g., Beta to VHS).

- Audio and video signals can be combined to produce one composite recording.

- Special effects such as a mosaic can be added to video recordings to protect a person's identity.

- Video recordings can be repaired, restored, or retrieved for playback and examination, if damage is not too extensive.

- Investigators should write-protect the original recording and never use the pause operation when viewing original video recordings.

- When submitting original video recordings to a lab, investigators should identify the locations of the images on the video recordings and describe the images. They should label the outer container "FRAGILE, SENSITIVE ELECTRONIC EQUIPMENT" or "FRAGILE, SENSITIVE AUDIO/VIDEO MEDIA" and "KEEP AWAY FROM MAGNETS OR MAGNETIC FIELDS."

Wood

Wood examinations can match sides, ends, and fractures; can determine wood species; and can compare wood particles found on clothing, vehicles, and other objects with wood from the incident scene.

- Submit wood in plastic or paper bags.

6.4 **INCIDENT SCENE SAFETY**

This section discusses the hazards, safety precautions, and personal protective equipment recommended for processing routine incident scenes. Security personnel should take care to consult applicable environmental and occupational health and safety laws as well as waste-disposal regulations.

6.4.1 **ROUTES OF EXPOSURE**

Personnel operating in or around contaminated environments must be aware of the various ways in which hazards may enter and harm the body.

Inhalation

Inhalation is the introduction of a substance into the respiratory system. Airborne contaminants may be in the form of a dust, aerosol, smoke, vapor, gas, or fume. Materials may be in a solid or liquid form and still represent an inhalation hazard because they produce vapors, mists, and fumes.

Proper work practices and adequate ventilation can minimize the risk of airborne contaminant inhalation. When working in areas with airborne contaminants, respiratory protection must be worn. Only certified personnel are allowed to wear respiratory protection.

Skin Contact

Contamination through the skin can result from direct contact or by absorption. The severity of the injury can depend on the concentration of the contaminant and the amount of exposure time. Systemic effects, such as dizziness, tremors, nausea, blurred vision, liver and kidney damage, shock, or collapse, can occur when the substances are absorbed through the skin and circulated throughout the body. Exposure can be prevented by using personal protective equipment (e.g., gloves, safety glasses, goggles, face shields, and protective clothing).

Ingestion

Ingestion involves introducing substances into the body through the mouth. Ingestion can cause severe damage to the mouth, throat, and digestive tract. To prevent entry of contaminants into the mouth, safe work practices, such as washing hands before eating, smoking, or applying cosmetics, must always be used. Personnel should not bring food, drink, or cigarettes into areas where contamination can occur, regardless of personal protection that may be worn.

Injection

The direct injection of contaminants into the body, either by needle sticks or mechanical injuries from contaminated glass, metal, or other sharp objects, can cause severe complications. Contaminants enter directly into the bloodstream and can spread rapidly. Extreme caution should be exercised when handling objects with sharp or jagged edges. Work gloves must be worn at all times.

6.4.2 **SAFETY**

The following sections discuss safety related to bloodborne pathogens, chemicals, light sources, confined spaces, and X-rays.

Bloodborne-Pathogen Safety

In the United States, regulations on bloodborne-pathogen safety from the Occupational Safety and Health Administration can be found in Title 29, Section 1910.1030, of the Code of Federal Regulations.

Fundamental to the bloodborne pathogens standard is the concept of universal precautions. It requires personnel to treat all blood, body fluids, or other potentially infectious materials as if infected with bloodborne diseases, such as hepatitis B virus (HBV), hepatitis C virus (HCV), and human immunodeficiency virus (HIV). The following protective measures should be taken to avoid direct contact with potentially infectious materials:

- Use barrier protection, such as disposable gloves, coveralls, and shoe covers, if contact with potentially infectious materials may occur. Change gloves when they are torn or punctured or when their ability to function as a barrier is compromised. Wear appropriate eye and face protection to protect against splashes, sprays, and spatters of potentially infectious materials.

- Wash hands after removing gloves or other personal protective equipment. Remove gloves and other personal protective equipment in a manner that will not result in contaminating unprotected skin or clothing.

- Do not eat, drink, smoke, or apply cosmetics where human blood, body fluids, or other potentially infectious materials are present, regardless of personal protection that may be worn.

- Place contaminated sharps in appropriate closable, leakproof, puncture-resistant containers when transported or discarded. Label the containers with a "BIOHAZARD" warning label.

- Do not bend, recap, remove, or otherwise handle contaminated needles or other sharps.

- Decontaminate equipment after use with a daily prepared solution of household bleach diluted 1:10 or 70 percent isopropyl alcohol or other appropriate disinfectant. Noncorrosive disinfectants are commercially available. It is important to allow sufficient contact time for complete disinfection.

- In addition to the preceding universal precautions, engineering controls and prudent work practices can reduce or eliminate exposure to potentially infectious materials. Some examples of engineering controls include puncture-resistant containers used for storage and disposal of sharps and paint stirrers and long-handled mirrors for use in locating and retrieving evidence in confined or hidden spaces.

Chemical Safety

Depending on the type of material encountered, a variety of health and safety hazards can exist:

- Flammable or combustible materials, such as gasoline, acetone, and ether, ignite easily when exposed to air and an ignition source, such as a spark or flame.

- Over time, some explosive materials, such as nitroglycerine and nitroglycerine-based dynamite, deteriorate to become chemically unstable. In particular, ether will form peroxides around the mouth of the vessel in which it is stored. All explosive materials are sensitive to heat, shock, and friction.

- Pyrophoric materials, such as phosphorus, sodium, and barium, can be liquid or solid and can ignite in air temperatures less than 130 degrees Fahrenheit (54 degrees Celsius) without an external ignition source.

- Oxidizers, such as nitrates, hydrogen peroxide, and concentrated sulfuric acid, are a class of chemical compounds that readily yield oxygen to promote combustion. They should not be stored with flammable and combustible materials or substances that could rapidly accelerate their decomposition.

- Corrosive materials can cause destruction to living tissue or objects, such as wood and steel. The amount of damage depends on the concentration and duration of contact.

In the United States, Material Safety Data Sheets on various chemicals provide guidance on hazardous properties, disposal techniques, personal protection, packaging and shipping procedures, and emergency preparedness.

Light-Source Safety

When using ultraviolet lights, lasers, and other light sources, the eyes must be protected from direct and indirect exposure. Not all laser beams are visible, and irreversible eye damage can result from exposure to direct or indirect light from reflected beams. Prolonged exposure to the skin should also be avoided.

Protective eyewear appropriate for the light source should be worn by all personnel in the vicinity. Goggles must have sufficient protective material and fit snugly to prevent light from entering at any angle. In the United States, the goggles must display the American National Standards Institute's mark denoting eye-protection compliance. Laser protective eyewear must be made of the appropriate optical density to protect against the maximum operating wavelength of the laser source.

Confined-Space Safety

A confined space is an enclosed area that is large enough for personnel to enter and work but that has limited or restricted means for entry and exit. Confined spaces (e.g., sewers, open pits, tank cars, and vats) are not designed for continuous occupancy. Confined spaces can expose personnel to hazards including toxic gases, explosive or oxygen-deficient atmospheres, electrical dangers, or materials that can engulf personnel entering the space.

Conditions in a confined space must be considered dangerous. Such spaces should not be entered until a confined-space permit has been issued. The atmosphere must be continuously monitored with a calibrated, direct-reading instrument for oxygen, carbon monoxide, flammable gases and vapors, and toxic air contaminants. Periodic readings from the monitor should be documented. Only certified confined-space personnel may operate in confined spaces. Rescue services must be immediately available.

The following practices must be followed when working in a confined space:

- Never enter before all atmospheric, engulfment, mechanical, and electrical hazards have been identified and documented. Relevant regulations from the U.S. Occupational Safety and Health Administration can be found in 29 CFR 1910.147, Control of Hazardous Energy (Lockout/Tagout).

- Provide ventilation. Ensure that ventilation equipment does not interfere with entry, exit, or rescue procedures.

- Provide barriers to warn unauthorized personnel and to keep entrants safe from external hazards.

- Provide constant communication between personnel entering the confined space and attendants.

- Put backup communication in place before entry.

- Wear appropriate personal protective equipment, such as self-contained breathing apparatus (SCBA), full-body harness, and head protection.

- Never attempt a rescue unless part of a designated rescue team.

- Personnel certified in first aid and cardiopulmonary resuscitation (CPR) must be on-site.

For additional information, refer to the Occupational Safety and Health Administration standard for Permit-Required Confined Spaces, 29 CFR 1910.146.

X-Ray Safety

Portable, handheld X-ray machines, often used to identify the contents of unknown packages, pose a risk for exposure to X-ray radiation at incident scenes.

- Shield the X-ray device, the questionable object, and the operator.

- Remove all nonessential personnel from the X-ray field.

- Limit the time that personnel are in the area of operation.

- Always wear assigned monitoring devices appropriate for X-ray radiation.

- Ensure that standard X-ray operating procedures are in place and followed and that adequate training has been provided in accordance with federal and state regulations.

6.4.3 **PERSONAL PROTECTIVE EQUIPMENT**

In all incident scenes, the selection of personal protective equipment must be done in coordination with a hazard-risk assessment completed by trained and qualified personnel. The hazard-risk assessment should identify the possible contaminants as well as the hazards associated with each product.

Hand Protection

Hand protection should be selected on the basis of the type of material being handled and the hazards associated with the material. Detailed information can be obtained from the manufacturer. The following list provides information about glove material types and functions:

- Nitrile provides protection from acids, alkaline solutions, hydraulic fluid, photographic solutions, fuels, lubricants, aromatics, petroleum, and chlorinated solvents. It also offers some resistance to cuts and snags.

- Neoprene offers resistance to oil, grease, acids, solvents, alkalies, bases, and most refrigerants.

- Polyvinyl chloride (PVC) is resistant to alkalies, oils, and limited concentrations of nitric and chromic acids.

- Latex (natural rubber) resists mild acids, caustics, detergents, germicides, and ketonic solutions. Latex will swell and degrade if exposed to gasoline or kerosene. When exposed to prolonged, excessive heat or direct sunlight, latex gloves can degrade.

- Powder-free gloves with reduced protein content will lower the risk of developing latex allergies. Personnel allergic to latex can usually wear nitrile or neoprene.

Guidelines for glove use include the following:

- Prior to donning, inspect the gloves for holes, punctures, and tears. Remove rings or other sharp objects that can cause punctures.

- When working with heavily contaminated materials, wear a double layer of gloves.

- Change gloves when torn or punctured or when their ability to function as a barrier is compromised.

- To avoid contaminating unprotected skin or clothing, remove disposable gloves by grasping the cuffs and pulling them off inside out. Discard disposable gloves in designated containers. Do not reuse.

Eye Protection

Appropriate eye protection, such as safety glasses and goggles, should be worn when handling biological, chemical, and radioactive materials. Face shields offer better protection when there is a potential for splashing or flying debris. Face shields must be worn in combination with safety glasses or goggles.

Contact lens users must wear safety glasses or goggles to protect the eyes. In the event of a chemical splash into the eye, it can be difficult to remove the contact lens to irrigate the eye, and contaminants can be trapped behind the contact lens.

Protective eyewear should be worn over prescription glasses. Safety glasses may be made to the wearer's eyeglass prescription.

Foot Protection

Shoes that completely cover and protect the foot are essential. Protective footwear should be used at incident scenes when there is a danger of foot injuries from falling or rolling objects, from objects piercing the sole, and from exposure to electrical hazards. The standard recognized by the Occupational Safety and Health Administration for protective footwear is the American National Standard for Personal Protection-Protective Footwear, ANSI Z41-1991. In some situations, non-permeable shoe covers can provide barrier protection to shoes and prevent the transfer of contaminants outside the incident scene.

Respiratory Protection

Certain incident scenes, such as bombings and clandestine laboratories, can produce noxious fumes and other airborne contaminants for which responders must use respiratory protection. In the United States, compliance with 29 CFR 1910.134, Respiratory Protection, is mandatory whenever respirators are used. Critical elements for the safe use of respirators include a written program, training, medical evaluation, fit testing, and a respirator-maintenance program.

Head Protection

In incident scenes where structural damage has occurred or may occur, protective helmets should be worn. The standard recognized by the Occupational Safety and Health Administration for protective helmets is ANSI Z89.1-1997, Requirements for Industrial Head Protection.

APPENDIX A

CRIME LAB ORGANIZATIONS

Security staff should consider the veracity and reliability of the labs and testing personnel or companies used to process and examine evidence. One way to find a professional laboratory is through an accrediting or other professional organization, such as the following:

American Academy of Forensic Sciences. Dedicated to the application of science to the law.

American Board of Forensic Entomology. Promotes the science of using insect evidence to uncover circumstances of interest to the law, often related to a crime.

American Society of Crime Laboratory Directors. Dedicated to providing excellence in forensic science through leadership and innovation.

Association for Crime Scene Reconstruction. Encourages the exchange of information and procedures useful in the reconstruction of crime scenes.

Canadian Society of Forensic Science. Maintains professional standards and promotes the study of forensic science.

Forensic Science Society UK. Dedicated to the application of science to the cause of justice.

International Association for Identification. Supports those engaged in forensic identification, investigation, and scientific examination of physical evidence.

International Association of Arson Investigators. Promotes fire investigation standards.

International Crime Scene Investigators. Helps law enforcement personnel involved in the processing of crime scenes.

APPENDIX B

SAMPLE POLICY ON COMPUTER EVIDENCE

SEIZURE AND DISCONNECTION OF COMPUTER EQUIPMENT

1. Isolate, photograph and document the computer system, phone and power connections as found. Confirm that the computer is not erasing data and check for physical traps.

2. Wear latex gloves at all times when handling computer and computer-related equipment in relationship to a criminal investigation.

3. Do not use fingerprint powder on the equipment.

4. Leave the computer off if it is found off.

5. If the computer is on, do not touch (or allow anyone to touch) the keyboard. Make a note of applications running on the screen. If necessary, you may move the mouse to activate the screen but DO NOT open any files or applications.

6. For standalone systems, do not shut the system down in a normal way. Unplug from the back of the machine, then from the power source.

   a. If the computer is a laptop and it is on, pull the battery first and then disconnect from the power source.

   b. For networked systems, a department computer crimes investigator will respond for assistance.

7. Photograph the back of the computer to record the cable connections.

8. Label all cables, indicating which cable is connected to which port on each device.

9. Photograph and document all attached devices (such as printers).

10. Make a note of anything unusual about the computer or related items in the vicinity (such as loose screws).

11. Disconnect all cables and attached devices.

12. Remove floppy disks and process as evidence.

13. Place evidence tape over the entrance to the disk drives and on the computer case in such a way that if someone were to use a drive or open the case, the tape would show tampering. Initial and date the edge of the tape. This will preserve the drives until an exact copy can be made for analysis so that the original drive is secured as evidence.

SEIZURE, PACKAGING, AND TRANSPORT OF COMPUTER ITEMS OR DEVICES

1. Seize other items that can store information, such as DVDs, CDs, flash memory (drives or cards), floppy disks, tapes, or cartridges.

2. Consider mobile phones, data bank watches, personal digital assistants, pagers, caller ID devices.

3. Check the area for notation of passwords.

4. Seize other devices attached to the computer, such as monitors, keyboards, mice, printers, external drives, cameras, modems, dongles, and power cords.

5. Seize any software and related manuals.

6. Package computers in original boxes and foam inserts, if available. If not, use other suitable boxes and bubble wrap or solid foam packing, not packing peanuts or shredded paper, which generate static electricity and dust.

7. Place separate storage media in boxes or paper bags. Do not use plastic bags, as they may generate static electricity.

8. Mark each item on the item itself for identification.

9. Seal, initial, and date each package.

10. Transport the evidence carefully, following these precautions:

    a. Transport the evidence inside the passenger area of the vehicle. Do not place it in the trunk next to a radio transmitter. Transmitters emit radio frequency energy, which can damage storage media.

    b. Consider turning off the vehicle radio during transport.

    c. Avoid exposing the evidence to extreme heat and cold.

    d. Photograph the scene after evidence has been removed.

11. Note any equipment that was not seized.

REFERENCES

American National Standards Institute. (1991). *Personal protection—Protective footwear.* ANSI Z41-1991. New York, NY: American National Standards Institute.

American National Standards Institute. (1997). *Requirements for industrial head protection.* ANSI Z89.1-1997. New York, NY: American National Standards Institute.

Code of Federal Regulations. (2007). *Bloodborne pathogens.* 29 CFR 1910.1030.

Code of Federal Regulations. (2007). *Control of hazardous energy (lockout/tagout).* 29 CFR 1910.147.

Code of Federal Regulations. (2007). *Hazardous materials table.* 49 CFR 172.101.

Code of Federal Regulations. (2007). *Permit-required confined spaces.* 29 CFR 1910.146.

Code of Federal Regulations. (2007). *Respiratory protection.* 29 CFR 1910.134.

Federal Bureau of Investigation. (2001). *Processing guide for developing latent prints.* Washington, DC: Federal Bureau of Investigation.
Available: http://www.fbi.gov/hq/lab/fsc/backissu/jan2001/lpu.pdf [2007, July 18].

Federal Bureau of Investigation. (2003). *Handbook of forensic services.* Washington, DC: Federal Bureau of Investigation.
Available: http://www.fbi.gov/hq/lab/handbook/forensics.pdf [2007, July 1].

International Air Transport Association. (2007). *Dangerous goods regulations manual.* Montreal, Canada: International Air Transport Association.

National Institute of Justice. (2003). *Eyewitness evidence: Trainer's manual for law enforcement.* Washington, DC: National Institute of Justice.
Available: http://www.ncjrs.gov/nij/eyewitness/188678.pdf [2007, July 1].

CHAPTER SEVEN

CANADIAN LAW
OF EVIDENCE

The law of evidence determines how facts may be proved in a court of law, and what facts may not be proved there.

(Cross, 1971)

Like the criminal law, the Canadian law of evidence was based on the common law of England, but over the years it has been codified by statute. Statutes that have committed the common-law rules of evidence to black and white include the Canada Evidence Act (1985) and the Canadian Charter of Rights and Freedoms (1982). The common law established restrictions on the government's right to search, the admissibility of confessions, the right against self-incrimination, and the prosecution's burden of proof in substantiating a criminal offence. Provinces and territories have also developed acts on admissibility of evidence at trials and judicial proceedings under their jurisdiction.

The Charter of Rights and Freedoms, however, only applies to governmental functions (criminal or administrative), and its rules on admissibility of evidence do not apply to private relationships, such as the employer/employee relationship in a civil action for wrongful dismissal or a labour arbitration hearing. Even in a governmental action, the court is free to admit evidence obtained in breach of the Charter if the court is satisfied that the administration of justice has not been brought into disrepute.

7.1 BASIC PRINCIPLES OF THE LAW OF EVIDENCE

The issue with the law of evidence is admissibility. A court will ask four questions to decide whether a piece of evidence will be allowed to be produced at trial:

1. Is the evidence relevant to the matter at hand?
2. Is it reliable?
3. Can it be authenticated?
4. Does the probative value override any prejudicial effect?

The decision of a court, arbitration panel, or other administrative review process is based on what evidence is proved or disproved. Evidence may take a variety of forms, such as the *viva voce* testimony (oral evidence) of an eyewitness; business or banking documents; video or photographic evidence; physical evidence, such as a weapon, DNA, or other biological or forensic material collected at a crime scene; computer-generated recreations of an accident; or even a view of the scene by a judge and jury. Rules based on statute or the common law outline whether and how evidence may be introduced at a trial or hearing. Much of the time taken during a trial or hearing is spent on objections raised by counsel related to whether certain evidence maybe introduced by opposing parties. Counsel may even object to questions put to a witness if there is a concern about the relevance or propriety of the question. The trier of law[1] then must make a ruling on whether the question will be allowed or whether testimony will be stricken from the trial record or otherwise disregarded.

7.2 INTRODUCTION OF EVIDENCE AT A TRIAL OR HEARING

Examination in Chief

Most evidence is entered at a trial or hearing through the *viva voce* testimony of a witness or by the witness's act of identifying or introducing a piece of evidence. The party calling the witness must do an "examination in chief" where the witness is asked questions related to his or her knowledge of relevant events at issue. In the examination in chief, the witness is introduced and his or her qualifications to testify are reviewed. For example, a Crown Prosecutor introducing a security officer might ask the officer to identify himself or herself and state why he or she is present. The officer may be an eyewitness to the offence or may introduce an exhibit, such as an item seized at the scene.

In the examination in chief, there can be no leading questions (those that would suggest a desired answer), although the court may allow a few exceptions where questions are being asked on undisputed matters so that the testimony can be speeded up. For example, the prosecutor may say, "I understand that you are a security officer for the ABC Company and that you were on duty the night of…"Another exception to the rule arises if the party conducting the examination in chief convinces the court that the witness is hostile or, in criminal matters, has made a prior inconsistent statement. For instance, if a witness gave a written statement to a security officer after an offence and then gives a different version at the trial, the prosecutor may be successful in introducing the written statement and then cross-examining the witness with leading questions.

Cross-Examination

Once the examination in chief of a witness is completed, the opposing party has the opportunity to conduct a cross-examination. Much more latitude is allowed in a cross-examination, and the party conducting it may ask direct and leading questions of the witness. The witness may be asked a question such as "Isn't it true that you did not have a good view of the accused at the time that you say the offence took place?"

---

[1] The trier of law is the judge, arbitration panel, or administrative tribunal that makes decisions on the admissibility of evidence. The trier of fact makes findings of fact as opposed to rulings of law. Although the trier of law and trier of facts are often the same person or body, the finder of fact may be the jury in a criminal or civil trial.

7.3 COMPETENCE AND COMPELLABILITY

In deciding whether a witness may testify, the trier of law assesses whether the witness presented is competent and compellable to give evidence. Competence refers to whether a witness has the legal capacity to testify, and compellability refers to whether the witness can be legally forced to testify. Competence may be impinged on such issues as mental incapacity or infancy. Where there is some doubt that a witness is competent, the trier of law will put questions to the witness to assess whether the witness understands the necessity to speak the truth once an oath is administered.

Several statutory and common-law provisions affect the compellability of witnesses. For example, those who are entitled to diplomatic immunity may be competent to testify but cannot be compelled to do so. Under the Charter of Rights and Freedoms, a person accused of a crime is not compelled to give evidence at his or her own trial (s. 11 (c)), although the Canada Evidence Act states that such a person is competent to give evidence (R.S. c. E-10 s. 4 (1)). An accused who chooses to testify is then subject to cross-examination by the prosecutor.

Under the Canada Evidence Act (S. 4 (3)), the spouse of an accused is not compellable to disclose any communication during their marriage but is competent to testify for the defence (S. 4 (1)). The act (S. 4 (2)) provides for exceptions where the spouse is charged with sexual offences under the Criminal Code. One last example of evidence that may not be compellable is communication between a solicitor and client. The communication is not admissible in court against the client. This exception does not protect the solicitor who is a party to the offence, nor does it apply to other professionals, such as doctors, psychiatrists, clergy, or accountants.

7.4 TYPES OF EVIDENCE

Direct and Circumstantial Evidence

Direct evidence is testimony from a witness about what he or she saw, heard, touched, tasted, or smelled. With direct evidence the trier of fact does not need to draw a presumption or inference. For example, the testimony of a security officer in a retail setting that he saw the accused take the item off the counter, place it in his pocket, and leave the store without paying for it is direct evidence. Circumstantial evidence can only be derived from a presumption or inference. Testimony that the security officer saw the accused pick up a rock and throw it and then heard the sound of breaking glass requires the inference that the rock broke the glass and that the accused committed vandalism. Even though the trier of fact must draw an inference from circumstantial evidence, such evidence is still admissible in court and, in fact, is often the only evidence put in at a trial to convict an accused. If the trier of fact can draw a reasonable inference from the circumstantial evidence, it may be sufficient to meet the burden of proof.

Primary and Secondary Evidence

Evidence may also be divided into primary and secondary categories. Primary evidence is original or firsthand and is often referred to as the "best evidence."It is the natural and most satisfactory means of proof (Black, 1991). Secondary evidence is, by nature, inferior to the primary or best evidence, but it may become admissible where the primary evidence is unavailable. Examples of secondary evidence include copies of a document, an affidavit of a witness who is unable to testify, or witness testimony about what was in a document that was lost or destroyed. Generally, the best-evidence rule requires that the primary evidence be introduced if it is available. The Canada Evidence Act, however, provides for the admission of documents or even copies of documents such as those kept by government, business, or banking without the oral evidence of a witness (R.S., c. E-10 s. 19–30).

7.5 THE RULE AGAINST HEARSAY

Hearsay evidence is testimony by a witness relating what others have said rather than what the witness knows personally. Courts will not hear testimony that is hearsay. For example, Security Officer Smith communicates on the radio to Security Officer Jones that he saw, on the video system, a male headed to the front door with a laptop computer. He describes the person, states that the person is not an employee, and says he suspects theft. Jones stops the person at the front door and confirms that he has no authority to take the laptop. The police are called and theft charges are laid. At trial, Jones may not testify about the conversation he had with Smith on the radio, but he may testify about stopping the person and recovering the laptop. Smith may be called to testify about what he saw on the video and the fact that he passed information to Jones. Each can testify about what he saw, said, and did but not what he was told by the other. The hearsay rule exists because the court should hear testimony from the person who uttered the original words. The rule also exists because opposing counsel cannot cross-examine a witness on the veracity of what he or she claims to have been told, but counsel can cross-examine the original speaker.

As in most rules of law, the exceptions to the rule are as important as the rule itself. The six exceptions to the hearsay rule are as follows:

1. **Government, Business, and Banking Documents**

    The Canada Evidence Act contains special provisions for the admission of government, business, and banking documents. The act allows them to be admitted into evidence as truth of their content even without a witness giving *viva voce* testimony of their accuracy.

    In one case, the notes of a private investigator who had died before a trial were allowed as evidence as an exception to the hearsay rule because they were business documents made in the ordinary course of business (*Conely v. Conely*, 1968).

2. Expert Evidence

A witness does not normally have the opportunity to give a personal opinion on any matter that may relate to the case. The witness is expected to testify about what he or she saw and heard, not about his or her opinion. One of the exceptions to the hearsay rule, however, is that opinion evidence may be accepted from someone who has been qualified as an expert witness. Expert opinion evidence would normally offend the hearsay rule because the expert is relying on research and a body of knowledge created by others and is therefore repeating the comments and opinions of others. Once the qualifications of the expert have been accepted by the court, however, the expert is permitted to provide opinion on his or her area of expertise. The courts have given the following reason for the rule (*Fullowka et al. v. Royal Oak Ventures, Inc. et al.*, 2004):

> Opinion evidence is deemed necessary where the Court requires expertise to assist in decision-making, that is, when a trier of fact would not know or have difficulty understanding non-everyday technical concepts and some areas in highly specialized fields known to but a few. Facts would be proven, the expert would apply his or her expert knowledge to only those facts and render an opinion for the benefit of the court.

3. *Res Gestae*

Res gestae statements are relevant statements made simultaneously with the facts at issue. They are another example of hearsay statements that may be admissible by way of another witness. For example, in one case (*R. v. Fowkes*), a police officer was in a room with a father and son when a shot came through the window. The son saw a face at the window and shouted out the nickname of the person he saw. The police officer did not see the face at the window but was allowed to testify with respect to the son's statement at trial to identify the person who fired the shot.

4. Dying Declarations

Another exception to the hearsay rule is a statement related to the cause of death made by a person who is dying. The statement would normally offend the hearsay rule because it is a statement made to a witness and repeated in court. To be admissible, the party tendering the evidence must show that the person making the original statement would have been a competent witness and that her or she was under apprehension of death.

5. Affidavits and Depositions

Many statutes and tribunal proceedings allow for affidavits or depositions to be produced in court as truth of their content.[2]

---

[2] For example, section 29 and 30 of the Canada Evidence Act, R.S., c. E-10.

6. **Admissions and Confessions**

A confession is a written or oral statement, not made in court, against the interest of the accused. The introduction of a confession as evidence would normally offend the hearsay rule because the confession is introduced by someone who heard the accused utter the words. Statements and confessions may be inculpatory or exculpatory. Inculpatory statements are those that directly incriminate the accused—for example, "I did it and I'm sorry."An exculpatory statement is a denial by the accused person, such as an excuse or a statement of innocence. A false exculpatory statement (such as a disprovable statement by the accused that "I took the tools but my foreman said I could") could be evidence of guilt.

For a confession to be admissible in court, three issues must be addressed:

1. **Is the statement relevant?**

Like any other form of evidence, a confession is not admissible in court if it is not relevant to the issue at hand. A relevant confession reflects on the guilt of the accused for the offence before the court. In some instances an admission of guilt to past, similar offences may be admissible as similar fact evidence. The court may decide to allow evidence of prior convictions if it is relevant to the guilt of the accused for the offence presently before the court. This rule may also apply outside criminal court. For example, in an investigation of harassment, the fact that the respondent committed similar acts of harassment in the past may be used in consideration of whether the act of harassment under investigation is founded and in the consideration of what discipline is appropriate.

2. **Was the statement voluntary?**

For a confession to be admissible as evidence, the party offering the confession must show that the statement was made voluntarily and without threat or promise. Many cases address the voluntary nature of confessions. The question is not whether the manner of receiving the confession was unfair but whether the confession is reliable. An accused may have confessed under a threat or promise for other benefits. The courts will ask whether the accused confessed to stop abuse or to gain from a promise made by the interrogators. A confession made without threat or promise is more reliable.

A threat may be as simple a statement as "Tell me what happened or we will go to your boss."Even mild threats and promises may cause a confession to be deemed non-voluntary and excluded from evidence. For example, a promise need not be something as obvious as "Tell me what happened and you will keep your job."It may be as simple as "Tell me what happened and things will go better for you."

3. Was the confession made to a person in authority?

A confession made to a person in authority is held to a higher standard during a *voir dire*.[3] Where the Crown is offering evidence of a confession made to a person in authority, it must not only prove that the confession was voluntary but also that the Charter rights of the accused were not breached. The definition of a person in authority goes beyond police officers and may include others whom the accused believes might be able to influencing the prosecution. A person in authority be an employer where the offence was against the company or a security officer acting on behalf of the company.[4]

The courts have identified the following as being "persons in authority":

- masters with their servants
- father of a rape victim when questioning the daughter's attacker
- government official dealing with aboriginals on a reserve
- captain of a vessel
- Crown Prosecutor
- parent of an accused where the parent is actively involved in questioning

Case law has held that the following are not "persons in authority":

- police informer
- physician with a patient
- bank manager in connection with a former employee

Criminal courts enter into a *voir dire* once the prosecutor indicates that a confession will be introduced as evidence. The purpose of the *voir dire* is simply to establish whether the confession was voluntary. Once the Crown has had the opportunity to introduce evidence of the voluntary nature of the confession, the defence counsel has the opportunity to rebut that evidence or to establish that the Charter rights of the accused were breached so the confession should not be received in evidence. The judge then makes a determination as to whether the confession should be admitted into evidence, and the trial continues. If the confession is ruled to be admissible, the police officer or other witness who received the confession will read it into evidence. In a jury trial, the jury is excluded during the *voir dire* and, if the confession is allowed into evidence, the jury is then allowed to decide on the guilt or innocence of the accused based on the confession and all the other evidence. Where a confession is made to someone who is not a person in authority, it is not necessary that a *voir dire* be held to establish the voluntary nature of the statement.

---

[3] "The preliminary examination which the court may make of one presented as a witness or juror, where his competency, interest, etc., is objected to" (Black, 1991).

[4] For further treatment of this issue, see Kaufman, 1974.

Decision to Caution the Accused During a Security Investigation

During an investigation, security may have occasion to question an employee or other accused person. If security staff have exercised an arrest, they are performing a "governmental function" and the suspect should be Charter cautioned. Where there is no arrest and the statement is being taken in the course of an internal investigation against an employee, security is not conducting a governmental function and the Charter of Rights and Freedoms does not apply. Security staff may then elect whether to provide the accused with a Charter caution. They must consider whether the prime reason for the investigation is to serve their employer or to provide the police with sufficient evidence to undertake a criminal prosecution. One factor is that in an internal investigation the employee has a duty to cooperate and be candid and forthright to any questions asked. Once a Charter caution has been issued, that duty no longer exists.

Judges' Rules

The Judges' Rules were initially drafted in Scotland to help police officers ensure that confessions would be admissible in court. In 1964, the rules were redrafted (Home Office, 1964). Although they were written long before the Charter of Rights and Freedoms, they are an excellent guide to security professionals taking a statement from someone who is a potential criminal accused. The rules provide (in part) as follows:

1. An accused cannot be compelled to remain for questioning if not under arrest.

2. The accused must be given the opportunity to contact a lawyer.

3. Once there is sufficient evidence to prefer a charge, the accused should be informed that he or she may be prosecuted and should be cautioned.

4. A record should be kept of the time and place at which the questioning and statement began and ended.

5. Questions and answers must be contemporaneously recorded.

6. A written statement should record the exact words spoken, and the accused should be asked to read it and make any corrections necessary.

7. Persons other than police officers who are charged with the duty of investigating offences or charging offenders shall, so far as may be practicable, comply with these rules.

Security professionals interviewing potentially accused persons should remember that the object of the interview is to learn the truth, not to induce a pattern of deceit or obtain answers that the questioner wants to hear. There should be no actual or implied threats or promises, and the accused should be given the opportunity to provide a full explanation. The accused should also be questioned in a language and phraseology that he or she understands. "Legalese" or technical terms unknown to the accused should be avoided. The interviewer should not be aggressive or abusive to the person being interviewed. An audio or video recording of the interview may provide better corroboration of the voluntary nature of the statement. This recording will confirm what was actually said by the accused and will clarify that no threats or promises were made.

7.6 DISCLOSURE REQUIREMENTS

R. v. Stinchcombe (1991) provides rules requiring criminal prosecutors to provide complete disclosure to the accused. Without the necessity of request, the accused is entitled to the following:

- a copy of his criminal record

- a copy of any statements that he or she made to a person in authority and that were recorded in writing or an opportunity to inspect such statements if they were recorded by electronic means

- inspection of any proposed evidence to be submitted, as well as a copy, where practical

- a copy of the "will state" statements prepared by the police

- any information known to the Crown that would be in the accused's favour

- criminal records of proposed witnesses

- the name and address of any person who might have information useful to the accused

7.7 BURDEN OF PROOF

The level of proof required at a trial or tribunal depends on the nature and seriousness of the case, the relevant statute, and the forum in which the case is heard. It is not surprising that society demands a higher burden of proof where the legal repercussions are greater. *Figure 7-1* shows the increasing levels of burdens of proof and the settings in which they apply.

One arbitration award explained the reason for the higher burden in dishonesty cases as follows (Fruehauf, 1954):

> The social effects upon one having been found guilty of stealing by an established arbitration tribunal may not be as far reaching as if a judicial body had made the finding; yet, the effects upon the public mind, which might be reasonably impressed by the fact that a formalized tribunal to settle industrial disputes issued judgment, would be far greater than if an employee were discharged by an employer on a charge of stealing and no impartial hearing were held.

In any labour arbitration case, the burden is on the employer to establish the breach of the employment relationship and to establish that discipline was appropriate under the circumstances. Arbitration panel rulings can only be appealed on the grounds of procedural error, and the panel is not bound by formal rules of evidence.

Balance of Probabilities

The balance of probabilities is the easiest burden for the plaintiff or employer to meet. It is applied at civil actions and at labour arbitration hearings that do not involve dishonesty (e.g., lateness, poor performance, etc.).

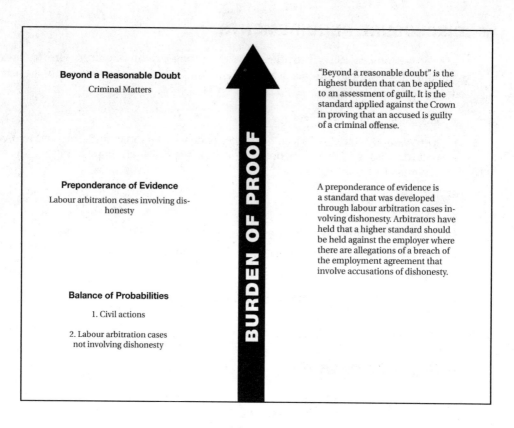

Beyond a Reasonable Doubt
Criminal Matters

Preponderance of Evidence
Labour arbitration cases involving dishonesty

Balance of Probabilities

1. Civil actions

2. Labour arbitration cases not involving dishonesty

BURDEN OF PROOF

"Beyond a reasonable doubt" is the highest burden that can be applied to an assessment of guilt. It is the standard applied against the Crown in proving that an accused is guilty of a criminal offense.

A preponderance of evidence is a standard that was developed through labour arbitration cases involving dishonesty. Arbitrators have held that a higher standard should be held against the employer where there are allegations of a breach of the employment agreement that involve accusations of dishonesty.

FIGURE 7-1

Burden of Proof

7.8 POLYGRAPH EVIDENCE

The polygraph is used by security and law enforcement organizations to test the veracity of a suspect. The instrument works by measuring changes in cardiovascular, respiratory, and electrodermal patterns of the suspect as he or she undergoes questioning. Questions at the beginning of the test establish standards, and the instrument then gives a diagnostic reading indicating the honesty or dishonesty of the individual in answering certain relevant questions. The fact that an accused passed or failed a polygraph test or that he or she agreed or refused to take the test is not admissible in evidence, but any confession provided following a polygraph test is admissible, subject to the usual rules of admissibility of confessions.

The courts have held that the ultimate decision on the credibility of a witness or accused lies with the trier of fact. Courts are therefore unwilling to accept polygraph results or the fact that an accused refused to take a polygraph test as proof of guilt at trial (*R. v. Beland*, 1987).

7.9 **ENTRAPMENT**

The courts exhibit concern when there is a suggestion that an investigator compelled an accused to commit a criminal offence when there was no reasonable ground to believe that the accused would have committed it in any event. The courts refer to this as "random virtue testing" (*R. v. Mack*, 1988). To counter this concern, the defence of entrapment has developed.

The defence of entrapment is sometimes raised in criminal proceedings or at labour arbitration hearings as a result of a security investigation. An accused who wishes to use the defence of entrapment must do so during the trial and must prove the defence on a balance of probabilities. Unless evidence of entrapment can be introduced through other witnesses, the accused must take the stand and introduce the defence during the examination in chief by the defence counsel. To prove the defence, the accused must show that the police or undercover operative went beyond providing the opportunity to commit the offence and actually induced the commission of the offence. To avoid the defence of entrapment, the investigator may only present the opportunity to one who arouses suspicion and may not induce the commission of the offence by pressuring, threatening, or deceiving the person. In some exceptional circumstances, the investigator may be able to avoid a suggestion of entrapment if he or she was testing "an area" where criminal activity was occurring.

To refute the defence of entrapment, the prosecutor must be able to show that

- the accused was already engaged in the particular criminal activity, or

- the physical location with which the person is associated is a place where the particular criminal activity was likely occurring.

In assessing whether entrapment has taken place, the court considers the following factors:[5]

- reasonableness of the suspicion

- availability of other investigative techniques

- whether an average person with both the strengths and weaknesses in the position of the accused would be induced to commit the crime

- persistence and number of attempts by the investigator before the accused agreed to commit the offence

- type of inducement used by the investigator, including deceit, fraud, trickery, or reward

- timing of the investigator's conduct—in particular, whether he or she instigated the offence or became involved in ongoing criminal activities

---

[5] In R. v. Barnes (1991), the Supreme Court held that the mere fact that the accused was previously involved in criminal activity is insufficient to establish "reasonable suspicion."

- whether the investigator's conduct involved an exploitation of human characteristics, such as friendship

- whether the investigator exploited a particular vulnerability of the person, such as a mental handicap or substance addiction

- harm or risk caused by the investigator (who may also have committed illegal acts) as compared to the accused

- existence of any threats implied or expressly made to the accused by the investigator or other agents

- whether the investigator's conduct is directed at undermining other constitutional values

Some forms of inducement are accepted by the courts without a declaration that entrapment has taken place. In *Nintendo of America v. 798824 Ont. Ltd.* (1991), a private investigator purchased a game cartridge from an employee of a company that had been served a notice of injunction. The court held that the private investigator had made no inducements or threats to the employee in purchasing the cartridge, and the investigator had turned over the evidence upon receiving it. Courts have also upheld evidence in theft cases where investigators have deliberately left valuables available or where marked bills were provided to a cashier to ascertain whether they were later taken from the cash (*R. v. Gallagher*, 1993). However, the courts may frown on some procedures, such as inducing a person who claims to be injured to pick up money or change a spare tire.

7.10 **VIDEO AND PHOTOGRAPHIC EVIDENCE**

Video and photographic evidence have become more prevalent in the courts. Video is used for transcribing the statement of witnesses or accused, recreating a scene, recording criminal activity, or depicting surveillance findings. Video and photographic evidence have long been accepted by the courts but with significant limitations related to reliability, relevance, and privacy.

Reliability

For video evidence to be admissible, the court must be convinced that it is reliable. If video surveillance is being introduced to show that the plaintiff or defendant was involved in a certain activity, the video must be clear enough to identify the person. In some cases, the plaintiff or defendant may allege that someone else is depicted in the tape (*Mitchell v. Trainor*, 1993).[6]

Video and photographic evidence must be verified by someone who can testify as to where and under what circumstances the evidence was obtained and state that it accurately depicts the scene that existed at the time it was obtained. Although this need not necessarily be the person who obtained the video or photographic evidence, obviously that person would be the best to introduce the evidence.

The courts have accepted digitally enhanced evidence under strict provisions that the original also be produced and that it is up to the court to draw conclusions from the manipulation of the original.

Relevance

For any evidence to be admissible in court, it must be relevant to the issue at trial. The test for video and photographic evidence is whether a witness would be permitted to describe the scene depicted by the evidence (*Simpson Timber Co. (Sask.) Ltd. v. Bonville*, 1986).

Prejudicial Effect Versus Probative Value and Privacy Issues

Video and photographic images may not be accepted into evidence even if they meet the preceding criteria—if the court finds that there is slight probative value and the prejudicial effect overrides the value of the evidence.

In one decision of the Federal Privacy Commissioner (PIPEDA Case #269, 2004), an employer hired a private investigator to conduct video surveillance on an employee. The employee had reported a number of work-related injuries and had requested

---

[6] The plaintiff admitted that some photographs introduced at court were of her but held that others were of her sister. The court found that all the pictures were of the plaintiff and that the private investigator's testimony that he had confirmed the observation through binoculars confirmed the finding.

workplace accommodation due to physical limitations. The company became increasingly suspicious of the complainant's claims, given his behaviour and the company's difficulties in obtaining updated medical information. The company had attempted to collect, directly from the complainant, accurate information regarding his ability to perform duties related to his employment, but he was uncooperative.

He was offered temporary positions in line with his physical limitations. He refused them and went on extended medical leave until his physician indicated that he was fit to return to work, with limitations. He returned to work but complained about his workstation. He was frequently absent and reported having other physical difficulties. The company's health officer requested an updated assessment from the employee's physician. She never received one, despite having requested one orally and in writing. The complainant continued to be dissatisfied with the position and workstation that the company provided. The company provided the employee with a rehabilitation program, but it was terminated due to lack of progress and the complainant's increasing physical discomfort. The company asked him to undergo an independent assessment, which he initially resisted. The conclusion of the independent medical assessor was that, while he had physical barriers, he also appeared to have non-physical barriers to returning to work. The assessors noted that it was unlikely that further functional testing would provide an accurate assessment of his true functional abilities.

The company hired a private investigation firm to conduct surveillance on the complainant to determine whether he had been truthful about his physical limitations. Following two weeks of surveillance, the private investigators provided the employer with a report and videotape. That information showed that the complainant had misrepresented the state of his health, and the company terminated his employment.

In the complaint to the Privacy Commissioner, the company argued that the decision to conduct video surveillance was a last resort to determine the veracity of the employee's claims. The company acknowledged that it had no formal policy or procedures in place to guide managers in such situations.

The industrial relations manager provided the investigation firm with direction about the complainant's limitations and instructed the investigators to monitor the employee's activities for several days or as required. The investigators followed the employee for a total of 139 hours over the course of two weeks and provided eight hours of videotape to the company. The tape showed the complainant performing activities that, in the company's medical practitioner's opinion, contradicted his claims of physical limitations.

The Assistant Commissioner's opinion pointed out that paragraph 7(1)(b) of the Personal Information Protection and Electronic Documents Act states that an organization may collect personal information without the knowledge or consent of the individual only if it is reasonable to expect that the collection with the knowledge or consent of the individual would compromise the availability or the accuracy of the information and the collection is reasonable for purposes related to investigating a breach of an agreement or a contravention of the laws of Canada or a province.

The Assistant Privacy Commissioner noted that the Office of the Privacy Commissioner considers video surveillance to be an extremely privacy-invasive form of technology. She noted that the very nature of the medium entails the collection of a great deal of personal information that may concern innocent third parties, may be extraneous, or may lead to judgments about the subject that have nothing to do with the purpose of collecting the information in the first place. She stated that resorting to video surveillance, especially on employees away from the work site, must be considered only in the most limited cases. She found that there was no question that the company had collected the complainant's personal information without his knowledge and consent.

The Assistant Commissioner noted that an organization must have substantial evidence to support the suspicion that the relationship of trust has been broken, must be able to show that it has exhausted all less-invasive means of obtaining the information required, and must limit the collection to the greatest extent possible.

The Assistant Commissioner noted that the company had, for nearly two years, attempted to accommodate the complainant with his workplace requirements. In June 2001, he was cleared to return to work with limitations, yet he continued to miss work for reasons related to his medical conditions. The company tried, unsuccessfully, to obtain up-to-date medical information. When the employee agreed to the independent assessment, the results did not refute the employer's growing suspicion that he was not accurately representing the state of his health.

The Assistant Commissioner was satisfied that the company's purpose was based on substantial evidence and that its surveillance was undertaken to determine whether the complainant was violating his employment contract by misrepresenting the state of his health. The Assistant Commissioner was also satisfied that the company had tried less privacy-invasive ways to gather the information it required. There were numerous attempts, orally and in writing, to obtain accurate medical information, but these met with resistance from the complainant. He was offered the opportunity to submit to the independent capacity assessment, which he did reluctantly. All these steps were considerably less privacy-invasive, but they did not dispel the organization's concerns. When the company took the step of hiring the private investigator, it outlined what information it was looking for, thereby focusing, as much as possible, the collection of personal information on the complainant.

The Assistant Commissioner stressed that while she was satisfied that the company only resorted to video surveillance after taking numerous measures to obtain the required information with the complainant's knowledge and consent, she recommended that the company formalize the steps it took by developing policy and practices that are privacy-conscious.

She suggested the policy should take into account the following guidance:

- Video surveillance is a last resort and should only be contemplated if all other avenues of collecting personal information have been exhausted.

- The decision to undertake video surveillance should be made at a very senior level of the organization.

- The private investigator should be instructed to collect personal information in accordance with PIPEDA.

In another complaint to the Privacy Commissioner, a railway employee complained that a supervisor had used a video camera installed for safety purposes to gather evidence of the employee leaving the work site early. The Commissioner found that the supervisor used the zoom lens on a video camera to watch the employee go off-site. The Commissioner held that the company failed to use less-intrusive methods first, such as ascertaining whether the employee had permission to go off-site. Accordingly, she found that the privacy complaint was founded.

In *Ferenczy v. MCI Medical Clinic* (2004), the Ontario Superior Court ruled that the admission of video evidence did not offend PIPEDA. The plaintiff had testified that it was difficult for her to grip a cup following the removal of a cyst from her hand by the defendant doctor. To counter her testimony, defence counsel introduced video of the plaintiff holding a coffee cup with her hand. Plaintiff's counsel argued that the admission of the evidence offended the privacy of the plaintiff. The court overruled this argument on a number of grounds. First, the court found that the private investigator was acting as an agent for the doctor. Second, the court found that the plaintiff had given implied consent because she had put her hand injury in issue by filing the lawsuit. The court stated:

> One who takes such a step (a law suit) surely cannot be heard to say that they do not consent to the gathering of information as to the nature and extent of their injury or the veracity of their claim by the person they have chosen to sue. Consent is not a defined term under the *Act*, and there is no indication in the *Act* that consent cannot be implied.

The treatment of video evidence in labour arbitrations can be demonstrated in *Re Steels Industrial Products and Teamsters Union Local 213 (Sidhu)* (1991). The arbitrator held that there were two questions to ask in relation to surveillance evidence:

- Was it reasonable, in all the circumstances, to request a surveillance?

- Was the surveillance conducted in a reasonable manner?

If the answer to either of the questions is "no," then the evidence should not be admitted. Some union–management contracts contain provisions excluding the use of video in the work site (Goldstein, 1991).

Video and photographic evidence may be excluded at a criminal trial where the suspect is able to establish a breach of the right to privacy under section 8 of the Charter of Rights and Freedoms or at a civil action or arbitration where the disputing party can establish a breach of provincial or federal privacy legislation. As a result of the decision in *R. v. Wong* (1991), police are required to obtain a court authorization before installing surreptitious video for criminal cases. Subject to privacy requirements, security staff do not require a court authorization where they can demonstrate reasonable grounds to believe that criminal or employment infractions are being committed.[7] The court or arbitrator will consider the balance between the probative value of the videotaped evidence and the prejudicial effect.

The Federal Privacy Commissioner has suggested that four questions be asked before undertaking video surveillance:

- Is the measure demonstrably necessary to meet a specific need?
- Is it likely to be effective in meeting that need?
- Is the loss of privacy proportional to the benefit gained?
- Is there a less privacy-invasive way of achieving the same end?

In *Re Doman Forest Products Ltd.* (1990), a British Columbia arbitrator considered a request for the admission of video evidence of an employee. The employee took sick leave because of the flu, and the employer hired a private investigator, who obtained videotape of the employee working at a construction site. When the employee returned to work, he told his employer that he had stayed at home to recuperate from the flu. The employee was terminated for cause and grieved his termination. The arbitrator stated that there was a need to balance the employee's right to privacy and the employer's right to investigate. He disallowed the video from evidence because there was a lack of reasonable cause to support the surveillance. The arbitrator found that the employer failed to confront the employee first with any suspicions about malingering and had set a trap for the employee. The arbitrator suggested that the employer should first have asked the employee about the nature of the illness, the effect it would have on his capacity to work, and whether the employee intended to do anything else while off sick. The arbitrator reinstated the employee with a 50 percent loss of pay. An example of the use of video evidence to disprove an injury claim can be found in *Alberta Wheat Pool v. Grain Workers Union, Local 333* (1995).

---

[7] See R. v. Swanarchuk (1990) for the distinction between security surveillance and law enforcement surveillance. The court held that video surveillance of employees in a Safeway washroom did not offend the Charter but would have if it was installed by the police.

7.11 **ADMISSION OF COMPUTER EVIDENCE**

Many employee investigations relate to inappropriate e-mails or Internet access. Courts and arbitration panels have held that employers have the right to monitor employee access to company computers and the Internet. If the information gathered in the monitoring of employee computer access is to be admissible as evidence, the employer should have a policy advising employees that their computer activity is being monitored in a reasonable manner and for appropriate cause.

7.12 **ADMISSIBILITY OF RECORDINGS OF PRIVATE COMMUNICATION**

The Criminal Code of Canada defines private communication in terms of an expectation of privacy (R.S., c. C-34, s. 183):

> "Private communication" means any oral communication, or any telecommunication, that is made by an originator who is in Canada or is intended by the originator to be received by a person who is in Canada and that is made **under circumstances in which it is reasonable for the originator to expect that it will not be intercepted** by any person other than the person intended by the originator to receive it, and includes any radio-based telephone communication that is treated electronically or otherwise for the purpose of preventing intelligible reception by any person other than the person intended by the originator to receive it.

Because of the definition, it is legal in Canada to record a conversation where there is one-party consent. An investigator using a hidden recorder may intercept communication where he or she is a party to it but may not legally leave a recorder in a room where he or she is not a party to the conversation. The police, however, must comply with the Charter of Rights and Freedoms and must obtain a court order to intercept private communications even where there is one-party consent.

Although investigators may legally record private communications to which they are parties, the recordings may or may not be admissible in civil court or arbitration hearings. As early as 1989 the courts found that the recording of a personal conversation may be an invasion of privacy even where it is being introduced by one of the parties to the conversation (*Ferguson and Wuckert v. McBee Technographics Inc.,* 1989).

The Criminal Code is slightly different in relation to interception of radio-based (or cellular) communication. There is an added requirement that the interception be done "maliciously or for gain" (R.S., c. C-34, s. 184.5 (1)). This requirement differentiates between a private investigator being paid to gather the cellular communication with a scanner and an in-house investigator gathering evidence of employee misconduct. In either case, admission of the evidence would be subject to an argument that reception of the evidence was a breach of the person's privacy.

7.13 **RELIABILITY OF PHYSICAL EVIDENCE**

In assessing the reliability of physical evidence, courts consider the continuity of the evidence. The party submitting the physical evidence must be able to establish that it is original and can be depended on as reliable evidence.

This chapter has provided the security professional with information on how evidence is introduced at a trial or hearing. It has considered the restrictions related to hearsay and exceptions to the hearsay rule. It has also considered restrictions on the introduction of confessions and appropriate means for receiving a confession from an accused person. It has addressed the varying burdens of proof, polygraph evidence and the defence of entrapment. Admissibility of video and photographic evidence was also considered, as was the admissibility of private communication and computer evidence.

REFERENCES

Alberta Wheat Pool v. Grain Workers Union, Local 333, [1995] 48 L.A.C. (4th) 332 (B.C.).

Black, H. C. (1991). *Black's law dictionary* (abridged 6th ed.). Eagan, MN: West Group.

Canada Evidence Act, R.S. 1985, c. C-5.

Canadian Charter of Rights and Freedoms, [1982] enacted as Schedule B to the Canada Act 1982 (U.K.), c. 11.

Conely v. Conely, [1968] 2 O.R. 677 (C.A.).

Criminal Code of Canada, R.S., c. C-34, s. 183 and s. 184.5 (1).

Cross, R., and Wilkins, N. (1971). An outline of the law of evidence. London: Butterworths.

Ferenczy v. MCI Medical Clinic, [2004] O.J. No. 1775.

Ferguson and Wuckert v. McBee Technographics Inc. et al., [1989] 2 W.W.R. 499.

Fruehauf–Carter Division and Int'l Union of Electrical Radio & Machinists, Talbot Lodge 61, (1954).

Fullowka et al v. Royal Oak Ventures Inc. et al, 2004 NMTSC 66.

Goldstein, E. (1991). *Visual evidence: A practitioner's manual.* Toronto: Carswell.

Home Office. (1964). Circular No. 31/1964, Appendix A.

Kaufman, F. (1974). *The admissibility of confessions in criminal matters* (2nd ed.). Toronto: Carswell.

Mitchell v. Trainor, [1993] 123 N.S.R. (2d) 361 (S.C.).

Nintendo of America v. 798824 Ont. Ltd., [1991] 41 F.T.R. 161 (F.C.T.D.).

Personal Information Protection and Electronic Documents Act (PIPEDA). (2000).

PIPEDA Case #269, issued April 23, 2004.

Re Doman Forest Products Ltd., New Westminster Division and International Woodworkers, Local I-357, [1990] 13 L.A.C. (4th) 275 (B.C.).

Re Steels Industrial Products and Teamsters Union Local 213 (Sidhu), [1991] 24 l.a.c. (4th) 259 (B.C.) (Blasina).

R. v. Barnes, [1991] 63 CCC (3d) 1 (SCC).

R. v. Beland, [1987] 2 S.C.R. 398.

R. v. Gallagher, [1993] A.J. No. 681 (P.C.).

R. v. Mack, [1988] 44 CCC (3d) 513 (SCC).

R. v. Fowkes, reported in J. Stephen, *Digest of the law of evidence* (12th ed.), Littleton, CO: Rothman, p. 8.

R. v. Stinchcombe, [1991] 3 S.C.R. 326, CanLII 45 (S.C.C.).

R. v. Swanarchuk, [1990] M.J. No. 686 (Q.B.).

R. v. Wong, [1991] 60 C.C.C. (3d) 460 (S.C.C).

Simpson Timber Co. (Sask.) Ltd. v Bonville, [1986] 5 W.W.R. 180 (Sask. Q.B.).

CHAPTER EIGHT

TESTIMONY

Testimonial evidence generally represents 80 percent of the evidence presented in court. Because of the incidents they encounter in their work, security employees are often called to give testimony. They may testify in formal or informal regulatory hearings; they may be interviewed by government authorities, give formal depositions, or appear before grand juries; or they may give testimony in civil or criminal courts at any level.

Security employees called to testify are usually paired with legal counsel, but during testimony counsel may be unable to assist or intercede. Moreover, the experience of testifying in a courtroom can be intimidating. Therefore, security employees should learn the rules and processes related to giving testimony.

Laws and rules regarding testimony vary from country to country (and even within countries), so it is impractical to address every variation in the legal treatment of testimony. For purposes of illustration, this document follows two U.S. codes: the Federal Code of Civil Procedures and the Federal Code of Criminal Procedures.

Security employees' testimony must always be truthful and at the same time follow court guidelines and counsel's strategy. A person who gives testimony—a witness—is usually either a fact witness or an opinion witness. (Security employees could be either.) Fact witness testimony is typically restricted to matters that the witness actually saw, heard, smelled, touched, or tasted. Hearsay—relating what some other person may have said—may or may not be admissible. (A typical hearsay exception regards reporting a person's "dying declaration," such as a crime victim's last words identifying the perpetrator.) To be accepted as an opinion witness, also known as an expert witness or forensic witness, one must demonstrate training, education, and experience in a specific subject. Such a witness may provide an opinion on the matter at hand, based on analysis of the evidence according to accepted scientific standards and scholarly research methods.

8.1 THE JOURNEY

Security employees can look on testimony as the end of a process that began with an earlier event. At any time after that event, from immediately to years later, they may be required to testify, even if they have left the job. From the first day on the job, they should realize that their observations, reports, or findings, coupled with their demeanor and their ability to articulate events, may be the key to the verdict.

8.1.1 PROCEDURE

Every security incident should be treated as if it could result in a courtroom appearance. This approach requires adherence to established procedures or at least consistent personal procedures. Security employees should mark evidence with their initials, the date, and a tracking or report number, in the same location whenever possible. If procedures are not followed, security employees should know why and be prepared to explain. Variations from procedure may occur due to weather, a situation's urgency, the type of evidence to be marked, and so on. Witnesses should be familiar with any evidence they claim to have marked. They should examine the evidence before taking the stand because its appearance may have changed and it may appear in a different order than expected.

8.1.2 REPORT

Security employees should provide all relevant reports and notes to counsel. It is also appropriate to educate counsel about the expected testimony. Witnesses should know their facts but not script their testimony.

8.1.3 TESTIMONY PREPARATION

Preparation begins long before thoughts of litigation. It starts with the accurate and timely capture of facts and impressions of the incident in a report or notes. Such documentation is much more credible than mental recollection, which is diminished and altered by time and events. Shortly before testimony, preparation may consist of a site visit and a review of notes, reports, photos, and diagrams. As part of the preparation, a thorough review of the case with prosecuting attorney will be conducted with the security representative to determine the strong and weak points of the case to be presented. The testimonial evidence the security professional will be presenting in court is call "parole" or "spoken word" and the attorney will want to make sure that it supports the case.

It is also normal to have a pre-trail meeting were opposing litigants get together to exchange information that each believes is necessary to their position. They will request a *duces tecum* (produce all tangible evidence) from each other as well as written questions called interrogatories. They also may wish to interview or interrogate certain witnesses, the complainant, and offender. Formal sworn depositions may also be taken, that are admissible in court.

8.2 COURTROOM PARTICIPANTS

Judges

Judges are public officials authorized to decide questions of law brought before a court and are the ultimate authority in regulating the litigation before them. In all trials, they are responsible for requiring adherence to procedural rules. In bench trials (those without a jury), judges also decide the outcome (guilt or innocence, fault or no fault).

Juries

Juries consist of jurors, selected citizens required to render a decision based on the facts presented to them. Jurors are not professional arbiters of fact. Typically their names are drawn from the voter rolls in a jurisdiction. Once sworn in the jury candidates are put through a legal process known as *voir dire* where the attorneys and/or judge ask questions to determine their suitability to be on the jury for the trial in question. Once the final jury members are selected, they receive instructions from the judge that includes what they may consider as evidence (relevancy, materiality and competency); give varying weight to different evidence; and then render a verdict within the boundaries of the applicable standard of proof.

Though charged with rendering a verdict based on fact, jurors, like most people, are influenced by their personality, culture, and life experience. For instance, in criminal cases, numerous studies have found black jurors less likely than white jurors to convict, especially when the defendant is black (Abshire and Bornstein, 2002). This cross-race effect may make it especially important for security witnesses to build a rapport with the jurors and show themselves as knowledgeable.

Witnesses may be able to communicate better with juries by using an interview technique called neuro-linguistic programming. People experience life through their senses (neurological); communicate primarily through spoken language (linguistic); and organize information and actions through a self-ordered mechanism called a program (programming). Through casual glances, witnesses can often detect how jurors view them and their answers. If witnesses detect a negative response, they can alter their delivery to improve communication. It may be that their body language signals laziness, lack of professionalism, or coldness, or perhaps the testimony is too wordy or filled with jargon.

Counsel

Counsel, attorneys, lawyers—these are advocates hired to represent their client to the best of their ability within the rules of procedure and bounds of integrity. It may be in their best interest to make witnesses look foolish or unprofessional, either in depositions (taking of sworn testimony before the trial) or in the courtroom. Counsel may also point out inconsistencies between testimony given before trial and testimony given at trial.

Witnesses

Security employees called to testify may serve as either fact witnesses or opinion/expert/forensic witnesses, and their testimony may be sought either to support or to contradict other evidence. For example, an individual with extensive experience, knowledge, and background in automobile paint may be recognized as an expert witness in an accident investigation. Suggestions on their attire, demeanor, and preparation are given below.

8.3 **TESTIFYING**

Security employees who will give testimony can take several steps to improve their effectiveness as witnesses. They should educate themselves about the following matters.

8.3.1 **PRE-TESTIMONY REVIEW**

Before testifying, in any venue, security employees should review their notes and discuss their testimony with counsel including any concerns they have about a weak point in the case. Attorneys have differing thoughts on strategies, presentation of witnesses, the form of the answer, and what should be said in direct examination or left unanswered until cross-examination (examination by opposing counsel). Typically, a security employee is just one part of the attorney's strategy. In some cases, the attorney may want the security employee to provide short answers, without superlatives, in response to questions. In other cases, the attorney may favor effusive, dramatically descriptive responses, but in all cases, answer only the questioned that is asked.

Proper pre-testimony review examines the following:

- notes and reports on the incident

- evidence that is available, accessible, and retrievable

- documentary evidence from any subsequent actions or hearings

If physical evidence will be used in court, the security employee should physically examine it during the pre-trial conference. That is the only way to ensure the evidence exists in its entirety as noted in descriptive documents and evidence tags. The security employee should also be prepared to testify on the gathering of the evidence and the chain of custody.

8.3.2 **INCIDENT SITE AND COURTROOM**

The security witness should visit the incident site—ideally, in conditions similar to those prevailing when the incident occurred (time of day, time of year, lighting, weather, etc.). Doing so can clarify elements of the report, put them in the proper perspective, and greatly enhance recollections of the incident.

It is also useful for a witness to visit a courtroom before giving testimony, especially if the upcoming appearance is the witness's first ever or first in that country. Observing the testimony of others, approaches of the different attorneys, actions of the judge, and conduct of the jurors will go far in removing the mystique surrounding trials.

8.3.3 PUBLIC PLACE DISCUSSIONS

Witnesses should avoid discussing cases in public places and with persons other than their side's attorney. When witnesses reveal their opinions in front of other witnesses, they raise the risk of impeachment problems (possibly due to a misinterpretation of their words) and may prematurely reveal their testimony to the opposition.

8.3.4 DEMEANOR AND ATTIRE

No matter what role they may play, witnesses should avoid being stiff, argumentative, arrogant, evasive, and uncaring, nor should they should not take questions personally. They should strive to be personable, charming, professional, polite, earnest, and knowledgeable. Security personnel who are testifying must also emphasize self-confidence.

Moreover, to be effective witnesses, security employees should dress appropriately for the jury and jurisdiction. A uniform may or may not appeal to the jury; a business suit may communicate arrogance. Whatever the style of dress, it should be neat, clean, respectable, and devoid of flashiness. Extravagant jewelry and numerous or exotic piercings may be off-putting.

8.3.5 QUESTIONING AND RESPONSE TECHNIQUES

Knowing what to expect of the opposition can help the security employee testify more effectively. During testimony, opposing counsel may well lay traps for witnesses. Security employees giving testimony should be aware of the following (McElheny, 2006):

- **Counsel might try to gauge the witness's ability to withstand serious cross-examination.** The witness should be prepared to testify and should keep in mind that he or she probably knows more than the attorney does about security response and reporting procedures.

- **An attorney might summarize a witness's answer in the attorney's words.** If that happens, the witness should not offer merely a yes answer. He or she can say, for example, that the attorney's summary is accurate only in the broadest terms and does not accurately capture what the witness said. The attorney's choice of words in the summary may change the witness's meaning.

- **Counsel might violate rules of evidence and seek hearsay, conversation information, rumors, and opinions.**

- **The attorney might ask for a witness's notes.** Witnesses often want to take notes or files to the stand, especially in complex cases. Before testifying, a witness should ask counsel whether to use notes and what to do if opposing counsel asks for them. If notes will be used, opposing counsel may have a right to receive a copy of them in advance. Any notes taken to the witness stand should be carefully organized. If opposing counsel takes the notes for a moment, the witness should not continue the testimony until the notes are returned. If opposing counsel shuffled them, the witness may politely ask the judge for time to put them back in order.

- **The attorney might ask trick questions.** For instance, in a case alleging inadequate security, opposing counsel might ask, "When you were working alone on the night of this incident, what is the first thing you did when Mary flagged you down on the employee parking lot to report she had been assaulted?" Perhaps the incident happened during the day, or several officers were on duty, or the witness proactively intervened instead of being flagged down. If the witness only replies, "I checked to see if she was injured and then called for an ambulance," the witness has allowed opposing counsel to make misstatements without clarification or objection. The misstatements may influence the jury.

A witness who does not understand a question should ask the attorney to speak up or clarify it. If the witness still does not understand the question clearly, the witness may state that he or she is confused; may ask whether he or she can give a qualified (limited and explained) answer; or may simply state that he or she cannot answer with a yes or no. Certainly the witness should refrain from answering the question that the witness merely *thinks* the attorney is asking. The attorneys and the judge may make comments, but the witness should do as the judge directs.

Witnesses should never guess on the witness stand nor volunteer information. If they do not know or cannot recall the answer, they should say so or ask if they can refer to their notes. However, continually saying "I can't recall" may damage their credibility. If the answers being solicited are not things the witness should know, the attorney for the witness's side will typically raise objections. Witnesses should not nod their heads in agreement or shake their heads in disagreement until opposing counsel has asked a question in its entirety.

Security employees who will give testimony should stay abreast of developments in the security field. They would appear uninformed, unprofessional, and unconvincing if opposing counsel raised a common and relevant security practice that they did not know about.

When answering questions, witnesses should emphasize self-confidence, speak clearly and give positive, direct, and definitive answers whenever possible. They may take their time in answering but should not obviously delay or deny the obvious. If they have to use technical terms that may be unfamiliar to the jury, they should immediately restate or explain them in ordinary language.

It may be undesirable for witnesses to make eye contact with the jury. Jurors might prefer that witnesses direct their answers to the attorney asking the questions so that jurors can evaluate the responses in a detached manner. A witness should ask his or her side's attorney, in advance, what to do if opposing counsel tells the witness to direct an answer to the jury or move closer to the jury box.

Regarding other body language and answering strategy issues, witnesses should do the following:

- Look comfortable but do not slouch, rest head on hand, chew gum, play with earrings or mustache, or move around in the chair.
- Ask for a restroom break or drink of water if needed.
- Speak authoritatively but not arrogantly.
- Answer questions directly but volunteer nothing.
- Be aware of time and distance distortions, as few people estimate accurately.
- Admit to meeting with counsel.
- Admit discussing the case with others (if true), if the discussions are not privileged,
- Keep an even temper even if opposing counsel appears to lose his or her temper.
- Stick to an answer even if opposing counsel repeats the question numerous times with increasing incredulity.
- Make opposing counsel ask simple questions, not multiple questions within a question.

8.3.6 INCONSISTENCIES

Lawyers are trained to look for inconsistencies in testimony and exploit them to their advantage. The following are types of inconsistencies that could lead a jury to believe a witness is dishonest:

- inconsistencies in the witness's own statement
- inconsistencies between the witness's different statements
- inconsistencies between the witness's statement and what others said
- inconsistencies between the witness's statement and other evidence

8.4 **EXPERT WITNESSES**

Unlike a fact witness, an expert witness is allowed to provide his or her opinion about what caused or could have prevented an incident. Acceptance as an expert witness typically requires such measures as experience, education, teaching, research, and publication of articles in the field. The legal requirements for expert witnesses are found in these three U.S. Supreme Court cases:

- *Daubert v. Merrell Dow Pharmaceuticals, Inc.* (1993), requires judges to determine whether expert scientific testimony is based on sound science before allowing it into evidence.

- *General Electric Co. v. Joiner* found that trial judges can specify the kind of scientific testimony that juries can hear.

- *Kumho Tire v. Carmichael Co.* expanded the scope of *Daubert*, requiring that any expert, scientific or otherwise, be scrutinized before testifying.

Whereas fact witnesses are typically requested or compelled to appear, expert witnesses are hired to provide their opinion.

The jurist controlling the case decides whether a person recommended and retained by counsel qualifies as an expert—that is, a person with knowledge not typically possessed by the layman or someone outside a defined field. In some jurisdictions, the judge appoints experts as additional resources for the judge and jury. However, in most jurisdictions, each side may retain its own experts. For example, in a lawsuit alleging inadequate security and an injury resulting from a violent act, experts might be retained to provide opinions (based on review of the facts of the case and analysis of relevant data) as to the who, what, when, where, how, and possibly why of the case. Other experts might be retained to testify on pure security issues, such as policies and procedures, personnel, technology, hardware, and design, as well as the relation of those issues to the incident. Still other experts might testify on criminological issues.

In sum, security employees can view testimony as a journey that begins with an incident; depends on procedures and reports; features judges, juries, counsel, and witnesses; requires pre-testimony review; and ends with testimony given with full knowledge of the techniques of testifying and the traps of opposing counsel.

REFERENCES

Abshire, J., & Bornstein, B. (2000). Juror sensitivity to the cross-race effect. *Law and Human Behavior*, 27(5), 471.

Daubert v. Merrell Dow Pharmaceuticals, 509 U.S. 579 (1993).

General Electric Co. v. Joiner, 522 U.S. 136 (1997).

Kumho Tire Co., Ltd. v. Carmichael, 526 US 137 (1999).

McElhaney, J. W. (2006, September). Deposition traps. *ABA Journal*, 92, 20.

INDEX

XYZ